NEW WEST
READER

NEW WEST
READER

Essays on an Ever-Evolving Frontier

NEW WEST
READER
Essays on an Ever-Evolving Frontier

Edited and introduced by

Philip Connors

NATION
BOOKS

NATION BOOKS • NEW YORK

NEW WEST READER
Essays on an Ever-Evolving Frontier

Published by
Nation Books
An Imprint of Avalon Publishing Group
245 West 17th St., 11th Floor
New York, NY 10011

AVALON
publishing group incorporated

Nation Books is a co-publishing venture of the Nation Institute and Avalon Publishing Group Incorporated.

Library of Congress Cataloging-in-Publication Data is available.

ISBN: 1-56025-648-6
ISBN 13: 978-1-56025-648-9

9 8 7 6 5 4 3 2 1

Book design by Jamie McNeely
Printed in the United States of America
Distributed by Publishers Group West

This book is dedicated to Shirley Dallman, Mike Fritz, and Dave Nimmer, who encouraged me to read and write

CONTENTS

IX   Introduction

1   Take My Saddle from the Wall: A Valediction
Larry McMurtry

35   Industrial Tourism and the National Parks
Edward Abbey

62   Redneck Secrets
William Kittredge

74   The Heart of the Game
Thomas McGuane

90   The Solace of Open Spaces
Gretel Ehrlich

105   Variations on a Theme by Crèvecoeur
Wallace Stegner

125   Illegal Aliens
Sharman Apt Russell

139   The Clan of One-Breasted Women
Terry Tempest Williams

150   All but the Waltz
Mary Clearman Blew

170   La Vida Loca
Jimmy Santiago Baca

175   Dust, or Erasing the Future: The Nevada
Test Site
Rebecca Solnit

207   The Maze and Aura
Jack Turner

230   Fifth World: The Return of Ma ah shra true ee,
the Giant Serpent
Leslie Marmon Silko

242   Believing in the American West
Patricia Nelson Limerick

265   The Unauthorized Autobiography of Me
Sherman Alexie

280   The Militia in Me
Denis Johnson

300   Creeks of Galiuro
Craig Childs

321   Spirit-Fried No-Name River Brown Trout:
A Recipe
David James Duncan

335   Brides of Place
Ellen Meloy

344   My Landlady's Yard
Dagoberto Gilb

349   About the Contributors

353   Permissions

357   Acknowledgments

INTRODUCTION

Living and Dreaming in the American West

Recently I spent a night in the heart of the White Sands National Monument, in southern New Mexico, a trip timed to the rising of a full moon. Sculpted by millennia of wind and water into sensuously curving dunes, the gypsum crystals of the Tularosa Basin reflected the light of the moon so intensely that midnight arrived like an otherwordly dawn. I stayed awake through the night, wandered the dunetops, tracked the paths of the armored stink beetles in the phosphorescent sand. Dappled in moonshadow, the gypsum fields were as cool and strange as the surface of the moon itself.

Toward morning I crawled in my sleeping bag for a nap before the sun rose and turned my lunar playground into a merciless desert. My wake-up call was swift and brutal. Directly above me, seemingly within arm's reach, a black fighter plane pierced my dreams. The roar made my eardrums hum like a plucked guitar string, and the jet left a trail on my retina as if the sky had been unzipped by the hand of God.

"In wildness is the preservation of the world," Thoreau famously wrote, and as I stumbled back to my vehicle in the glare of the sunrise I wondered what the bard of American wilderness would have made of White Sands at the turn of the twenty-first century. In the White Sands Missile Range, that portion of the Tularosa Basin adjacent to the national monument (and off limits to you and me), men have been rehearsing the annihilation of the Earth for more than sixty years. In one of the gnarlier landscapes left in the Lower Forty-eight, bleached earless lizards skitter within walking distance of the original Ground Zero. Kit fox lope among the detritus of unexploded ordnance. And the stink beetles leave their tiny tracks among the dunes while some of man's most sophisticated instruments of death stalk the sky.

In wildness is the preservation of the world. I couldn't jar the phrase from my brain. Too many encounters with eco-friendly postcards and Sierra Club come-ons. But another phrase begged to answer it: "I am become death, the destroyer of worlds," the first words uttered by J. Robert Oppenheimer when he saw that ghostly eyeball known as the Trinity explosion. Travelers for centuries had called the stretch of country encompassing White Sands and Trinity the *Jornada del Muerto*, the Journey of Death. Who could resist the dark whiff of prophecy in that name for a place where the Unites States government simultaneously preserves and bombards the landscape?

This is the theater of irony and paradox we live amid here in the modern West.

At our worst, our response to such complexities shapes itself into a simple-minded rage. It would be easy enough to raise a belated one-finger salute to the fighter jet and mumble a few fruitless words about the depredations of the military-industrial complex. I wouldn't be surprised if on that fine, clear morning I did just that. A certain kind of righteous anger, particularly toward agents of the federal government, has never been expunged from the Westerner's DNA. Instead it mutates, seeking its full expression in new and interesting ways.

Part of our confusion, which too often results in that impotent anger, is the fault of our stories. No other region of the country has been fed so many myths about itself with such repetition. For every *Gone With the Wind*, I offer you twenty John Wayne morality plays. In the second half of the nineteenth century alone, nearly two thousand novels about Buffalo Bill were published. This incessant mythmaking is dangerous insofar as it gives us no understanding of our reality, past or present, and no useful clues about how to deal with our shortcomings. We're constantly being told we have no shortcomings. We are the children of God, with the good fortune to have found ourselves in God's country. And at Trinity, we became a kind of God ourselves.

The dominant narrative of the Western experience involved decent folk who'd fled a society of hopeless corruption, always somewhere to the east, and arrived in a New World Eden, intent on turning a slice of it into something suitable in the plans of a Christian God—a manicured homestead, prosperous and tame, oozing good sense and rectitude. Alas, there were a few corrupt souls in the neighborhood—heedless savages, horse thieves, men with pistols on their hips—and our good pilgrims had no choice but to confront the bad guys on their terms, often with the aid of a taciturn hero on horseback. Violence, regrettable but necessary, ensued. The good guys were wounded but lived; the bad guys died in the dirt, a blood sacrifice to civilization. Meadows bloomed with wildflowers, and the creeks flowed strong and clear. The taciturn stranger had the decency to saddle and ride by morning, having left nothing but a silver bullet as a calling card.

Just how pervasive do these myths remain? Consider that two of our most recent four presidents, elected with the votes of patriotic millions, shaped their public personae with all the tropes of the dominant Western icon, the cowboy. At its purest, the myth of the cowboy exalts action over thought, threat over mutual understanding, and righteous violence as the ultimate response to conflict. What these modern-day, world-historical avatars of an old and hollow myth never seem to understand—or perhaps understand quite cunningly, and cynically—is that the myth was just that, a myth. Cowboys in the Old West punched cows, not masked bandits with a taste for salty aphorism; they led a sweaty life of subsistence nomadism so ascetic in its material comforts that it serves as the exact antithesis of the American Dream. A further confusion of the mythos equated the cowboy with the gun-slinger, when in fact the latter was customarily a shiftless mercenary or a lawless maniac. In the real Old West, men who lived by a code of righteous violence did not live long. Often as not they died from an unchivalrous shot in the back.

My first encounter with the West was an instructive disappointment. I was twelve years old at the time, and my family drove from Minnesota, where we'd just lost our farm in a swamp of debt, to a resort in Vail, Colorado, for an Amway convention. For a week we played the uniquely American role of drive-by pioneers. My parents hoped that in the thin and bracing air of the Rockies we would decode at last the hidden formula to the American Dream—which, in the world of Amway, meant fusing a transformative love of Jesus Christ with the simple financial miracle of selling soap to family and friends, who would then be recruited to sell more soap to family and friends. I wasn't much interested in Amway at the time, except as a means to allow me a glimpse of the world I'd come to love in the novels of Louis L'Amour. Fifty of them sat on a shelf in our farmhouse, and I'd read them all twice in my impatience to get my hands on his other fifty. As we drove into the Front Range of the Rockies, I scanned the horizon for a familiar image from those books—a little fenced homestead, a cabin with smoke curling out the chimney, a horse tied to a wooden rail. Instead, we slid off the interstate, took our lunch at McDonald's, and later that evening checked into the fanciest hotel I'd ever seen. All that week I spent my mornings swimming in the heated pool, and afternoons I wandered through the hotel conference rooms, seeking abandoned buffet lines, where I might pluck a couple of cold chicken wings from the clutch of congealed grease. Instead of being shown a world of pioneer self-sufficiency, I was stuck in a tony resort town that catered first and foremost to the whims of the idle Eastern rich (and those, like my family, who envied them). Another manifestation of the Western experience, though one not explored in the novels of Louis L'Amour.

The West is as much an idea as a place, particularly if you're somewhere east of it. The itch to move westward, whether for exploration or settlement, for reasons spiritual or material, is even older than America itself. Modernity enhanced the means and speed of transport and made it a more crowded place once you were there; modernity, in the form of the U.S. military, also nearly extinguished the people who had lived there for millennia within the constraints of prevailing resources, a loss of cultural memory that haunts us to this day.

Cabeza de Vaca was the first man to write an account of his exploits in the American West. In 1527, he sailed from Spain on a mission to explore and colonize the North American mainland. He was second in command of a crew of three hundred, which triumphantly landed near Tampa Bay, Florida, in 1528. The triumph did not last. Shipwrecks, disease, starvation, and conflict with the natives eventually reduced the crew to four, including de Vaca, who for years endured slavery and then a career as a solitary, wandering trader among various tribes in what we now call Texas.

Upon reuniting with the other three survivors of the expedition, de Vaca set out for the Spanish settlements of Mexico. Along the last stretch of the journey he was greeted as a faith healer; the natives, apprised of his approach, would bring their sick to meet him. By de Vaca's account, a laying on of hands, an *Ave Maria*, and a sign of the cross were generally sufficient to cure all who submitted to his ministrations. Shaman, peacemaker, herald of the coming order, de Vaca was the first European superstar in the New World. His account of the journey, written for the king of Spain, remains to this day a strange and wondrous document, an underknown treasure of American literature, whose Anglophilic keepers tend to forget that the Spanish came before Jamestown.

In its day, de Vaca's story touched off a frenzy among rival explorers, who focused not on what de Vaca had seen but what he had purportedly missed. Somewhere beyond the edge of his route, which may have taken him as far west as southern New Mexico and Arizona, lay the Seven Cities of Cibola, a golden empire of untold riches—so the rumor went. Never mind that de Vaca's story recounted myriad forms of physical deprivation and emotional hardship, with nary a glimpse of wealth worth the effort required to plunder it. The bottom line: he hadn't gone far enough West. The real West lay just over the horizon.

De Vaca's literary effort thus set a pattern that continued well into modern times. Not only did it give birth in North America to the captivity narrative, a favorite of writers and readers for subsequent centuries, it established the first-person explorer as the ultimate literary persona of the West. Lewis and Clark's journals, John Wesley Powell's observations on water in the West, John Muir's rambles and ruminations through the California wilderness—all were anticipated by de Vaca's story. Yet de Vaca's authority, grounded in close observation and intense experience, was ignored or denigrated by those who wanted to believe in a different kind of West. It was the same for Powell and Muir: rain would follow the plow, never mind the West's aridity; wilderness didn't need political protection, not when we had it in such abundance.

The desire for a soothing fiction has always, in the West, been stronger than the collective stomach for reality. Zane Grey and Louis L'Amour didn't manufacture this desire out of thin air, like a couple of whiz-kid ad executives. They simply cashed in on a predilection for fantasy that predated them by centuries.

I don't mean to sound superior on the subject of Western dreaming. Few of us here are entirely immune to the old yearnings, least of all me. I've hitchhiked across the Northern Rockies in the dead of winter for the sheer Kerouacian thrill of it; I transferred to the University of Montana in Missoula after reading *A River Runs Through It*, hopeful I'd inhale, like secondhand smoke, a bit of the native genius that produced that modern masterpiece. As a boy I imagined a wilderness life of manly self-sufficiency, a log cabin built with my own two hands, a trusty mule in the corral. Perhaps I'd take up whittling and trade my stylish canes once a year in town for supplies to last the winter. Or maybe I'd prospect in the hills back of my homestead, pickax slung over my shoulder, unearthing the occasional gold nugget of a purity not seen since the Klondike. I'd teach myself to make venison jerky, and in the evenings, warmed with a nip of moonshine I cooked up in the still behind the corral, I'd play mournful songs on the mandolin, with self-accompaniment on harmonica, while the sun went down like a bloody yolk over the mesas to the west.

Instead, I left Montana straight out of college for a job at the *Wall Street Journal*. It helps to have a sense of humor about the divergent lines of life and dream.

And it doesn't hurt to have faith and flexibility. Four summers ago, the alchemy of luck, timing, and one key friend in a very high place bequeathed me the most romantic job still available in the United States of America: fire lookout with the U.S. Forest Service. The literary pedigree is impressive: Norman Maclean, Gary Snyder, Kerouac, and Abbey. So are the views, eighty miles in all directions from my particular perch, Mexico to the south, Arizona to the west. The nearest road is a six-mile walk. When the occasional day hikers stumble up, I act the part of living exhibition in the Museum of the American Frontier: bearded, steely-eyed, taciturn, binoculars slung jauntily over my shoulder (in place of the pickax). And they love it. It tickles them enormously that someone still gets to live like this.

I do not mention the helicopter that delivers propane every spring for my refrigerator and stove. Nor that I listen to NPR in the afternoons so as not to lose touch with events in the wider world. Nor even that the only wild turkey I've ever bagged—despite their abundance near my post—comes bottled at 101 proof. (Much more convenient than brewing it oneself.) I entertain myself in the evenings not with a mandolin—I have no musical talent whatsoever—but with novels of urban anomie and Major League baseball on the AM radio. I know to some of my fellow citizens, particularly those of an acquisitive nature, the deprivations of the job still sound almost primeval—no telephone, no electricity, no running water, not to mention no health insurance or 401(k)—but Grizzly Adams I am not.

Still, this is a finer perch than most from which to consider the ambiguities and ironies of life in the modern West. Beyond my window lies the first stretch of country in the world to be officially designated wilderness, thanks to the foresight of Aldo Leopold. The example of the Gila Wilderness led, forty years later, to the capstone of the American preservation movement, the Wilderness Act. Meanwhile, in the Gila, wolves and grizzlies were exterminated to make the land safe for cattle, and as a result the deer population exploded so radically a road was blazed through the heart of Leopold's wilderness for the convenience of motorized hunting.

There are those who argue a wilderness without cattle is utterly worthless as a natural resource; and there are those who believe a wilderness without large predators is a wilderness in name only. These two camps have been at war for decades. They can barely talk to each other. There remain bars where to wear a pair of sandals is to invite a beating. Recently, as the Fish and Wildlife Service has pursued a plan to reintroduce the Mexican gray wolf to the Gila, ranchers have cried betrayal, while environmentalists have tentatively cheered. Except the poor wolves keep straying beyond the man-made line on the map meant to encompass their habitat, and must be rounded up and let loose again within their proscribed turf. Nobody is thrilled about how the plan has played out—perhaps least of all the wolves—but such is the devil's bargain we struck when we invented the concept of "managed wilderness."

In fact, the peak on which I type this might aptly be renamed Devil's Bargain Vista. Forty miles to the east you'll find the man-made lake of Elephant Butte, a bulge in the Rio Grande made possible by an impressive dam. Last year, after an eight-year drought, the level of the lake dropped precipitously, and what had been prime beachfront property was suddenly a desert lot with a dim view of murky water. Powell's old warning still unheeded.

Forty miles to the southwest you'll see a mammoth, man-made hole in the ground called the Santa Rita mine, on which the town of Silver City has long depended for prosperity. The town of Santa Rita once did too, until it was swallowed by the pit. When the price of copper is up, the bars in Silver City fill with big spenders, and money washes through the whole community. When the price of copper falls, the layoffs hit and the big spenders suddenly survey an economy where the most stable job is as a greeter at the local Wal-Mart.

Rolling away in all directions is the Gila National Forest itself, the biggest devil's bargain of all, managed for "multiple uses," many of them in direct conflict with one another. The hunters, the fishermen, the ranchers, the bird-watchers, the backpackers, the motorized sightseers—none have ever entirely made peace with the presence of all the others, and maybe they never will. The only thing they agree on is that this chunk of country, 3.3 million acres, some of it as wild as you could yet hope to find in the continental U.S., is worth fighting over. Each group dreams of exactly how the Gila should be shaped to approach an ideal of health and happiness for man and creature, and each dreams with a righteous fervor that borders on the religious.

The dreaming never ends.

What follows are some of the contemporary writers who've done the most to help the West think about itself in a grown-up way. This is not to say they lack humor or playfulness. These folks are dreamers of a sort themselves. They have a fully developed sense of irony, but one that doesn't curdle their vision. Many of them have worked extensively in fiction. Some are poets, and others have even written for the movies. But all of them have enlarged our understanding of what it means to live and dream in the American West, and they've often done it most provocatively by telling true stories.

Some magnificent fiction has been written by Western writers in recent decades—by Cormac McCarthy, Marilynne Robinson, and Norman Maclean, among others—but it seems clear to me that the example of de Vaca, Lewis and Clark, Powell, and Muir still remains vital for contemporary Western writers, and I wanted to explore what those writers had been up to in the form of the personal essay over the last forty years. We like to be outdoors—that much is clear from our nonfiction. We like the look and sound and smell and feel of the world, and we have an abiding need to make sense of our place in it. Given that the personal narrative is intrinsic to the DNA of the region's writers, my aim is to highlight the stylistic and intellectual fecundity of the form. This book is not meant to be an imitation *Best American Essays*, confined by region. It is not meant to be a monument or a canonization. In a few instances, these pieces have been pried loose from larger works whose resonance can best be grasped in their original context. In other words, this anthology is a signpost that points the way to further reading for those interested in the culture of the new West.

A note on geography: you will find nothing here from or about California or points north on the Pacific Coast. Their urban density and surfeit of annual rainfall, I believe, make these places distinct from the arid, more sparsely populated mountain West. I've also mostly left out writers from the shortgrass plains east of the Rockies. The sight and smell and color of mountain landforms, even of foothills, marks for me the beginning of the West, despite what climatologists may tell us about average annual precipitation and the isohyetal line of twenty inches, beyond which conventional agriculture becomes dicey and, some argue, the West truly begins.

Such a boundary may reveal more about my own personal dream of the West, as it was influenced by John Ford movies, than it does about a real difference in outlook and style in writers working in various places west of the Mississippi. I seriously doubt it, but if scholars tell me my literary mapmaking is strongly subjective, I will have no choice but to plead guilty.

—P.C.
Gila National Forest
May 2005

NEW WEST
READER

TAKE MY SADDLE FROM THE WALL: A VALEDICTION

Larry McMurtry

I am quite as often split in my feelings about the McMurtrys as I am in my feelings about Texas. They pertain, of course, both to the Old Texas and the New, but I choose them here particularly because of another pertinence. All of them gave such religious allegiance as they had to give to that god whose principal myth was the myth of the Cowboy, the ground of whose divinity was the Range. They were many things, the McMurtrys, but to themselves they were cowboys first and last, and the rituals of that faith they strictly kept.

Now the god has departed, thousands of old cowboys in his train. Among them went most of the McMurtrys, and in a few more years the tail-end of the train will pass from sight. All of them lived to see the ideals of the faith degenerate, the rituals fall from use, the principal myth become corrupt. In my youth, when they were old men, I often heard them yearn aloud for the days when the rituals had all their power, when they themselves had enacted the pure, the original myth, and I know that they found it bitter to leave the land to which they were always faithful to the strange and godless heirs that they had bred. I write of them here not to pay them homage, for the kind of homage I could pay they would neither want nor understand; but as a gesture of recognition, a wave such as riders sometimes give one another as they start down opposite sides of a hill. The kind of recognition I would hope to achieve is a kind that kinsmen are so frequently only able to make in a time of parting.

I have never considered genealogy much of an aid to recognition, and thus have never pursued my lineage any distance at all. I remember my McMurtry grandparents only dimly, and in very slight detail, and only a few of the many stories I have heard about them strike me as generative. My grandfather, William Jefferson McMurtry, was the first man I ever saw who wore a mustache—a heavy grey one—and when I think of him I think first of that mustache. He died when I was four and only three stories about him have stuck in my mind.

The first was that he was a drunkard in his middle age, and that my grandmother, burdened with many children and unburdened by any conveniences, had found his drunkenness tiresome and threatened to leave him if he didn't stop drinking. The threat was undoubtedly made in earnest, and he took it so immediately to heart that he stopped drinking then and there, with a jug half-full of whiskey hanging in the saddle room of the barn. The jug of whiskey hung untouched for nineteen years, until the nail rusted out and it fell.

I remember, too, that it was said he could stand on the back porch of the ranch-house and give a dinner call that his boys could hear plainly in the lower field, two miles away. As a boy, riding across the lower field, I would sometimes look back at the speck of the ranch-house and imagine that I heard the old man's dinner call carrying across the flats.

My grandmother's name was Louisa Francis. By the time I was old enough to turn outward, she had turned inward and was deaf, chair-bound, and dying. She lived until I was nine, but I cannot recall that we ever communicated. She was a small woman, wizened by hardship, and I thought her very stern. One day when I was in my teens I went down the crude stone steps to the spring that had been for years the family's only source of water, and it occurred to me that carrying water up those steps year after year would make a lady stern. The children all spoke of William Jefferson as if they had liked him and got on with him well enough, but they spoke of Louisa Francis as one speaks of the Power. I have since thought that an element in her sternness might have been a grim, old-lady recognition that the ideal of the family was in the end a bitter joke; for she had struggled and kept one together, and now, after all, they had grown and gone and left her, and in that hard country what was there to do but rock to death?

William Jefferson, however, sustained himself well to the end, mostly, I judge, on inquisitiveness. Since eleven of the twelve children were gone, my father bore the brunt of this inquisitiveness, and one can imagine that it became oppressive at times. When my father returned to the ranch late at night from a trip or a dance the old man would invariably hear his car cross the rattly cattleguard and would hasten out in the darkness to get the news, as it were. Generally the two would meet halfway between the barn and the backyard gate, William Jefferson fresh with queries and midnight speculations on the weather or this or that, my father—mindful that the morning chores were just over the hill—anxious to get to bed. By the time Grandfather died the habit had grown so strong that three years passed before my father could walk at night from the barn to the backyard gate without encountering the ghost of William Jefferson somewhere near the chicken house.

Pioneers didn't hasten to West Texas like they hastened to the southern and eastern parts of the state. At first glance, the region seemed neither safe nor desirable; indeed, it wasn't safe, and it took the developing cattle industry to render it desirable. My grandparents arrived in 1877 and prudently paused for ten years in Denton County, some sixty miles west of Dallas and not quite on the lip of the plains. The fearsome Comanche had been but recently subdued—in fact, it was still too early to tell whether they *were* subdued. The last battle of Adobe Walls was fought in the Panhandle in 1874, and Quanah Parker surrendered himself and his warriors in 1875. The very next year, sensing a power vacuum, Charles Goodnight drove his herds into the Palo Duro; Satanta, the last great war chief of the Kiowa, killed himself in prison in 1878. Remnants of the two nations trickled into the reservation for the next few years; there were occasional minor hostilities on the South Plains as late as 1879. The Northern Cheyenne broke out in 1878—who could be sure the Comanches wouldn't follow their example? To those brought up on tales of Comanche terror the psychological barrier did not immediately fall. The Comanche never committed themselves readily to the reservation concept, and for a time there remained the chance that one might awaken in the night in that lonely country to find oneself and one's family being butchered by a few pitiless, reactionary warriors bent on a minor hostility.

At any rate, in the eighties William Jefferson and Louisa Francis and their first six children moved a hundred miles farther west, to Archer County, where, for three dollars an acre, they purchased a half-section of land. They settled near a good seeping spring, one of the favorite watering places on a military road that then ran from Fort Belknap to Buffalo Springs. The forts that the road connected soon fell from use, but cattle drivers continued to use the trail and the spring for many years. The young McMurtry boys had only to step out their door to see their hero figures riding past.

Indeed, from the pictures I have seen of the original house, they could have ignored the door altogether and squeezed through one of the walls. Life in such a house, in such a country, must surely have presented formidable difficulties, and the boys (there were eventually nine, as against three girls) quite sensibly left home as soon as they had mastered their directions.

The median age for leave-taking seems to have been seventeen, and the fact that the surrounding country was rapidly filling up with farmers merely served as an added incentive to departure. The cowboy and the farmer are genuinely inimical types: they have seldom mixed easily. To the McMurtrys, the plow and the cotton-patch symbolized not only tasks they loathed but an orientation toward the earth and, by extension, a quality of soul which most of them not-so-covertly despised. A "one-gallus farmer" ranked very low in their esteem, and

there were even McMurtrys who would champion the company of Negroes and Mexicans over the company of farmers—
particularly if the farmers happened to be German. The land
just to the north of the McMurtry holdings was settled by an
industrious colony of German dairymen, and the Dutchmen
(as they were called) were thought to be a ridiculous and
unsightly thorn in the fair flesh of the range.

In later years two or three of the McMurtry brothers increased
their fortunes through farming, but this was a fact one seldom
heard bruited about. Indeed, I heard no discussion of the
matter until fairly recently, when one of the farms sold for an
even million dollars, a figure capable of removing the blight
from almost any scutcheon.

The cowboy's contempt of the farmer was not unmixed with
pity. The farmer walked in the dust all his life, a hard and
ignominious fate. Cowboys could perform terrible labors
and endure bone-grinding hardships and yet consider themselves the chosen of the earth; and the grace that redeemed
it all in their own estimation was the fact that they had gone
a-horseback. They were riders, first and last. I have known
cowboys broken in body and twisted in spirit, bruised by
debt, failure, loneliness, disease and most of the other afflic-
tions of man, but I have seldom known one who did not consider himself phenomenally blessed to have been a cowboy,
or one who could not cancel half the miseries of existence by
dwelling on the horses he had ridden, the comrades he had
ridden them with, and the manly times he had had. If the
cowboy is a tragic figure, he is certainly one who will not
accept the tragic view. Instead, he helps his delineators wring

pathos out of tragedy by ameliorating his own loss into the heroic myth of the horseman.

To be a cowboy meant, first of all, to be a horseman. The writer J. Frank Dobie was quite right when he pointed out that the seat of the cowboy's manhood is the saddle. I imagine, too, that he understood the consequences of that fact for most cowboys and their women, but if so he was too kindly a man to spell out the consequences in his books. I would not wish to make the point crudely, but I do find it possible to doubt that I have ever known a cowboy who liked women as well as he liked horses, and I know that I have never known a cowboy who was as comfortable in the company of women as he was in the company of his fellow cowboys.

I have pointed out elsewhere that I did not believe this was the result of repressed homosexuality, but of a commitment to a heroic concept of life that simply takes little account of women. Certainly the myth of the cowboy is a very efficacious myth, one based first of all upon a deep response to nature. Riding out at sunup with a group of cowboys, I have often felt the power of that myth myself. The horses pick their way delicately through the dewy country, the brightness of sunrise has not yet fallen from the air, the sky is blue and all-covering, and the cowboys are full of jokes and morning ribaldries. It is a fine action, compelling in itself and suggestive beyond itself of other centuries and other horsemen who have ridden the earth.

Unfortunately, the social structure of which that action is a part began to collapse almost a hundred years ago, and the day of the cowboy is now well into its evening. Commitment to the myth today carries with it a terrible emotional price—very often the cowboy becomes a victim of his own ritual. His women, too, are victims, though for the most part acquiescent victims. They usually buy the myth of cowboying and the ideal of manhood it involves, even though both exclude them. A few even buy it to the point of attempting to assimilate the all-valuable masculine qualities to themselves, producing that awful phenomenon, the cowgirl.

If, as I suggested earlier, the cowboy is a tragic figure, one element of the tragedy is that he is committed to an orientation that includes but does not recognize the female, which produces, in day-to-day life, an extraordinary range of frustrations. Curiously, the form the cowboy's recognition does take is literary: he handles women through a romantic convention. The view is often proffered by worshippers of the cowboy that he is a realist of the first order, but that view is an extravagant and imperceptive fiction. Cowboys are romantics, extreme romantics, and ninety-nine out of a hundred of them are sentimental to the core. They are oriented toward the past and face the present only under duress, and then with extreme reluctance.

People who think cowboys are realists generally think so because the cowboy's speech is salty and apparently straightforward, replete with the wisdom of natural men. What that generally means is that cowboy talk sounds shrewd and perceptive, and so it does. In fact, however, both the effect and the intention of much cowboy talk is literary: cowboys are aphorists. Whenever possible, they turn their observations into aphorisms. Some are brilliant aphorists, scarcely inferior to Wilde or La Rochefoucauld; one is proud to steal from them. I plucked a nice one several years ago, to wit: "A woman's love is like the morning dew: it's just as apt to fall on a horseturd as it is on a rose." In such a remark the phrasing is worth more than the perception, and I think the same might be said for the realism of most cowboys. It is a realism in tone only: its insights are either wildly romantic, mock-cynical, or solemnly sentimental. The average cowboy is an excellent judge of horseflesh, only a fair judge of men, and a terrible judge of women, particularly "good women." Teddy Blue stated it succinctly forty years ago:

> *I'd been traveling and moving around all the time and I can't say I ever went out of my way to seek the company of respectable ladies. We (cowboys) didn't consider we were fit to associate with them on account of the company we kept. We didn't know how to talk to them anyhow. That was what I meant by saying the cowpunchers was afraid of a decent woman. We were so damned scared that we'd do or say something wrong . . .*

That was written of the nineteenth century cowboy, but it would hold good for most of their descendants, right down to now. Most of them marry, and love their wives sincerely, but since their sociology idealizes women and their mythology excludes her, the impasse which results is often little short of tragic. Now, as then, the cowboy escapes to the horse, the range, the work, and the company of comrades, most of whom are in the same unacknowledged fix.

Once more I might repeat what cannot be stressed too often: that the master symbol for handling the cowboy is the

---

* *We Pointed Them North*, p. 188

symbol of the horseman.* The gunman had his place in the mythology of the West, but the cowboy did not realize himself with a gun. Neither did he realize himself with a penis, nor with a bankroll. Movies fault the myth when they dramatize gunfighting, rather than horsemanship, as the dominant skill. The cowboy realized himself on a horse, and a man might be broke, impotent, and a poor shot and still hold up his head if he could ride.

Holding up the head had its importance too, for with horsemanship went pride, and with that, stoicism. The cowboy, like Mithridates, survived by preparing for ill and not for good— after all, it sometimes took only a prairie-dog hole to bring a man down. Where emotion was concerned, the cowboy's ethic was Roman: emotion, but always emotion within measure. A uncle of mine put it as nicely as one could want. This one was no McMurtry, but an uncle-by-marriage named Jeff Dobbs. He had been a cowboy and a Texas Ranger, and when he had had enough of the great world he retired to the backwoods of Oklahoma to farm peanuts and meditate on the Gospels. He was a self-styled Primitive Baptist, which meant that he had a theology all his own, and he had honed his scriptural knife to a fine edge in some forty years of nightly arguments with his wife, my Aunt Minta. Neither of them ever yielded a point, and

---

* *Singing Cowboy,* ed. Margaret Larkin, Oak Publications, New York, 1963, p. 60. See in this regard the well-known song "My Love Is a Rider," a song said to have been composed by Belle Starr: *He made me some presents among them a ring. The return that I made him was a far better thing. 'Twas a young maiden's heart I would have you all know, He won it by riding his bucking bronco. Now listen young maidens where e're you reside, Don't list to the cowboy who swings the rawhide. He'll court you and pet you and leave you and go Up the trail in the spring on his bucking bronco.*

when my aunt was killed I don't think they even agreed on the book of Zechariah.

One morning not unlike any other, Aunt Minta went out in her car, was hit by a truck, and killed instantly. At this time I was in graduate school in Houston, doctoral longings in me, and I wrote Uncle Jeff to offer condolence. His reply is *echt-cowboy:*

Will answer your welcome letter.

Was glad to heare from you again, well it has rained a-plenty here the last week, the grass is good and everything is lovely . . .

Would like for you to visit me, we could talk the things over that we are interested in. What does PhD stand for? to me its post-hole digger, guess that would be about what it would stand for with all the other old Texas cowpokes . . .

I never could understand why a man wanted to spend all his life going to school, ide get to thinking about the Rancho Grandy, and get rambling on my mind, freedom to quote O. M. Roberts:

To what avail the plow or sail or land.

Or life if freedom fail . . .

going to school was always like being in jail to me, life is too short, sweet and uncertain to spend it in jail.

Well, Larry, am still having trouble with my sore eye, I have had it five months now, it looks like pinkeye to me, might have took it from the pink-eyed cow.

Yes it was an awful tragidy to have Mint crushed in the smashup, my car was a total loss too.

Things like that will just hoppen though. It is lonesome dreary out here in the backwoods by myself.

Don't ever join the army, if you do you will have to stay in for four

years, that would be a long time to stay in the danged army, this con-
scription is not according to the constitution of the U.S. its involuntary
servitude which is slavery . . .

Well I have just had a couple of Jehovah's witnesses visit me but I
soon got them told, I think they are as crazy as a betsie bug and I don't
like to be bothered with them, with this sore eye I am in a bad humour
most of the time anyway, yours truly

Jeff Dobbs

I doubt that Seneca himself could have balanced the car and the wife that simply, and this about one week after she was gone.

But mention of horses and horsemanship brings me back to the McMurtrys, all of whom were devoted to the horse. Indeed, so complete was their devotion that some of them were scarcely competent to move except on horseback. They walk reluctantly and with difficulty, and clearly do not care to be dependent upon their own legs for locomotion. That a person might walk for pleasure is a notion so foreign to them that they can only acquaint it with lunacy or a bad upbringing.

Much as their walking leaves to be desired, it is infinitely to be preferred to their driving. A few of them developed a driver's psychology and a driver's skills, but most of them remained unrepentent horsemen to the end; and an unrepentent horseman at the wheel of a Cadillac is not the sort of person with whom one cares to share a road. That their names are not writ large in the annals of the Highway Patrol is only due to the fact that they lived amid the lightly habited wastes of West Texas and were thus allowed a wider margin of error than most mortals get.

As horsemen their talents varied, but only one or two were without flair. When it came to riding broncs, Jim, the second eldest, was apparently supreme. If he ever saw a horse he was afraid of no one ever knew about it, and in early Archer County his only rival as a bronc-rider was a legendary cowpuncher named Nigger Bones Hook. If the latter's skills were as remarkable as his name he must indeed have been a rider to contend with, but there are those who consider Uncle Jim his equal. Unfortunately, Uncle Jim overmatched himself early in his life and as a consequence was reduced to riding wheelchairs for some forty years. When he was fifteen, William Jefferson let him ride a strong, wild bronc that had been running loose for some years; Uncle Jim stayed on him, but he was not experienced enough to ride him safely, and before the ride was over his head was popping uncontrollably. When the horse exhausted himself neither it nor Uncle Jim were able to bring their heads back to a normal position. William Jefferson took both hands and set his son's head straight, but Uncle Jim's neck was broken and he left the field that day with a pinched nerve which would eventually result in a crippling arthritis. Despite the kickback from that one early ride he went on to acquire a large ranch, a wife and family, a couple of banks and a commensurate fortune. The horse that crippled him never raised its head again and died within two days.

When Jim reached the Panhandle in 1900 he was far from done as a rider; indeed, his most celebrated feat was recorded shortly thereafter. He hired on with the ROs, a ranch owned by an extraordinary and very eccentric Englishman named Alfred Rowe, who was later to go down on the *Titanic.* Uncle Jim's wages were fifteen dollars a month. One day Rowe bought seventeen

horses from the army, all incorrigibles that had been con-
demned as too wild to be ridden. Rowe offered Uncle Jim a
dollar a head to ride them, and he rode them all that same afternoon, after which, convinced that he had made his fortune, he
soon went into business for himself.

Roy McMurtry was apparently the only one of the nine boys
to rival Jim's skill with a bucking horse, but few of the others
were loath to try their hand (or their seat) with a bronc. It is quite
clear that riding was the physical skill most crucially connected
with the entrance into manhood. In the spring of 1910 Johnny
McMurtry, then still in his teens, borrowed a horse and made
his way to the Panhandle, looking for a job as a cowboy. He
immediately found one with his brothers Charley and Jim, who
were then partners in an operation which at times involved as
many as 4,000 cattle. One would have thought that with that
many cattle to hassle, a young and extraordinarily willing
brother would have been an entirely welcome addition to the
staff; but McMurtrys, like most cattlemen, take willingness for
granted and judge solely on performance. On almost his first
drive Johnny came near to achieving permanent disgrace
through a lapse in horsemanship. Some eight hundred nervous
yearlings were involved; the older brothers were in the process
of calming them after several rather hectic stampedes, one of
which had flattened a six-wire fence. The cattle were almost
quiet when the lapse occurred; the account I quote is from an
unpublished memoir left me by Uncle Johnny:

> I rode up the bank of Sadler Creek on an old silly horse, he got to pitching
> and pitched under a cottonwood tree and dragged me off, then into the
> herd he went and stampeded them again, Jim didn't see it so thought the

*horse had pitched me off, he caught him and brought him back to me, he
was as mad as a gray lobo wolf with hydrophobia, he told me that if I
couldn't ride that horse I had better go back to Archer County and catch
rabbits for a living, that was about the only horse I had that I could really
ride pitching and I was proud of it and was down right insulted for Jim
to think I couldn't ride him . . .*

The distinction between being drug off and being pitched off
might seem obscure to many, but not to a young man whose
ego-needs were closely bound up with horsemanship.

At any rate, all the McMurtrys could ride well enough to get
themselves out of Archer County at an early age. Invariably,
the direction they rode was northwest, toward the open and
still comparatively empty plains of the Panhandle. Specifically
they rode to the town of Clarendon, near the Palo Duro
canyon, a town which in those days serviced and supplied most
of the great Panhandle ranches, among them the JAs and the
ROs. For better or worse, Clarendon was their Paris. Charlie
arrived in '96, Bob in '99, Jim in 1900, Ed in 1902, Roy in 1920,
Lawrence, Grace and May at dates now unremembered, Jo and
Jeff in 1916, and Margaret in 1919. Even the old folks went to
Clarendon for a time (1919–1925), but doubtless found it impossible to live peacefully with so many of their children about,
and soon retreated to the balmier latitudes of Archer County,
my father with them.

That that bare and windy little town on the plains should
have been so much to my family I find a bit sad, but not inexplicable. Youth is youth and a heyday a heyday, wherever one
spends it, and it would appear that at the turn of the century

Clarendon was to cowboys what Paris was soon to be for writers. It was the center of the action. If one merely wanted to cowboy, there were the great ranches; and if one was more ambitious the plains was the one place where land in quantity could still be had cheap.

In time the McMurtrys got—and no doubt earned—their share of that land. Most of them started as twenty-dollar-a-month cowboys and quit when they were far enough ahead to buy some land of their own. Seven of the boys and two of the girls lived out their lives within a hundred miles of Clarendon, and in time the nine boys between them owned almost a hundred and fifty thousand acres of Texas land and grazed on it many many thousand head of cattle.

I do not intend here to attempt to describe the McMurtrys one by one. In truth, I didn't know them all that well, not as individuals, and individual character sketches would be neither very interesting nor very authoritative. Most of them were old men when I was very young, and I almost never saw them singly or for any length of time. When I saw them I saw them as a family, grouped with their wives and multitudinous progeny at the family reunions which were held more or less annually from the late forties until the middle sixties. Most of the reunions were held in Clarendon, or, to be more accurate, were held at the Clarendon Country Club, which fact alone is indicative enough of the direction the family had moved.

The Country Club sits some fifteen miles to the northwest of Clarendon, on a ridge not far from the Salt Fork of the Red. Fifteen miles is a short trot in that country, and the wives of the local elite would think nothing of driving that far for some minor social function, though as I remember the clubhouse about the only social functions to which it could be adapted were dancing and drinking. Once long ago some cousins and I discovered a couple of rusty slot-machines in a broom closet, indicating that that particular form of gambling had, in those regions at least, passed out of vogue. There was a swimming pool (the one essential of all country clubs), a grove of trees for shade, a windmill for water, and a pond, I suppose, for decor. Of the sights and sounds which one associates with big-city country clubs in Texas—the polished foliage, the liveried staff, the well-parked rows of Mercedes and Lincolns, the tinkle of ice and the ploop of badly hit tennis balls—there was nothing.

Thus, when I saw the McMurtrys, I saw them on the ground that had always held them, the great ring of the plains, with the deep sky and the brown ridges and the restless grass being shaken by the wind as it passed on its long journey from the Rockies south. Teddy Blue mayhap and Old Man Goodnight surely had left their horsetracks on that ridge; there one might have witnessed the coming and going of the god. One by one the old men arrived, in heavy cars with predominantly heavy wives, followed now and then by cautious offspring in Chevrolets. The day was given over to feasting and anecdotage, in almost equal division. The barbecuing was entrusted to a Negro and a County Agent and generally consisted of about a hundred chickens (for the women and youngsters) and a side of beef (for the men, who, being cattlemen, scorned all other meat if beef were available). Vegetables were irrelevant, but there was usually a washpot full of beans, and of course, twenty or thirty cakes brought by the twenty or thirty wives. Later, should the season be opportune, a pickup full of watermelons might arrive, easily sufficient to bloat such children as were not already bloated on soda pop.

Gourmandry was encouraged, indeed, almost demanded, and I recall one occasion when the son of someone's hired hand put all the young McMurtrys to shame by consuming twenty-six Dr. Peppers in the course of a single day.

In the forenoon the family normally split itself into three groups, the division following the traditional dividing line of Western gatherings: men, women, and children, or each to his own kind. After lunch everyone was too stuffed to move and mingled freely if somewhat heavily. My hundred or so cousins and I found generally that we could do without one another with no ill effects, and in the afternoons I picked my way gingerly among the bulging uncles and aunts, eavesdropping on such conversations as interested me. With most of my uncles I had no rapport at all. To their practiced eye it must have been evident from the first that I was not going to turn out to be a cattleman. For one thing, I wasn't particularly mean, and in the West the mischief quotient is still a popular standard for measuring the appearance of approvable masculine qualities in a youngster. Any boy worth his salt was expected to be a nuisance, if not to the adults at least to the weaker members of his own age group. I was a weaker member myself; indeed, though I don't remember it, I believe at some early and very primitive reunion I was cast into a hog wallow or pelted with ordure or something; though the atrocity may be apocryphal it would not have been out of keeping with the spirit of such occasions. Mean kids meant strength in time of need, and how could the elders be sure that a bookish and suspiciously observant youngster like myself might not in time disgrace the line? I knew from an early age that I could never meet their standard, and since in those days theirs was the only standard I knew existed

I was the more defensive around them. Indeed, scared. One was mild and two were gentle: the rest, with one exception, were neither harder nor softer than saddle leather. The one exception, was, in my estimation, harder than your average saddle. Tolerance was a quality I think no McMurtry ever understood, much less appreciated, and though one or two of them came to understand mercy it was never the family's long suit.

Strength was quite obviously the family's long suit: strength of body, strength of will, and, over it all, strength of character. One of my difficulties with them was that their strength of character was totally and inflexibly committed to a system of values that I found not wholly admirable. The talk beneath the reunion tent was the talk of men whose wills had begun to resent their weakening bodies. They had all, like Hector, been tamers of horses once—adventure and physical hardship had been the very ground of their manhood. The talk was often of the hardships of their youth, hardships that time with its strange craft had turned into golden memories. As I listened and grew older I became, each year, more sharply aware of the irony of the setting: that those men, who in their youth had ridden these same plains and faced their winds and dangers, should in their age buy so puny a symbol as the Clarendon Country Club, the exultantly unbourgeois and undomestic ideal of the Cowboy expiring in the shade of that most bourgeois and most domestic institution. To give them credit, though, I doubt that any of them were happy about it.

Of all the hardship stories I heard, the one which remains most resonant in my mind is the story of the molasses barrel. It was, for all witnesses, a traumatic event. Late one fall, not long after the turn of the century, William Jefferson had gone to the small town of Archer City to purchase the winter's provisions. Archer City was eighteen miles from the ranch, a tedious trip by wagon. He returned late in the afternoon, and among the supplies he brought back was an eighty-pound barrel of good sorghum molasses, in those days the nearest thing to sugar that could be procured. Such sweetening as the family would have for the whole winter was in the barrel, and all gathered around to watch it being unloaded. Two of the boys rolled the barrel to the back of the wagon and two more reached to lift it down, but in the exchange of responsibilities someone failed to secure a hold and the barrel fell to the ground and burst. Eighty pounds of sweetness quivered, spread out, and began to seep unrecoverably into the earth. Grace, the oldest girl, unable to accept the loss, held her breath and made three desperate circles of the house before anyone could recover himself sufficiently to catch her and pound her on the back. Indeed, the story was usually told as a story on Grace, for most of them had suppressed the calamity so effectively that they could not remember how anyone else had responded. They could speak with less emotion of death and dismemberment than of that moment when they stood and watched the winter's sweetness soak into the chicken yard.*

---

*It now appears that the uncle who first told me this sad story had added a few flowers of his own. What "really happened," it seems, is that the barrel of molasses had a wooden spigot, and was unloaded safely and laid across two support beams so that when the spigot was opened the molasses would drain into the molasses pitcher. Unfortunately, a sow came along one day, walked under the barrel, and rooted the spigot out. The molasses drained from the barrel and ran down a footpath all the way to the lots. The catastrophe was thus discovered and the children lined up beside the path to weep. As with many family stories, I think I prefer the fiction to the truth.

• • •

Uncle Johnny, the seventh boy, was born in 1891. He was my favorite uncle and in many ways the family's darling, and I should like to write of him in some detail. Of them all, he fought the suburb most successfully, and hewed closest to the nineteenth century ideal of the cowboy. He was the last to be domesticated, if indeed he ever was domesticated, and at one point he almost abandoned the struggle to be a rancher in order to remain a free cowboy. Indeed, according to the memoir he left me, the desire to be a cowboy was his first conscious desire:

> *Dad had built two log barns and we boys would climb on top of those barns and watch the herds go by, never since then have I wanted to be anything except a cowboy . . .*

By the time he was twelve he could chop cotton well enough to consider himself financially independent, and after only a month or two of labor was able to buy a secondhand saddle. By that time he had completed such textbooks as the little schoolhouse on Idiot Ridge possessed, and he was not again impeded by education until 1909, when Louisa Francis persuaded him to enroll in a business college in McKinney. The school was teeming with chiggers, but Uncle Johnny applied himself grimly and in only four months acquired a diploma stating that he was a Bachelor of Accounts. He was the only McMurtry to achieve such eminence, and was also, ironically, the only McMurtry ever to go formally broke.

As soon as his course was finished he had to begin to think about paying for it. He went home, borrowed a horse, and headed for the Panhandle, equipped with his original secondhand saddle and seven dollars in cash. He meant to hire on with the JAs, but stopped by first to visit Charley and Jim at their ranch on the Salt Fork of the Red. They were shrewd men and doubtless knew a good thing when they saw it riding up. They hired him immediately at twenty dollars a month and keep, which meant, apparently, that he was allowed to eat whatever small vermin he could catch. Not that Uncle Johnny cared: at this time his eagerness for the cowboy life was little short of mystical. He was willing to forgo eating, if necessary, and fortunately had never much liked to sleep either. Fortunately, since to his brothers 3 A.M. was traditionally the end of the night.

He worked for Charley and Jim three years, much of that time in a bachelor camp on the baldies, as the high plains were then called. His possessions consisted of a saddle, shirt, pants, and chaps, two quilts, a six-shooter, and a horse called Sugar-in-the-Gourd. In coolish weather his brothers generously provided him with a tepee, a small stove, and a bucket of sourdough. He spent his wages on cattle—there being nothing else in his vicinity to spend them on—and when his brothers phased him out in 1913 he had paid off the business college and was fifteen hundred dollars to the good.

The yen to work for a really big ranch was still strong in him, so he drifted southwest to the Matadors and hired on with them two days before the wagons pulled out for the spring roundup in 1913. The Matador, like the ROs, was English-owned; they then ran 50,000 head of cattle on slightly over a half-million acres of land. By August Uncle Johnny had helped in the rounding up and shipping of some 19,000 steers, and by early December had assisted in the branding of 11,000 calves.

From the minute he saw the Matador wagons he seemed to

realize that he had found his blood's country, and he often said that if he could choose three years to live over they would be the years he had spent with the Matadors. Much of the memoir is devoted to those years, and to the men he worked with: Weary Willie Drace, his wagon-boss, Rang Thornton, Pelada Vivian, and the Pitchfork Kid, names which mean nothing now. In speaking of their departed comrades, men once renowned but soon to be forgotten, old cowboys invariably draw upon the same few images, all of them images taken from their work. Thus, here is Teddy Blue, speaking of the men who had gone with him in the seventies up the long trail to the Yellowstone:

> *Only a few of us are left now, and they are scattered from Texas to Canada. The rest have left the wagon and gone ahead across the big divide, looking for a new range. I hope they find good water and plenty of grass. But wherever they are is where I want to go.* *

And here, a generation later, is Uncle Johnny, speaking of his buddy the Pitchfork Kid:

> *His equal will never be seen on earth again and if he is camping the wagon and catching beeves in the great perhaps and I am fortunate enough to get there I won't be foolish enough to try and run ahead of him and catch the beef, I know it can't be done . . .*

By October of 1915 he had increased his savings to $2500 and he decided to take the leap from cowboying to ranching, clearly one of the harder decisions he ever made:

---

* *We Pointed Them North*, p. 230.

I left the wagon at the Turtle Hole, I have never before or since hated to do anything as bad as I hated to leave that wagon and to this day when I go down through there I am filled with nostalgia, just looking at the old red hill in Croton, the breaks on the Tongue River and the Roaring Springs, if I had known that leaving was going to be that hard I would have stayed and worn myself out right there . . .

Where he went was a ranch in the sandy country south of Muleshoe, near the New Mexico line, and he stayed there the rest of his life. He struggled for more than ten years to keep the first ranch he bought, lost it and went stone broke in 1930, struggled back, and died owning several thousand acres, several hundred cows, and a Cadillac.

I saw Uncle Johnny's ranch for the first time when I was in my early teens and went there for a reunion. Three times in all he managed to capture the reunion for Muleshoe, and for the children of the family those were high occasions, quite different in quality from anything Clarendon offered. To begin with, Uncle Johnny lived far out in the country—and such country. I thought the first time I saw it that only a man who considered himself forsaken of God would live in such country, and nothing I have found out since has caused me to alter that view. The more I saw of it the more I knew that he had been well-punished for casting over the Edenic simplicity of the Matador wagons.

Then too, the house in which he lived, or, at least, in which he might have lived, was a bit out of the ordinary. It was a towering three-story edifice, reminiscent of the house in *Giant*. Every grain of paint had long since been abraded away by the blowing sand. The house had been built by an extremely eccentric New York architect, who must also have considered himself forsaken of God. Indeed, in the long run he probably was, for solitude and his wife's chirpings eventually drove him mad and he came in one morning from chopping wood, called her into the basement, and killed her on the spot with the flat of his axe, or so legend had it. No one had ever bothered to remove the basement carpet, and the spot, or splotch, remained. Nothing could have had a more Dostoevskian impact on such simple Texas kids as we were than that large irregular stain on the basement rug. A good part of every Muleshoe reunion was given over to staring at it, while we mentally or in whispers tried to reconstruct the crime.

When we grew tired of staring at the spot we usually turned our attentions to the player piano. The architect had apparently been as nostalgic for Gotham as Uncle Johnny was for the Matador wagons, since the piano was equipped with duplicate rolls of "The Sidewalks of New York" and a number of other ditties that must have evoked really choking memories amid those wastes. There were also a few spiritual items such as "The Old Rugged Cross," meant, no doubt, for his wife's Bible group. Over the years Uncle Johnny had developed a keen distaste for the piano, or perhaps for the selection of rolls, and he was always dashing in and attempting to lock it, an endeavour in which he was somehow never successful.

He himself appeared not to care for the house, and slept in the little bunk-house. The only sign that he ever inhabited the big house was that the bed in the master bedroom had eleven quilts on it, compensation, no doubt, for having wintered on the baldies with one blanket, one soogan and a wagon sheet. He generally had in his employ a decrepit cook of sorts (male) and one or two desperately inept cowboys, usually Mexican. These slept in the bunkhouse too, or did if they were allowed the leisure to sleep. All the McMurtrys were near-fanatic workers, but Uncle Johnny was by all accounts the most relentless in this regard. His brothers often said, with a certain admiration, that Johnny never had learned how much a horse or a human being could stand. Such humans as worked for him stood as much as he could stand, or else left; and he had to an extraordinary degree that kind of wiry endurance which is fairly common in the cow country. His health broke when he was thirty-three and he was partially crippled the rest of his life, but it hardly seems to have slowed him down. He could not be kept in bed more than five hours a night, and even with one leg virtually useless sometimes branded as many as eight hundred cattle in one day; once, indeed, he vaccinated 730 off the end of a calf-dragger's rope in one afternoon.

In the last ten years of his life he sustained an almost incredible sequence of injuries, one following on another so rapidly that he could scarcely get from one hospital to the next without something nearly fatal happening to him. His arthritis was complicated by the fact that his right leg had been broken numerous times. Horses were always falling with him and on him, or throwing him into trees, or kicking him across corrals. The McMurtrys seemed to consider that these minor injuries were no more than he deserved, for being too tight to buy good horses instead of young half-broken broncs. He appreciated good horses, of course, but when he had something to do would get on any horse that stood to hand. One leg was broken almost a dozen times in such manner, and near the end he was so stiff that he had his cowboys wire him on his horses with baling wire, a lunatic thing to do considering the roughness of the country and the temperament of most of the horses he rode.

In the late fifties he got cancer of the throat and had his entire larynx removed. For awhile he spoke with an electric voice-box, a device which rendered his dry, wry wit even dryer and wryer. He soon grew dissatisfied with that, however, and learned to speak with an esophageal voice; it left him clear but barely audible and greatly reduced his effectiveness as a raconteur. No sooner was he home from the hospital after his throat operation than he got out to shut a gate and let his own pickup run over him, crushing one hip and leg horribly. He managed to dig himself out and crawl back to his ranch, and was immediately flown back to the same hospital.

In time he recovered and went home to Muleshoe and got married, this in his sixty-fifth year. The day after his wedding, so I am told, he and Aunt Ida, his bride, spent some eleven hours horseback, sorting out a herd of cattle he had bought in Louisiana. Two years later, while on their way to Lubbock, a car ran into them on the highway and broke them both up like eggshells. Aunt Ida got a broken back and knee, Uncle Johnny two broken knees and a bad rebreakage of his crippled leg. In time they both recovered, but Uncle Johnny was scarcely home before he allowed a whole feed-house full of hundred-pound sacks of cattle feed to fall on top of him, breaking his leg yet again.

In the days of the Muleshoe reunions, most of these disasters were still in the future, and he was very much his vigorous self. He owned a Cadillac at this time, but did almost all of his driving in an army surplus jeep of ancient vintage, so ancient, in fact, that it lacked both roof and seats. The small matter of the seat Uncle Johnny took care of by turning a syrup-bucket upside down in the floorboards and balancing a piece of two-by-four across it. This worked well enough for day-to-day driving, but once when he set out to haul a trailerful of pigs to Lubbock the arrangement proved imperfect. The pigs turned over the trailer, the wrench threw Uncle Johnny off the syrup bucket, and jeep, trailer, uncle and swine ended up in a heap in the bar-ditch. He was not much hurt in the accident but was very out of temper before he managed, afoot and with only one usable leg, to get the seven wild pigs rounded up again.

Few of the McMurtrys were devoid of temper and he was not one of those who lacked it, yet I think no child ever sensed his temper. Children found him extraordinarily winning, the perfect uncle and instant confidant. He brought a quality to uncleship that only certain childless men can bring—adult, and yet not domestic. I had always supposed him a truly gentle man and was very shocked, one night, to hear him say that the way to handle Mexicans was to kick loose a few of their ribs every now and then. I had only to reflect on that awhile to realize that I had never known a cowboy who was also a truly gentle man. The cowboy's working life is spent in one sort of violent activity or other; an ability to absorb violence and hardship is part of the proving of any cowboy, and it is only to be expected that the violence will extend itself occasionally from animals to humans, and particularly to those humans that class would have one regard as animals.

One of the more dramatic manifestations of Uncle Johnny's temper occurred just prior to the last of the Muleshoe reunions. For nostalgia's sake he grazed a few animals of even greater vintage than his jeep, among them a large male elk and an aging buffalo bull. The two animals were never on very good terms, and indeed the old buffalo was regarded as a great nuisance by everyone attached to the ranch. A few days before the reunion someone, Uncle Johnny most likely, made the mistake of leaving the elk and the buffalo alone in the same pen for an hour. The two soon joined in battle, and the battle raged freely for quite some time, neither combatant able to gain a clear advantage. When Uncle Johnny happened on the scene, half of his corrals had been flattened and much of the rest knocked hopelessly awry. Enraged, he at once found in favor of the elk and shot the buffalo dead on the spot. An hour later, when he was somewhat cooler, the Scotch took precedence over the Irish in him and he decided that it might be a novelty (as it would certainly be an economy) to barbecue the buffalo and serve him to the clan. He thus set free the fatted calf that had been meant for that fate and had the buffalo towed to the barbecue pit. It was barbecued, I believe, for forty-eight hours and on the day of the reunion its flesh proved precisely consistent with the McMurtry character: neither harder nor softer than saddle leather. How long one should have had to chew it to break down its resistance I did not find out.

There is yet one more story about Uncle Johnny, and it is the story which slides the panel, as Mr. Durrell might put it. We have seen him so far as the dashing young cowboy and the lovable family eccentric, and I should probably have always thought of him in those terms if the last story had not come to me. It came as I left for college and was offered as a safeguard and an admonition.

While still young, Uncle Johnny had the misfortune to catch what in those days was called a social disease. Where he got it one can easily imagine: some grim clapboard house on the plains, with the wind moaning, Model A's parked in the grassless yard, and the girls no prettier than Belle Starr. His condition became quite serious, and had my father not gone with him to a hospital and attended him during a prolonged critical period he might well have died.

Instead, he recovered, and in gratitude gave my father a present. Times were hard and Uncle Johnny poor but the present was a pair of spurs with my father's brand mounted on them in gold—extraordinary spurs for this plain country.

Since then, my father has worn no other spurs, and for a very long time Uncle Johnny took on himself the cloth of penance—the sort of penance appropriate to the faith he held. For all McMurtrys and perhaps all cowboys are essentially pantheists: to them the Almighty is the name of drought, the Good Lord the name of rain and grass. Nature is the only deity they really recognize, and nature's order the only order they hold truly sacred.

The most mysterious and most respected part of nature's order was the good woman. Even the most innocent cowboy was scarcely good enough for a good woman, and the cowboy who was manifestly not innocent might never be good enough, however much he might crave one. Instead, he might choose just such a setting as Uncle Johnny chose: a country forsaken of God and women, the rough bunkhouse, the raw horses and the unused mansion, the sandstorms and the blue northers—accoutrements enough for any penance.

At sixty-five he married a woman he had known for a very long time. When he began to court her he discovered, to quote the memoir, that "she was a much better woman than I was entitled to." Even after they married it was some time before he considered himself quite worthy to occupy the same house with her. Perhaps when he did, he let the penance go. Despite the series of injuries, his optimism grew, he bought new land, began to talk of a long-postponed world cruise, and wrote on the last page of his memoir:

I have had my share of fun and am still having it, we have a lot of plans for the future and expect to carry them out . . .

Ruin had not taught him well at all. A short while after the feed fell on him he learned that he had cancer of the colon. From that time on he was in great pain. His will to live never weakened, indeed, seemed to increase, but this time the cancer was inexorable and he died within three years, his world cruise untaken.

In July of 1965, eight months before he died, Uncle Johnny attended the last reunion. It was held at the Clarendon Country Club, on a fine summer day, and as reunions went, it was a quiet, sparsely attended affair. There was a light turnout of cousins and no more than a dozen or two small children scattered about. The food was catered this time, and just as well, too; the Homeric magnificence of some of the earlier feasts would have been largely wasted on the tired and dyspeptic McMurtrys who managed to drag themselves to the plains that day. Charlie and Jim were dead, several of the others were sick, and most of the survivors had long since ruined their digestions.

The talk was what the talk had always been, only the tones

had more audible cracks and the rhythms were shorter. Once I saw Uncle Bob, who was just recovering from a broken hip, trying to talk to Uncle Johnny, who was still recovering from his final broken leg. It was a fine paradigm of the existential condition, for the two brothers were standing on a windy curve of the ridge, moving their mouths quite uselessly. Uncle Johnny had almost no voice and Uncle Bob even less hearing, and indeed, had they been able to communicate they would probably only have got in a fight and injured themselves further, for they were not always in accord and it was rumoured that only a few months earlier they had encountered one another on the streets of Amarillo and almost come to blows.

Uncle Johnny, all day, was in very great pain, and only the talk and the sight of the children seemed to lift him above it. Finally it was three o'clock and the white sun began to dip just slightly in its arch. It was time for he and Aunt Ida to start the two-hundred-mile drive back to Muleshoe. Uncle Johnny reached for his white Stetson and put it on and all of his brothers and sisters rose to help him down the gentle slope to the Cadillac. Most of the women were weeping, and in the confusion of the moment Aunt Ida had forgotten her purse and went back to the tables to get it, while Uncle Johnny, helped by the lame and attended by the halt, worked his way around the open door of the car and stood there a few minutes, kissing his sisters goodbye. Though he was seventy-five and dying there was yet something boyish about him as he stood taking leave of the family. He stood in the frame that had always contained him, the great circular frame of the plains, with the wind blowing the grey hair at his temples and the whole of the Llano Estacado at his back. When he smiled at the children who were near, the pain left his face for a second, and he gave them the look that had always been his greatest appeal—the look of a man who saw life to the last as a youth sees it, and who sees in any youth all that he himself had been.

The family stood awkwardly around the car, looking now at Uncle Johnny, now at the shadow-flecked plains, and they were as close in that moment to a tragic recognition as they would ever be: for to them he had always been the darling, young Adonis, and most of them would never see him alive again. There were no words—they were not a wordy people. Aunt Ida returned with her purse and Uncle Johnny's last young grin blended with his grimace as he began the painful task of fitting himself into the car. In a few minutes the Cadillac had disappeared behind the first brown ridge, and the family was left with its silence and the failing day.

There, I think, this remembrance should end: with that place and that group, witnesses both to the coming and going of the god. Though one could make many more observations about the place, about the people, about the myth, I would rather stop there, on the sort of silence where fiction starts. Texas soaks up commentary like the plains soak up a rain, but the images from which fiction draws its vibrancy are often very few and often silent, like those I have touched on in this essay. The whiskey jug hanging in the barn for nineteen years; the children, rent with disappointment around the puddle of molasses; the whorehouse and the gold-mounted spurs. And Uncle Jeff, alone in the backwoods with his bad eye and his memories of the Rancho Grandy; and Uncle Johnny, riding up the Canadian in 1911 on a horse called Sugar-in-the-Gourd, and, only four years later, riding away bereft from the Roaring Springs, the dream of innocence and fullness never to be redeemed.

Those images, as it happens, all come from Old Texas, but it would not be hard to find in today's experience, or tomorrow's, moments that are just as eloquent, just as suggestive of gallantry or strength or disappointment. Indeed, had I more taste for lawsuits I would list a few for balance. Texas is rich in unredeemed dreams, and now that the dust of its herds is settling the writers will be out on their pencils, looking for them in the suburbs and along the mythical Pecos. And except to paper riders, the Pecos is a lonely and a bitter stream.

I have that from men who rode it and who knew that country round—such as it was, such as it can never be again.

INDUSTRIAL TOURISM AND THE NATIONAL PARKS

Edward Abbey

I like my job. The pay is generous; I might even say munificent: $1.95 per hour, earned or not, backed solidly by the world's most powerful Air Force, biggest national debt, and grossest national product. The fringe benefits are priceless: clean air to breathe (after the spring sandstorms); stillness, solitude and space; an unobstructed view every day and every night of sun, sky, stars, clouds, mountains, moon, cliffrock and canyons; a sense of time enough to let thought and feeling range from here to the end of the world and back; the discovery of something intimate—though impossible to name—in the remote.

The work is simple and requires almost no mental effort, a good thing in more ways than one. What little thinking I do is my own and I do it on government time. Insofar as I follow a schedule it goes about like this:

For me the work week begins on Thursday, which I usually

spend in patrolling the roads and walking out the trails. On Friday I inspect the campgrounds, haul firewood, and distribute the toilet paper. Saturday and Sunday are my busy days as I deal with the influx of weekend visitors and campers, answering questions, pulling cars out of the sand, lowering children down off the rocks, tracking lost grandfathers and investigating picnics. My Saturday night campfire talks are brief and to the point. "Everything all right?" I say, badge and all, ambling up to what looks like a cheerful group. "Fine," they'll say; "how about a drink?" "Why not?" I say.

By Sunday evening most everyone has gone home and the heavy duty is over. Thank God it's Monday, I say to myself the next morning. Mondays are very nice. I empty the garbage cans, read the discarded newspapers, sweep out the outhouses and disengage the Kleenex from the clutches of cliffrose and cactus. In the afternoon I watch the clouds drift past the bald peak of Mount Tukuhnikivats. (*Someone* has to do it.)

Tuesday and Wednesday I rest. Those are my days off and I usually set aside Wednesday evening for a trip to Moab, replenishing my supplies and establishing a little human contact more vital than that possible with the tourists I meet on the job. After a week in the desert, Moab (pop. 5,500, during the great uranium boom), seems like a dazzling metropolis, a throbbing dynamo of commerce and pleasure. I walk the single main street st visit to Times Square. (Wow, I'm thinking, this is great.)

After a visit to Miller's Supermarket, where I stock up on pinto beans and other necessities, I am free to visit the beer joints. All of them are busy, crowded with prospectors, miners, geologists, cowboys, truckdrivers and sheepherders, and the talk is loud, vigorous, blue with blasphemy. Although differences of opinion have been known to occur, open violence is rare, for these men treat one another with courtesy and respect. The general atmosphere is free and friendly, quite unlike the sad, sour gloom of most bars I have known, where nervous men in tight collars brood over their drinks between out-of-tune TV screens and a remorseless clock. Why the difference?

I have considered the question and come up with the following solution:

1. These prospectors, miners, etc. have most of them been physically active all day out-of-doors at a mile or more above sea level; they are comfortably tired and relaxed.

2. Most of them have been working alone; the presence of a jostling crowd is therefore not a familiar irritation to be borne with resignation but rather an unaccustomed pleasure to be enjoyed.

3. Most of them are making good wages and/or doing work they like to do; they are, you might say, happy. (The boom will not last, of course, but this is forgotten. And the ethical and political implications of uranium exploitation are simply unknown in these parts.)

4. The nature of their work requires a combination of skills and knowledge, good health and self-reliance, which tends to inspire self-confidence; they need not doubt their manhood. (Again, everything is subject to change.)

5. Finally, Moab is a Mormon town with funny ways.

Hard booze is not sold across the bar except in the semi-private "clubs." Nor even standard beer. These hard-drinking fellows whom I wish to praise are trying to get drunk on three-point two! They rise somewhat heavily from their chairs and barstools and tramp, with frequency and a squelchy, sodden noise, toward the pissoirs at the back of the room, more waterlogged than intoxicated.

In the end the beer halls of Moab, like all others, become to me depressing places. After a few games of rotation pool with my friend Viviano Jacquez, a reformed sheepherder turned dude wrangler (a dubious reform), I am glad to leave the last of those smoky dens around midnight and to climb into my pickup and take the long drive north and east back to the silent rock, the unbounded space and the sweet clean air of my outpost in the Arches.

Yes, it's a good job. On the rare occasions when I peer into the future for more than a few days I can foresee myself returning here for season after season, year after year, indefinitely. And why not? What better sinecure could a man with small needs, infinite desires, and philosophic pretensions ask for? The better part of each year in the wilderness and the winters in some complementary, equally agreeable environment —Hoboken perhaps, or Tijuana, Norales, Juareg . . . one of the border towns. Maybe Tonopah, a good tough Nevada mining town with legal prostitution, or possibly Oakland or even New Orleans—some place grimy, cheap (since I'd be living on unemployment insurance), decayed, hopelessly corrupt. I idle away hours dreaming of the wonderful winter to come, of the chocolate-covered mistress I'll have to rub my back, the journal spread open between two tall candles in massive silver candlesticks, the scrambled eggs with green chile, the crock of homebrew fermenting quietly in the corner, etc., the nights of desperate laughter with brave young comrades, burning bill-boards, and defacing public institutions. . . . Romantic dreams, romantic dreams.

For there is a cloud on my horizon. A small dark cloud no bigger than my hand. Its name is Progress.

The ease and relative freedom of this lively job at Arches follow from the comparative absence of the motorized tourists, who stay away by the millions. And they stay away because of the unpaved entrance road, the unflushable toilets in the campgrounds, and the fact that most of them have never even heard of Arches National Monument. (Could there be a more genuine testimonial to its beauty and integrity?) All this must change.

I'd been warned. On the very first day Merle and Floyd had mentioned something about developments, improvements, a sinister Master Plan. Thinking that *they* were the dreamers, I paid little heed and had soon forgotten the whole ridiculous business. But only a few days ago something happened which shook me out of my pleasant apathy.

I was sitting out back on my 33,000-acre terrace, shoeless and shirtless, scratching my toes in the sand and sipping on a tall iced drink, watching the flow of the evening over the desert. Prime time: the sun very low in the west, the birds coming back to life, the shadows rolling for miles over rock and sand to the very base of the brilliant mountains. I had a small fire going near the table—not for heat or light but for the fragrance of the juniper and the ritual appeal of the clear flames. For symbolic reasons. For ceremony. When I heard a faint sound over my shoulder I looked and saw a file of deer watching from fifty yards away, three does and a velvet-horned buck, all dark against the sundown sky. They began to move. "Come on over," I said, "have a drink." They declined, moving off with casual, unhurried grace, quiet as phantoms, and disappeared beyond the rise. Smiling, thoroughly at peace, I turned back to my drink, the little fire, the subtle transformations of the immense landscape before me. On the program: rise of the full moon.

It was then I heard the discordant note, the snarling whine of a jeep in low range and four-wheel-drive, coming from an unexpected direction, from the vicinity of the old foot and horse trail that leads from Balanced Rock down toward Courthouse Wash and on to park headquarters near Moab. The jeep came in sight from beyond some bluffs, turned onto the dirt road, and came up the hill toward the entrance station. Now, operating a motor vehicle of any kind on the trails of a national park is strictly forbidden, a nasty bureaucratic regulation which I heartily support. My bosom swelled with the righteous indignation of a cop: by God, I thought, I'm going to write these sons of bitches a ticket. I put down the drink and strode to the housetrailer to get my badge.

Long before I could find the shirt with the badge on it, however, or the ticket book, or my shoes or my park ranger hat, the jeep turned in at my driveway and came right up to the door of my trailer. It was a gray jeep with a U.S. Government decal on the side—Bureau of Public Roads—and covered with dust. Two empty water bags flapped at the bumper. Inside were three sunburned men in twill britches and engineering boots, and a pile of equipment: transit case, tripod, survey rod, bundles of wooden stakes. *(Oh no!)* The men got out, dripping with dust, and the driver grinned at me, pointing to his parched open mouth and making horrible gasping noises deep in his throat.

"Okay," I said, "come on in."

It was even hotter inside the trailer than outside, but I opened the refrigerator and left it open and took out a pitcher filled with ice cubes and water. As they passed the pitcher back and forth I got the full and terrible story, confirming the worst of my fears. They were a survey crew, laying out a new road in the Arches.

And when would the new road be built? Nobody knew for sure; perhaps in a couple of years, depending on when the Park Service would be able to get the money. The new road—to be paved, of course—would cost somewhere between half a million and one million dollars, depending on the bids, or more than fifty thousand dollars per linear mile. At least enough to pay the salaries of ten park rangers for ten years. Too much money, I suggested—they'll never go for it back in Washington.

The three men thought that was pretty funny. Don't worry, they said, this road will be built. I'm worried, I said. Look, the party chief explained, you *need* this road. He was a pleasant-mannered, soft-spoken civil engineer with an unquestioning dedication to his work. A very dangerous man. Who *needs* it? I said; we get very few tourists in this park. That's why you need it, the engineer explained patiently; look, he said, when this road is built you'll get ten, twenty, thirty times as many tourists in here as you get now. His men nodded in solemn agreement, and he stared at me intently, waiting to see what possible answer I could have to that.

"Have some more water," I said. I had an answer all right but I was saving it for later. I knew that I was dealing with a madman.

As I type these words, several years after the little episode of the gray jeep and the thirsty engineers, all that was foretold has come to pass. Arches National Monument has been developed. The Master Plan has been fulfilled. Where once a few adventurous people came on weekends to camp for a night or two and enjoy a taste of the primitive and remote, you will now find serpentine streams of baroque automobiles pouring in and out, all through the spring and summer, in numbers that would have seemed fantastic when I worked there: from 3,000 to 30,000 to 300,000 per year, the "visitation," as they call it, mounts ever upward. The little campgrounds where I used to putter around reading three-day-old newspapers full of lies and watermelon seeds have now been consolidated into one master campground that looks, during the busy season, like a suburban village: elaborate housetrailers of quilted aluminum crowd upon gigantic camper-trucks of Fiberglass and molded plastic; through their windows you will see the blue glow of television and hear the studio laughter of Los Angeles; knobby-kneed oldsters in plaid Bermudas buzz up and down the quaintly curving asphalt road on motorbikes; quarrels break out between campsite neighbors while others gather around their burning charcoal briquettes (ground campfires no longer permitted—not enough wood) to compare electric toothbrushes. The Comfort Stations are there, too, all lit up with electricity, fully equipped inside, though the generator breaks down now and then and the lights go out, or the sewage backs up in the plumbing system (drain fields were laid out in sand over a solid bed of sandstone), and the water supply sometimes fails, since the 3,000-foot well can only produce about 5gpm—not always enough to meet the demand. Down at the beginning of the new road, at park headquarters, is the new entrance station and visitor center, where admission fees are collected and where the rangers are going quietly nuts answering the same three basic questions five hundred times a day: (1) Where's the John? (2) How long's it take to see this place? (3) Where's the Coke machine?

Progress has come at last to the Arches, after a million years of neglect. Industrial Tourism has arrived.

What happened to Arches Natural Money-mint is, of course, an old story in the Park Service. All the famous national parks have the same problems on a far grander scale, as everyone knows, and many other problems as yet unknown to a little subordinate unit of the system in a backward part of southeastern Utah. And the same kind of development that has so transformed Arches is under way, planned or completed in many more national parks and national monuments. I will mention only a few examples with which I am personally familiar:

The newly established Canyonlands National Park. Most of the major points of interest in this park are presently accessible, over passable dirt roads, by car—Grandview Point, Upheaval Dome, part of the White Rim, Cave Spring, Squaw Spring campground and Elephant Hill. The more difficult places, such as Angel Arch or Druid Arch, can be reached by jeep, on horseback or in a one- or two-day hike. Nevertheless the Park Service had drawn up the usual Master Plan calling for modern paved highways to most of the places named and some not named.

Grand Canyon National Park. Most of the south rim of this park is now closely followed by a conventional high-speed highway and interrupted at numerous places by large asphalt parking lots. It is no longer easy, on the South Rim, to get away from the roar of motor traffic, except by descending into the canyon.

Navajo National Monument. A small, fragile, hidden place containing two of the most beautiful cliff dwellings in the Southwest—Keet Seel and Betatakin. This park will be difficult to protect under heavy visitation, and for years it was understood that it would be preserved in a primitive way so as to screen out those tourists unwilling to drive their cars over some twenty miles of dirt road. No longer so: the road has been paved, the campground enlarged and "modernized," and the old magic destroyed.

Natural Bridges National Monument. Another small gem in the park system, a group of three adjacent natural bridges tucked away in the canyon country of southern Utah. Formerly you could drive your car (over dirt roads, of course) to within sight of and easy walking distance—a hundred yards?—of the most spectacular of the three bridges. From there it was only a few hours walking time to the other two. All three could easily be seen in a single day. But this was not good enough for the developers. They have now constructed a paved road into the heart of the area, between the two biggest bridges.

Zion National Park. The northwestern part of this park, known as the Kolob area, has until recently been saved as almost virgin wilderness. But a broad highway, with banked curves, deep cuts and heavy fills, that will invade this splendid region, is already under construction.

Capitol Reef National Monument. Grand and colorful scenery in a rugged land—south-central Utah. The most beautiful portion of that park was the canyon of the Fremont River, a great place for hiking, camping, exploring. And what did the authorities do? They built a state highway through it.

Lee's Ferry. Until a few years ago a simple, quiet, primitive place on the shores of the Colorado, Lee's Ferry has now fallen under the protection of the Park Service. And who can protect it against the Park Service? Powerlines now bisect the scene; a 100-foot pink water tower looms against the red cliffs; tract-style houses are built to house the "protectors"; natural campsites along the river are closed off while all campers are now herded into an artificial steel-and-asphalt "campground" in the hottest, windiest spot in the area; historic buildings are razed by bulldozers to save the expense of maintaining them while at the same time hundreds of thousands of dollars are spent on an unneeded paved entrance road. And the administrators complain of *vandalism.*

I could easily cite ten more examples of unnecessary or destructive development for every one I've named so far. What has happened in these particular areas, which I chance to know a little and love too much, has happened, is happening, or will soon happen to the majority of our national parks and national forests, despite the illusory protection of the Wilderness Preservation Act, unless a great many citizens rear up on their hind legs and make vigorous political gestures demanding implementation of the Act.

There may be some among the readers of this book, like the earnest engineer, who believe without question that any and all forms of construction and development are intrinsic goods, in the national parks as well as anywhere else, who virtually identify quantity with quality and therefore assume that the greater the quantity of traffic, the higher the value received. There are some who frankly and boldly advocate the eradication of the last remnants of wilderness and the complete subjugation of nature to the requirements of—not man—but industry. This is a courageous view, admirable in its simplicity and power, and with the weight of all modern history behind it. It is also quite insane. I cannot attempt to deal with it here.

There will be other readers, I hope, who share my basic assumption that wilderness is a necessary part of civilization and that it is the primary responsibility of the national park system to preserve *intact and undiminished* what little still remains.

Most readers, while generally sympathetic to this latter point of view, will feel, as do the administrators of the National Park Service, that although wilderness is a fine thing, certain compromises and adjustments are necessary in order to meet the ever-expanding demand for outdoor recreation. It is precisely this question which I would like to examine now.

The Park Service, established by Congress in 1916, was directed not only to administer the parks but also to "provide for the enjoyment of same in such manner and by such means as will leave them unimpaired for the enjoyment of future generations." This appropriately ambiguous language, employed long before the onslaught of the automobile, has been understood in various and often opposing ways ever since. The Park Service, like any other big organization, includes factions and factions. The Developers, the dominant faction, place their emphasis on the words *"provide for the enjoyment."* The Preservers, a minority but also strong, emphasize the words *"leave them unimpaired."* It is apparent, then, that we cannot decide the question of development versus preservation by a simple referral to holy writ or an attempt to guess the intention of the founding fathers; we must make up our own minds and decide for ourselves what the national parks should be and what purpose they should serve.

The first issue that appears when we get into this matter, the most important issue and perhaps the only issue, is the one called *accessibility.* The Developers insist that the parks must be made fully accessible not only to people but also to their machines, that is, to automobiles, motorboats, etc. The Preservers argue, in principle at least, that wilderness and motors are incompatible and that the former can best be experienced, understood, and enjoyed when the machines are left behind where they belong—on the superhighways and in the parking lots, on the reservoirs and in the marinas. What does accessibility mean? Is there any spot on earth that men have not proved accessible by the simplest means—feet and legs and heart? Even Mt. McKinley, even Everest, have been surmounted by men on foot. (Some of them, incidentally, rank amateurs, to the horror and indignation of the professional mountaineers.) The interior of the Grand Canyon, a fiercely hot and hostile abyss, is visited each summer by thousands and thousands of tourists of the most banal and unadventurous type, many of them on foot—self-propelled, so to speak—and the others on the backs of mules. Thousands climb each summer to the summit of Mt. Whitney, highest point in the forty-eight United States, while multitudes of others wander on foot or on horseback through the ranges of the Sierras, the Rockies, the Big Smokies, the Cascades and the mountains of New England. Still more hundreds and thousands float or paddle each year down the currents of the Salmon, the Snake, the Allagash, the Yampa, the Green, the Rio Grande, the Ozark, the St. Croix and those portions of the Colorado which have not yet been destroyed by the dam builders. And most significant, these hordes of nonmotorized tourists, hungry for a taste of the difficult, the original, the real, do not consist solely of people young and athletic but also of old folks, fat folks, pale-faced office clerks who don't know a rucksack from a haversack, and even children. The one thing they all have in common is the refusal to live always like sardines in a can—they are determined to get outside of their motorcars for at least a few weeks each year.

This being the case, why is the Park Service generally so anxious to accommodate that other crowd, the indolent millions born on wheels and suckled on gasoline, who expect and demand paved highways to lead them in comfort, ease and safety into every nook and corner of the national parks? For the answer to that we must consider the character of what I call Industrial Tourism and the quality of the mechanized tourists— the Wheelchair Explorers—who are at once the consumers, the raw material and the victims of Industrial Tourism.

Industrial Tourism is a big business. It means money. It includes the motel and restaurant owners, the gasoline retailers, the oil corporations, the road-building contractors, the heavy equipment manufacturers, the state and federal engineering agencies and the sovereign, all-powerful automotive industry. These various interests are well organized, command more wealth than most modern nations, and are represented in Congress with a strength far greater than is justified in any constitutional or democratic sense. (Modern politics is expensive—power follows money.) Through Congress the tourism industry can bring enormous pressure to bear upon such a slender reed in the executive branch as the poor old Park Service, a pressure which is also exerted on every other possible level—local, state, regional—and through advertising and the well-established habits of a wasteful nation.

When a new national park, national monument, national seashore, or whatever it may be called is set up, the various forces of Industrial Tourism, on all levels, immediately expect action—meaning specifically a road-building program. Where trails or primitive dirt roads already exist, the Industry expects —it hardly needs to ask—that these be developed into modern paved highways. On the local level, for example, the first thing that the superintendent of a new park can anticipate being asked, when he attends his first meeting of the area's Chamber of Commerce, is not "Will roads be built?" but rather "When does construction begin?" and "Why the delay?"

(The Natural Money-Mint. With supersensitive antennae these operatives from the C. of C. look into red canyons and see only green, stand among flowers snorting out the smell of money, and hear, while thunderstorms rumble over mountains, the fall of a dollar bill on motel carpeting.)

Accustomed to this sort of relentless pressure since its founding, it is little wonder that the Park Service, through a process of natural selection, has tended to evolve a type of administration which, far from resisting such pressure, has usually been more than willing to accommodate it, even to encourage it. Not from any peculiar moral weakness but simply because such well-adapted administrators are themselves believers in a policy of economic development. "Resource management" is the current term. Old foot trails may be neglected, back-country ranger stations left unmanned, and interpretive and protective services inadequately staffed, but the administrators know from long experience that millions for asphalt can always be found; Congress is always willing to appropriate money for more and bigger paved roads, anywhere—particularly if they form loops. Loop drives are extremely popular with the petroleum industry—they bring the motorist right back to the same gas station from which he started.

Great though it is, however, the power of the tourist business would not in itself be sufficient to shape Park Service policy. To all accusations of excessive development the administrators can reply, as they will if pressed hard enough, that they are giving the public what it wants, that their primary duty is to serve the public not preserve the wilds. "Parks are for people" is the public-relations slogan, which decoded means that the parks are for people-in-automobiles. Behind the slogan is the assumption that the majority of Americans, exactly like the managers of the tourist industry, expect and demand to see their national parks from the comfort, security, and convenience of their automobiles.

Is this assumption correct? Perhaps. Does that justify the continued and increasing erosion of the parks? It does not. Which brings me to the final aspect of the problem of Industrial Tourism: the Industrial Tourists themselves.

They work hard, these people. They roll up incredible mileages on their odometers, rack up state after state in two-week transcontinental motor marathons, knock off one national park after another, take millions of square yards of photographs, and endure patiently the most prolonged discomforts: the tedious traffic jams, the awful food of park cafeterias and roadside eateries, the nocturnal search for a place to sleep or camp, the dreary routing of One-Stop Service, the endless lines of creeping traffic, the smell of exhaust fumes, the ever-proliferating Rules & Regulations, the fees and the bills and the service charges, the boiling radiator and the flat tire and the vapor lock, the surly retorts of room clerks and traffic cops, the incessant jostling of the anxious crowds, the irritation and restlessness of their children, the worry of their wives, and the long drive home at night in a stream of racing cars against the lights of another stream racing in the opposite direction, passing now and then the obscure tangle, the shattered glass, the patrolman's lurid blinker light, of one more wreck.

Hard work. And risky. Too much for some, who have given up the struggle on the highways in exchange for an entirely different kind of vacation—out in the open, on their own feet, following the quiet trail through forest and mountains, bedding down at evening under the stars, when and where they feel like it, at a time when the Industrial Tourists are still hunting for a place to park their automobiles.

Industrial Tourism is a threat to the national parks. But the chief victims of the system are the motorized tourists. They are being robbed and robbing themselves. So long as they are unwilling to crawl out of their cars they will not discover the treasures of the national parks and will never escape the stress and turmoil of the urban-suburban complexes which they had hoped, presumably, to leave behind for a while.

How to pry the tourists out of their automobiles, out of their back-breaking upholstered mechanized wheelchairs and onto their feet, onto the strange warmth and solidity of Mother Earth again? This is the problem which the Park Service should confront directly, not evasively, and which it cannot resolve by simply submitting and conforming to the automobile habit. The automobile, which began as a transportation convenience, has become a bloody tyrant (50,000 lives a year), and it is the responsibility of the Park Service, as well as that of everyone else concerned with preserving both wilderness and civilization, to begin a campaign of resistance. The automotive combine has almost succeeded in strangling our cities; we need not let it also destroy our national parks.

It will be objected that a constantly increasing population makes resistance and conservation a hopeless battle. This is true. Unless a way is found to stabilize the nation's population, the parks cannot be saved. Or anything else worth a damn. Wilderness preservation, like a hundred other good causes, will be forgotten under the overwhelming pressure of a struggle for mere survival and sanity in a completely urbanized, completely industrialized, ever more crowded environment. For my own part I would rather take my chances in a thermonuclear war than live in such a world.

Assuming, however, that population growth will be halted at a tolerable level before catastrophe does it for us, it remains permissible to talk about such things as the national parks. Having indulged myself in a number of harsh judgments upon the Park Service, the tourist industry, and the motoring public, I now feel entitled to make some constructive, practical, sensible proposals for the salvation of both parks and people.

(1) No more cars in national parks. Let the people walk. Or ride horses, bicycles, mules, wild pigs—anything—but keep

the automobiles and the motorcycles and all their motorized relatives out. We have agreed not to drive our automobiles into cathedrals, concert halls, art museums, legislative assemblies, private bedrooms and the other sanctums of our culture; we should treat our national parks with the same deference, for they, too, are holy places. An increasingly pagan and hedonistic people (thank God!), we are learning finally that the forests and mountains and desert canyons are holier than our churches. Therefore let us behave accordingly.

Consider a concrete example and what could be done with it: Yosemite Valley in Yosemite National Park. At present a dusty milling confusion of motor vehicles and ponderous camping machinery, it could be returned to relative beauty and order by the simple expedient of requiring all visitors, at the park entrance, to lock up their automobiles and continue their tour on the seats of good workable bicycles supplied free of charge by the United States Government.

Let our people travel light and free on their bicycles— nothing on the back but a shirt, nothing tied to the bike but a slicker, in case of rain. Their bedrolls, their backpacks, their tents, their food and cooking kits will be trucked in for them, free of charge, to the campground of their choice in the Valley, by the Park Service. (Why not? The roads will still be there.) Once in the Valley they will find the concessioners waiting, ready to supply whatever needs might have been overlooked, or to furnish rooms and meals for those who don't want to camp out.

The same thing could be done at Grand Canyon or at Yellowstone or at any of our other shrines to the out-of-doors. There is no compelling reason, for example, why tourists need to drive their automobiles to the very brink of the Grand Canyon's south rim. They could *walk* that last mile. Better yet, the Park Service should build an enormous parking lot about ten miles south of Grand Canyon Village and another east of Desert View. At those points, as at Yosemite, our people could emerge from their steaming shells of steel and glass and climb upon horses or bicycles for the final leg of the journey. On the rim, as at present, the hotels and restaurants will remain to serve the physical needs of the park visitors. Trips along the rim would also be made on foot, on horseback, or—utilizing the paved road which already exists—on bicycles. For those willing to go all the way from one parking lot to the other, a distance of some sixty or seventy miles, we might provide bus service back to their cars, a service which would at the same time effect a convenient exchange of bicycles and/or horses between the two terminals.

What about children? What about the aged and infirm? Frankly, we need waste little sympathy on these two pressure groups. Children too small to ride bicycles and too heavy to be borne on their parents' backs need only wait a few years—if they are not run over by automobiles they will grow into a lifetime of joyous adventure, if we save the parks and *leave them unimpaired for the enjoyment of future generations.* The aged merit even less sympathy: after all they had the opportunity to see the country when it was still relatively unspoiled. However, we'll stretch a point for those too old or too sickly to mount a bicycle and let them ride the shuttle buses.

I can foresee complaints. The motorized tourists, reluctant to give up the old ways, will complain that they can't see enough without their automobiles to bear them swiftly (traffic permitting) through the parks. But this is nonsense. A man on foot, on horseback or on a bicycle will see more, feel more, enjoy more in one mile than the motorized tourists can in a hundred miles. Better to idle through one park in two weeks than try to race through a dozen in the same amount of time. Those who are familiar with both modes of travel know from experience that this is true; the rest have only to make the experiment to discover the same truth for themselves.

They will complain of physical hardship, these sons of the pioneers. Not for long; once they rediscover the pleasures of actually operating their own limbs and senses in a varied, spontaneous, voluntary style, they will complain instead of crawling back into a car; they may even object to returning to desk and office and that drywall box on Mossy Brook Circle. The fires of revolt may be kindled—which means hope for us all.

(2) No more new roads in national parks. After banning private automobiles the second step should be easy. Where paved roads are already in existence they will be reserved for the bicycles and essential in-park services, such as shuttle buses, the trucking of camping gear and concessioners' supplies. Where dirt roads already exist they too will be reserved for nonmotorized traffic. Plans for new roads can be discarded and in their place a program of trail-building begun, badly needed in some of the parks and in many of the national monuments. In mountainous areas it may be desirable to build emergency shelters along the trails and bike roads; in desert regions a water supply might have to be provided at certain points—wells drilled and handpumps installed if feasible.

Once people are liberated from the confines of automobiles there will be a greatly increased interest in hiking, exploring, and back-country packtrips. Fortunately the parks, by the mere elimination of motor traffic, will come to seem far bigger than they are now—there will be more room for more persons, an astonishing expansion of space. This follows from the interesting fact that a motorized vehicle, when not at rest, requires a volume of space far out of proportion to its size. To illustrate: imagine a lake approximately ten miles long and on the average one mile wide. A single motorboat could easily circumnavigate the lake in an hour; ten motorboats would begin to crowd it; twenty or thirty, all in operation, would dominate the lake to the exclusion of any other form of activity; and fifty would create the hazards, confusion, and turmoil that makes pleasure impossible. Suppose we banned motorboats and allowed only canoes and rowboats; we would see at once that the lake seemed ten or perhaps a hundred times bigger. The same thing holds true, to an even greater degree, for the automobile. Distance and space are functions of speed and time. Without expending a single dollar from the United States Treasury we could, if we wanted to, multiply the area of our national parks tenfold or a hundredfold—simply by banning the private automobile. The next generation, all 250 million of them, would be grateful to us.

(3) Put the park rangers to work. Lazy scheming loafers, they've wasted too many years selling tickets at toll booths and sitting behind desks filling out charts and tables in the vain effort to appease the mania for statistics which torments the Washington office. Put them to work. They're supposed to be rangers—make the bums range; kick them out of those overheated air-conditioned offices, yank them out of those overstuffed patrol cars, and drive them out on the trails where they should be, leading the dudes over hill and dale, safely into and back out of the wilderness. It won't hurt them to

work off a little office fat; it'll do them good, help take their minds off each other's wives, and give them a chance to get out of reach of the boss—a blessing for all concerned.

They will be needed on the trail. Once we outlaw the motors and stop the road-building and force the multitudes back on their feet, the people will need leaders. A venturesome minority will always be eager to set off on their own, and no obstacles should be placed in their path; let them take risks, for godsake, let them get lost, sunburnt, stranded, drowned, eaten by bears, buried alive under avalanches—that is the right and privilege of any free American. But the rest, the majority, most of them new to the out-of-doors, will need and welcome assistance, instruction and guidance. Many will not know how to saddle a horse, read a topographical map, follow a trail over slickrock, memorize landmarks, build a fire in rain, treat snakebite, rappel down a cliff, glissade down a glacier, read a compass, find water under sand, load a burro, splint a broken bone, bury a body, patch a rubber boat, portage a waterfall, survive a blizzard, avoid lightning, cook a porcupine, comfort a girl during a thunderstorm, predict the weather, dodge falling rock, climb out of a box canyon, or pour piss out of a boot. Park rangers know these things, or should know them, or used to know them and can relearn; they will be needed. In addition to this sort of practical guide service the ranger will also be a bit of a naturalist, able to edify the party in his charge with the natural and human history of the area, in detail and in broad outline.

Critics of my program will argue that it is too late for such a radical reformation of a people's approach to the out-of-doors, that the pattern is too deeply set, and that the majority of Americans would not be willing to emerge from the familiar luxury of their automobiles, even briefly, to try the little-known and problematic advantages of the bicycle, the saddle horse, and the footpath. This might be so; but how can we be sure unless we dare the experiment? I, for one, suspect that millions of our citizens, especially the young, are yearning for adventure, difficulty, challenge—they will respond with enthusiasm. What we must do, prodding the Park Service into the forefront of the demonstration, is provide these young people with the opportunity, the assistance, and the necessary encouragement.

How could this most easily be done? By following the steps I have proposed, plus reducing the expenses of wilderness recreation to the minimal level. Guide service by rangers should, of course, be free to the public. Money saved by *not* constructing more paved highways into the parks should be sufficient to finance the cost of bicycles and horses for the entire park system. Elimination of automobile traffic would allow the Park Service to save more millions now spent on road maintenance, police work and paper work. Whatever the cost, however financed, the benefits for park visitors in health and happiness—virtues unknown to the statisticians—would be immeasurable.

Excluding the automobile from the heart of the great cities has been seriously advocated by thoughtful observers of our urban problems. It seems to me an equally proper solution to the problems besetting our national parks. Of course it would be a serious blow to Industrial Tourism and would be bitterly resisted by those who profit from that industry. Exclusion of automobiles would also require a revolution in the thinking of Park Service officialdom and in the assumptions of most

American tourists. But such a revolution, like it or not, is precisely what is needed. The only foreseeable alternative, given the current trend of things, is the gradual destruction of our national park system.

Let us therefore steal a slogan from the Development Fever Faction in the Park Service. The parks, they say, are for people. Very well. At the main entrance to each national park and national monument we shall erect a billboard one hundred feet high, two hundred feet wide, gorgeously filigreed in brilliant neon and outlined with blinker lights, exploding stars, flashing prayer wheels and great Byzantine phallic symbols that gush like geysers every thirty seconds. (You could set your watch by them.) Behind the fireworks will loom the figure of Smokey the Bear, taller than a pine tree, with eyes in his head that swivel back and forth, watching You, and ears that actually twitch. Push a button and Smokey will recite, for the benefit of children and government officials who might otherwise have trouble with some of the big words, in a voice ursine, loud and clear, the message spelled out on the face of the billboard. To wit:

HOWDY FOLKS. WELCOME. THIS IS YOUR NATIONAL PARK, ESTAB-
LISHED FOR THE PLEASURE OF YOU AND ALL PEOPLE EVERYWHERE.
PARK YOUR CAR, JEEP, TRUCK, TANK, MOTORBIKE, SNOWMOBILE,
JETBOAT, AIRBOAT, SUBMARINE, AIRPLANE, JETPLANE, HELICOPTER,
HOVERCRAFT, WINGED MOTORCYCLE, ROCKETSHIP, OR ANY OTHER
CONCEIVABLE TYPE OF MOTORIZED VEHICLE IN THE WORLD'S
BIGGEST PARKINGLOT BEHIND THE COMFORT STATION IMMEDIATELY
TO YOUR REAR. GET OUT OF YOUR MOTORIZED VEHICLE, GET ON
YOUR HORSE, MULE, BICYCLE OR FEET, AND COME ON IN.
ENJOY YOURSELVES. THIS HERE PARK IS FOR people.

The survey chief and his two assistants did not stay very long. Letting them go in peace, without debate, I fixed myself another drink, returned to the table in the backyard and sat down to await the rising of the moon.

My thoughts were on the road and the crowds that would pour upon it as inevitably as water under pressure follows every channel which is opened to it. Man is a gregarious creature, we are told, a social being. Does that mean he is also a herd animal? I don't believe it, despite the character of modern life. The herd is for ungulates, not for men and women and their children. Are men no better than sheep or cattle, that they must live always in view of one another in order to feel a sense of safety? I can't believe it.

We are preoccupied with time. If we could learn to love space as deeply as we are now obsessed with time, we might discover a new meaning in the phrase to *live like men.*

At what distance should good neighbors build their houses? Let it be determined by the community's mode of travel: if by foot, four miles; if by horseback, eight miles; if by motorcar, twenty-four miles; if by airplane, ninety-six miles.

Recall the Proverb: "Set not thy foot too often in thy neighbor's house, lest he grow weary of thee and hate thee."

The sun went down and the light mellowed over the sand and distance and hoodoo rocks "pinnacled dim in the intense inane." A few stars appeared, scattered liberally through space. The solitary owl called.

Finally the moon came up, a golden globe behind the rocky fretwork of the horizon, a full and delicate moon that floated lightly as a leaf upon the dark slow current of the night. A face that watched me from the other side.

The air grew cool. I put on boots and shirt, stuffed some cheese and raisins in my pocket, and went for a walk. The moon was high enough to cast a good light when I reached the place where the gray jeep had first come into view. I could see the tracks of its wheels quite plainly in the sand and the route was well marked, not only by the tracks but by the survey stakes planted in the ground at regular fifty-foot intervals and by streamers of plastic ribbon tied to the brush and trees.

Teamwork, that's what made America what it is today. Teamwork and initiative. The survey crew had done their job; I would do mine. For about five miles I followed the course of their survey back toward headquarters, and as I went I pulled up each little wooden stake and threw it away, and cut all the bright ribbons from the bushes and hid them under a rock. A futile effort, in the long run, but it made me feel good. Then I went home to the trailer, taking a shortcut over the bluffs.

REDNECK SECRETS

William Kittredge

ack in my more scattered days there was a time when I decided the solution to all life's miseries would begin with marrying a nurse. Cool hands and commiseration. She would be a second-generation Swedish girl who left the family farm in North Dakota to live a new life in Denver, her hair would be long and silvery blonde, and she would smile every time she saw me and always be after me to get out of the house and go have a glass of beer with my buckaroo cronies.

Our faithfulness to one another would be legendary. We would live near Lolo, Montana, on the banks of the Bitterroot River where Lewis and Clark camped to rest on their way West, "Traveler's Rest," land which floods a little in the spring of the year, a small price to pay for such connection with mythology. Our garden would be intricately perfect on the sunny uphill side of our sixteen acres, with little wooden flume boxes to turn the irrigation water down one ditch or another.

We would own three horses, one a blue roan Appaloosa, and haul them around in our trailer to jackpot roping events on summer weekends. I wouldn't be much good on horseback, never was, but nobody would care. The saddle shed would be tacked to the side of our doublewide expando New Moon mobile home, and there would be a neat little lawn with a white picket fence about as high as your knee, and a boxer dog called Aces and Eights, with a great studded collar. There would be a .357 magnum pistol in the drawer of the bedside table, and on Friday night we would dance to the music of old-time fiddlers at some country tavern and in the fall we would go into the mountains for firewood and kill two or three elk for the freezer. There would be wild asparagus along the irrigation ditches and morels down under the cottonwoods by the river, and we would always be good.

And I would keep a journal, like Lewis and Clark, and spell bad, because in my heart I would want to be a mountain man—"We luved aft the movee in the bak seet agin tonite."

We must not gainsay such Western dreams. They are not automatically idiot. There are, after all, good Rednecks and bad Rednecks. Those are categories.

So many people in the American West are hurt, and hurting. Bad Rednecks originate out of hurt and a sense of having been discarded and ignored by the Great World, which these days exists mostly on television, distant and most times dizzily out of focus out here in Redneck country,

Bad Rednecks lose faith and ride away into foolishness, striking back. The spastic utility of violence. The other night in a barroom, I saw one man turn to another, who had been pestering him with drunken nonsense. "Son," he said, "you better calm yourself, because if you don't, things are going to get real Western here for a minute."

Real Western. Back in the late '40's when I was getting close to graduating from high school, they used to stage Saturday night prizefights down in the Veterans Auditorium. Not boxing matches but prizefights, a name which rings in the ear something like *cockfight.* One night the two main-event fighters, always heavyweights, were some hulking Indian and a white farmer from a little dairy-farm community.

The Indian, I recall, had the word "Mother" carved on his hairless chest. Not tattooed, but carved in the flesh with a blade, so the scar tissue spelled out the word in livid welts. The white farmer looked soft and his body was alabaster, pure white, except for his wrists and neck, which were dark, burned-in-the-fields red, burnished red. While they hammered at each other we hooted from the stands like gibbons, rooting for our favorites on strictly territorial and racial grounds, and in the end were all disappointed. The white farmer went down like thunder about three times, blood snorting from his nose in a delicate spray and decorating his whiteness like in, say, the movies. The Indian simply retreated to his corner and refused to go on. It didn't make any sense.

We screeched and stomped, but the Indian just stood there looking at the bleeding white man, and the white man cleared his head and looked at the Indian, and then they both shook their heads at one another, as if acknowledging some private news they had just then learned to share. They both climbed out of the ring and together made their way up the aisle. Walked away.

Real Western. Of course, in that short-lived partnership of the downtrodden, the Indian was probably doomed to a lifetime on the lower end of the seesaw. No dairy farms in a pastoral valley, nor morning milking and school boards for him. But that is not the essential point in this equation. There is a real spiritual equivalency between Redmen and Rednecks. How sad and ironic that they tend to hit at each other for lack of a real target, acting out some tired old scenario. Both, with some justice, feel used and cheated and disenfranchised. Both want to strike back, which may be just walking away, or the bad answer, bloody noses.

Nobody is claiming certain Rednecks are gorgeous about their ways of resolving the pain of their frustrations. Some of them will indeed get drunk in honkytonks and raise hell and harass young men with long hair and golden earrings. These are the bad Rednecks.

Why bad? Because they are betraying themselves. Out-of-power groups keep fighting each other instead of what they really resent: power itself. A Redneck pounding a hippie in a dark barroom is embarrassing because we see the cowardice. What he wants to hit is a banker in broad daylight.

But things are looking up. Rednecks take drugs; hippies take jobs. And the hippie carpenters and the 250-pound, pig-tailed lumberjacks preserve their essence. They are still isolated, outrageous, lonely, proud and mean. Any one of them might yearn for a nurse, a doublewide, a blue roan Appaloosa, and a sense of place in a country that left him behind.

Like the Indian and the buffalo on the old nickel, there are two sides to American faith. But in terms of Redneck currency, they conflict. On the one side there is individualism, which in its most radical mountain-man form becomes isolation and loneliness: the standard country-and-western lament. It will lead to dying alone in your motel room: whether gored, boozed or smacked makes little difference. On the other side there are family and community, that pastoral society of good people inhabiting the good place on earth that William Bradford and Thomas Jefferson so loved to think about.

Last winter after the snowmobile races in Seeley Lake, I had come home to stand alongside my favorite bar rail and listen to my favorite skinny Redneck barmaid turn down propositions. Did I say *home?* Anyway, standing there and feeling at home, I realized that good Redneck bars are like good hippie bars: they are community centers, like churches and pubs in the old days, and drastically unlike our singles bars where every person is so radically on his or her own.

My skinny barmaid friend looked up at one lumberjack fellow, who was clomping around in his White logger boots and smiling his most winsome. She said, "You're just one of those boys with a sink full of dishes. You ain't looking for nothing but someone dumb enough to come and wash your dishes. You go home and play your radio."

A sink full of dirty dishes. And laundry. There are aspects of living alone that can be defined as going out to the J.C. Penney store and buying $33 worth of new shorts and socks and t-shirts because everything you own is stacked up raunchy and stinking on the far side of the bed. And going out and buying paper plates at K-mart because you're tired of eating your meals crouched over the kitchen sink. You finally learn about dirty dishes. They stay dirty. And those girls, like

my skinny friend, have learned a thing or two. There are genuine offers of solace and companionship, and there are dirty
dishes and nursing. And then a trailer house, and three babies
in three years, diapers, and he's gone to Alaska for the big
money. So back to barmaiding, this time with kids to support,
babysitters. Go home and play your radio.

There is, of course, another Montana. Consider these remarks
from the journals of James and Granville Stewart, 1862:

> JANUARY 1, 1862. *Snowed in the forenoon. Very cold in the afternoon.*
> *Raw east wind. Everybody went to grand ball given by John Grant at*
> *Grantsville and a severe blizzard blew up and raged all night. We danced*
> *all night, no outside storm could dampen the festivities.*
>
> JANUARY 2. *Still blowing a gale this morning. Forty below zero and*
> *the air is filled with driving, drifting snow. After breakfast we laid down*
> *on the floor of the several rooms, on buffalo robes that Johnny furnished,*
> *all dressed as we were and slept until about two-o'clock in the afternoon,*
> *when we arose, ate a fine dinner, then resumed dancing which we kept up*
> *with unabated pleasure . . . danced until sunrise.*
>
> JANUARY 3. *The blizzard ceased about daylight, but it was very cold*
> *with about fourteen inches of snow badly drifted in places and the ground*
> *bare in spots. We estimated the cold at about thirty-five below, but for-*
> *tunately there was but little wind. After breakfast all the visitors left for*
> *home, men, women, and children, all on horseback. Everyone got home*
> *without frost bites.*

Sounds pretty good. But Granville Stewart got his. In the great
and deadly winter of 1886–1887, before they learned the need of
stacking hay for winter, when more than one million head of

cattle ran the Montana ranges, he lost two-thirds of his cow herd. Carcasses piled in the coulees and fence corners come springtime, flowers growing up between the ribs of dead longhorn cattle, and the mild breezes reeking with decay. A one-time partner of Stewart's, Conrad Kohrs, salvaged 3,000 head out of 35,000. Reports vary, but you get the sense of it.

Over across the Continental Divide to where the plains begin on the east side of the Crazy Mountains, in the Two Dot country, on bright mornings you can gaze across the enormous swale of the Musselshell, north and east to the Snowy Mountains, fifty miles distant and distinct and clear in the air as the one mountain bluebell you picked when you came out from breakfast.

But we are not talking spring, we are talking winter and haystacks. A man we know, let's call him Davis Patten, is feeding cattle. It's February, and the snow is drifting three feet deep along the fence lines, and the wind is carrying the chill factor down to about thirty below. Davis Patten is pulling his feed sled with a team of yellow Belgian geldings. For this job, it's either horses or a track-layer, like a Caterpillar D-6. The Belgians are cheaper and easier to start.

Davis kicks the last remnant of meadow hay, still greenish and smelling of dry summer, off the sled to the trailing cattle. It's three o'clock in the afternoon and already the day is settling toward dark. Sled runners creak on the frozen snow. The gray light is murky in the wind, as though inhabited, but no birds are flying anywhere. Davis Patten is sweating under his insulated coveralls, but his beard is frozen around his mouth. He heads the team toward the barns, over under the cottonwood by the creek. Light from the kitchen windows shows through the bare limbs. After he has fed the team a bait of oats, Davis and his wife Loretta will drink coffee laced with bourbon.

Later they watch television, people laughing and joking in bright Sony color. In his bones Davis recognizes, as most of us do, that the principal supporting business of television is lies, truths that are twisted about a quarter turn. Truths that were never truths. Davis drifts off to sleep in his Barca-Lounger. He will wake to the white noise from a gray screen.

It is important to have a sense of all this. There are many other lives, this is just one, but none are the lives we imagine when we think of running away to Territory.

Tomorrow Davis Patten will begin his day chopping ice along the creek with a splitting maul. Stock water, a daily chore. Another day with ice in his beard, sustained by memories of making slow love to Loretta under down comforters in their cold bedroom. Love, and then quickfooting it to the bathroom on the cold floors, a steaming shower. Memories of a bed that reeks a little of child making.

The rewards of the life, it is said, are spiritual, and often they are. Just standing on land you own, where you can dig any sort of hole you like, can be considered a spiritual reward, a reason for not selling out and hitting the Bahamas. But on his winter afternoons Davis Patten remembers another life. For ten years, after he broke away from Montana to the Marines, Davis hung out at the dragster tracks in the San Joaquin Valley, rebuilding engines for great, roaring, ass-busting machines. These days he sees their striped red-and-white dragchutes flowering only on Sunday afternoons. The "Wide World of Sports." Lost horizons. The intricate precision of cam shaft adjustments.

In the meantime, another load of hay.

• • •

Up in towns along the highline, Browning and Harlem and Malta, people are continually dying from another kind of possibility. Another shot of Beam on the rocks and Annie Greensprings out back after the bars are closed. In Montana they used to erect little crosses along the highways wherever a fatality occurred. A while back, outside Browning, they got a dandy. Eleven deaths in a single car accident. *Guinness Book of World Records.* Verities. The highway department has given up the practice of erecting crosses: too many of them are dedicated to the disenfranchised.

Out south of Billings the great coal fields are being strip-mined. Possibilities. The history of Montana and the West, from the fur trade to tomorrow, is a history of colonialism, both material and cultural. Is it any wonder we are so deeply xenophobic, and regard anything east of us as suspect? The money and the power always came from the East, took what it wanted, and left us, white or Indian, with our traditions dismantled and our territory filled with holes in the ground. Ever been to Butte? About half the old town was sucked into a vast open-pit mine.

Verities. The lasting thing we have learned here, if we ever learn, is to resist the beguilements of power and money. Hang on to your land. There won't be any more. Be superstitious as a Borneo tribesman. Do not let them photograph our shy, bare-breasted beauties as they wash clothes along the stream bank. Do not let them steal your soul away in pictures, because they will if they get a chance, just as Beadle's Nickel-Dime Library westerns and Gene Autry B-movies gnawed at the soul of this country where we live. Verities have to be earned, and they take time in the earning—time spent gazing out over your personal wind-glazed fields of snow. Once earned, they inhabit you in complex ways you cannot name, and they cannot be given away. They can only be transmogrified— transformed into something surreal or fantastic, unreal. And ours have been, and always for the same reason: primarily the titillation of those who used to be Easterners, who are everywhere now.

These are common sentiments here in the mountain West. In 1923 Charlie Russell agreed to speak before the Great Falls Booster Club. After listening to six or seven booster speeches, he tore up his own talk and spoke. This is what he said:

> *In my book a pioneer is a man who turned all the grass upside down, strung bob-wire over the dust that was left, poisoned the water and cut down the trees, killed the Indian who owned the land, and called it progress. If I had my way, the land here would be like God made it, and none of you sons of bitches would be here at all.*

So what are we left with? There was a great dream about a just and stable society, which was to be America. And there was another great dream about wilderness individuals, mountain men we have called them, who would be the natural defenders of that society. But our society is hugely corrupt, rich and impossibly complex, and our great simple individuals can define nothing to defend, nothing to reap but the isolation implicit in their stance, nothing to gain for their strength but loneliness. The vast, sad, recurrent story which is so centrally American. Western Rednecks cherish secret remnants of those dreams, and still try to live within them. No doubt a foolish enterprise.

But that's why, full of anger and a kind of releasing joy, they plunge their Snowcats around frozen lakes at 90 miles an hour, coming in for a whiskey stop with eyes glittering and icicles bright in their whiskers, and why on any summer day you can look into the sky over Missoula and see the hang-gliding daredevils circling higher than the mountains. That's why you see grown men climbing frozen waterfalls with pretty colored ropes.

And then there seems to be a shooting a week in the doublewide village. Spastic violence. You know, the husband wakes up from his drunk, lying on the kitchen floor with the light still burning, gets himself an Alka-Seltzer, stumbles into the living room, and there is Mother on the couch with half her side blown away. The 12-gauge is carefully placed back where it belongs on the rack over the breakfront. Can't tell what happened. Must have been an intruder.

Yeah, the crazy man inside us. Our friends wear Caterpillar D-9 caps when they've never pulled a friction in their lives, and Buck knives in little leather holsters on their belts, as if they might be called upon to pelt out a beaver at any moment. Or maybe just stab an empty beer can. Ah, wilderness, and suicidal nostalgia.

Which gets us to another kind of pioneer we see these days, people who come to the country with what seems to be an idea that connection with simplicities will save their lives. Which simplicities are those? The condescension implicit in the program is staggering. If you want to feel you are being taken lightly, try sitting around while someone tells you how he envies the simplicity of your life. What about Davis Patten? He says he is staying in Montana, and calling it home. So am I.

Despite the old Huckleberry Finn—mountain man notion of

striking out for the territory, I am going to hang on here, best I can, and nourish my own self. I know a lovely woman who lives up the road in a log house, on what is left of a hard-earned farmstead. I'm going to call and see if she's home. Maybe she'll smile and come have a glass of beer with me and my cronies.

THE HEART OF THE GAME

Thomas McGuane

Hunting in your own back yard becomes with time, if you love hunting, less and less expeditionary. This year, when Montana's eager frosts knocked my garden on its butt, the hoe seemed more like the rifle than it ever had before, the vegetables more like game.

My son and I went scouting before the season and saw some antelope in the high plains foothills of the Absaroka Range, wary, hanging on the skyline; a few bands and no great heads. We crept around, looking into basins, and at dusk met a tired cowboy on a tired horse followed by a tired blue-heeler dog. The plains seemed bigger than anything, bigger than the mountains that seemed to sit in the middle of them, bigger than the ocean. The clouds made huge shadows that traveled on the grass slowly through the day.

Hunting season trickles on forever; if you don't go in on a cow with anybody, there is the dark argument of the empty deep-freeze against headhunting ("You can't eat horns!"). But nevertheless, in my mind, I've laid out the months like playing cards, knowing some decent whitetails could be down in the river bottom and, fairly reliably, the long windy shots at antelope. The big buck mule deer—the ridge-runners—stay up in the scree and rock walls until the snow drives them out; but they stay high long after the elk have quit and broken down the hay corrals on the ranches and farmsteads, which, when you're hunting the rocks from a saddle horse, look pathetic and housebroken with their yellow lights against the coming of winter.

Where I live, the Yellowstone River runs straight north, then takes an eastward turn at Livingston, Montana. This flowing north is supposed to be remarkable; and the river doesn't do it long. It runs mostly over sand and stones once it comes out of the rock slots near the Wyoming line. But all along, there are deviations of one sort or another: canals, backwaters, sloughs; the red willows grow in the sometime-flooded bottom, and at the first elevation, the cottonwoods. I hunt here for the white-tail deer which, in recent years, have moved up these rivers in numbers never seen before.

The first morning, the sun came up hitting around me in arbitrary panels as the light moved through the jagged openings in the Absaroka Range. I was walking very slowly in the edge of the trees, the river invisible a few hundred yards to my right but sending a huge sigh through the willows. It was cold and the sloughs had crowns of ice thick enough to support me. As I crossed one great clear pane, trout raced around under my feet and a ten-foot bubble advanced slowly before my cautious steps. Then passing back into the trees, I found an active game trail, cut cross-lots to pick a better stand, sat in a good vantage place under a cottonwood with the ought-six across my knees. I thought, running my hands up into my sleeves, this is lovely but I'd rather be up in the hills; and I fell asleep.

I woke up a couple of hours later, the coffee and early-morning drill having done not one thing for my alertness. I had drooled on my rifle and it was time for my chores back at the ranch. My chores of late had consisted primarily of working on screenplays so that the bank didn't take the ranch. These days the primary ranch skill is making the payment; it comes before irrigation, feeding out, and calving. Some rancher friends find this so discouraging they get up and roll a number or have a slash of tanglefoot before they even think of the glories of the West. This is the New Rugged.

The next day, I reflected upon my lackadaisical hunting and left really too early in the morning. I drove around to Mission Creek in the dark and ended up sitting in the truck up some wash listening to a New Mexico radio station until my patience gave out and I started out cross-country in the dark, just able to make out the nose of the Absaroka Range as it faced across the river to the Crazy Mountains. It seemed maddeningly up and down slick banks, and a couple of times I had game clatter out in front of me in the dark. Then I turned up a long coulee that climbed endlessly south, and started in that direction, knowing the plateau on top should hold some antelope. After half an hour or so, I heard the mad laughing of coyotes, throwing their voices all around the inside of the coulee, trying to panic rabbits and making my hair stand on end despite my affection for them. The stars tracked overhead into the first pale light and it was nearly dawn before I came up on the bench. I could hear cattle below me and I moved along an edge of thorn trees to break my outline, then sat down at the point to wait for shooting light.

I could see antelope on the skyline before I had that light; and by the time I did, there was a good big buck angling across from me, looking at everything. I thought I could see well enough, and I got up into a sitting position and into the sling. I had made my moves quietly, but when I looked through the scope the antelope was 200 yards out, using up the country in bounds. I tracked with him, let him bounce up into the reticle, and touched off a shot. He was down and still, but I sat watching until I was sure.

Nobody who loves to hunt feels absolutely hunky-dory when the quarry goes down. The remorse spins out almost before anything and the balancing act ends on one declination or another. I decided that unless I become a vegetarian, I'll get my meat by hunting for it. I feel absolutely unabashed by the arguments of other carnivores who get their meat in plastic with blue numbers on it. I've seen slaughterhouses, and anyway, as Sitting Bull said, when the buffalo are gone, we will hunt mice, for we are hunters and we want our freedom.

The antelope had piled up in the sage, dead before he hit the ground. He was an old enough buck that the tips of his pronged horns were angled in toward each other. I turned him downhill to bleed him out. The bullet had mushroomed in the front of the lungs, so the job was already halfway done. With antelope, proper field dressing is critical because they can end up sour if they've been run or haphazardly hog-dressed. And they sour from their own body heat more than from external heat.

The sun was up and the big buteo hawks were lifting on the

thermals. There was enough breeze that the grass began to have directional grain like the prairie and the rim of the coulee wound up away from me toward the Absaroka. I felt peculiarly solitary, sitting on my heels next to the carcass in the sagebrush and greasewood, my rifle racked open on the ground. I made an incision around the metatarsal glands inside the back legs and carefully removed them and set them well aside; then I cleaned the blade of my hunting knife with handfuls of grass to keep from tainting the meat with those powerful glands. Next I detached the anus and testes from the outer walls and made a shallow puncture below the sternum, spread it with the thumb and forefinger of my left hand, and ran the knife upside down to the bone bridge between the hind legs. Inside, the diaphragm was like the taut lid of a drum and cut away cleanly, so that I could reach clear up to the back of the mouth and detach the windpipe. Once that was done I could draw the whole visceral package out onto the grass and separate out the heart, liver, and tongue before propping the carcass open with two whittled-up sage scantlings.

You could tell how cold the morning was, despite the exertion, just by watching the steam roar from the abdominal cavity. I stuck the knife in the ground and sat back against the slope, looking clear across to Convict Grade and the Crazy Mountains. I was blood from the elbows down and the antelope's eyes had skinned over. I thought, This is goddamned serious and you had better always remember that.

There was a big red enamel pot on the stove; and I ladled antelope chili into two bowls for my son and me. He said, "It better not be too hot."

"It isn't."

"What's your news?" he asked.

"Grandpa's dead."

"Which grandpa?" he asked. I told him it was Big Grandpa, my father. He kept on eating. "He died last night."

He said, "I know what I want for Christmas."

"What's that?"

"I want Big Grandpa back."

It was 1950-something and I was small, under twelve say, and there were four of us: my father, two of his friends, and me. There was a good belton setter belonging to the one friend, a hearty bird hunter who taught dancing and fist-fought at any provocation. The other man was old and sick and had a green fatal look in his face. My father took me aside and said, "Jack and I are going to the head of this field"—and he pointed up a mile and a half of stalks to where it ended in the flat woods— "and we're going to take the dog and get what he can point. These are running birds. So you and Bill just block the field and you'll have some shooting."

"I'd like to hunt with the dog." I had a 20-gauge Winchester my grandfather had given me, which got hocked and lost years later when another of my family got into the bottle; and I could hit with it and wanted to hunt over the setter. With respect to blocking the field, I could smell a rat.

"You stay with Bill," said my father, "and try to cheer him up."

"What's the matter with Bill?"

"He's had one heart attack after another and he's going to die."

"When?"

"Pretty damn soon."

I blocked the field with Bill. My first thought was, I hope he doesn't die before they drive those birds onto us; but if he does, I'll have all the shooting.

There was a crazy cold autumn light on everything, magnified by the yellow silage all over the field. The dog found birds right away and they were shooting. Bill said he was sorry but he didn't feel so good. He had his hunting license safety-pinned to the back of his coat and fiddled with a handful of 12-gauge shells. "I've shot a shitpile of game," said Bill, "but I don't feel so good anymore." He took a knife out of his coat pocket. "I got this in the Marines," he said, "and I earned it for four years in the Pacific. The handle's drilled out and weighted so you can throw it. I want you to have it." I took it and thanked him, looking into his green face, and wondered why he had given it to me. "That's for blocking this field with me," he said. "Your dad and that dance teacher are going to shoot them all. When you're not feeling so good, they put you at the end of the field to block when there isn't shit-all going to fly by you. They'll get them all. They and the dog will."

We had an indestructible tree in the yard we had chopped on, nailed steps to, and initialed; and when I pitched that throwing knife at it, the knife broke in two. I picked it up and thought, *This thing is jinxed.* So I took it out into the crab-apple woods and put it in the can I had buried, along with a Roosevelt dime and an atomic-bomb ring I had sent away for. This was a small collection of things I buried over a period of years. I was sending them to God. All He had to do was open the can, but they were never collected. In any case, I have long known that if I could understand why I wanted to send a broken knife I believed to be jinxed to God, then I would be a long way toward what they call a personal philosophy as opposed to these hand-to-mouth metaphysics of who said what to who in some cornfield twenty-five years ago.

We were in the bar at Chico Hot Springs near my home in Montana: me, a lout poet who had spent the day floating under the diving board while adolescent girls leapt overhead; and my brother John, who had glued himself to the pipe which poured warm water into the pool and announced over and over in a loud voice that every drop of water had been filtered through his bathing suit.

Now, covered with wrinkles, we were in the bar, talking to Alvin Close, an old government hunter. After half a century of predator control he called it "useless and half-assed."

Alvin Close killed the last major stock-killing wolf in Montana. He hunted the wolf so long he raised a litter of dogs to do it with. He hunted the wolf futilely with a pack that had fought the wolf a dozen times, until one day he gave up and let the dogs run the wolf out the back of a shallow canyon. He heard them yip their way into silence while he leaned up against a tree, and presently the wolf came tiptoeing down the front of the canyon into Alvin's lap. The wolf simply stopped because the game was up. Alvin raised the Winchester and shot it.

"How did you feel about that?" I asked.

"How do you think I felt?"

"I don't know."

"I felt like hell."

Alvin's evening was ruined and he went home. He was seventy-six years old and carried himself like an old-time army officer, setting his glass on the bar behind him without looking.

• • •

You stare through the plastic at the red smear of meat in the supermarket. What's this it says here? *Mighty Good? Tastee? Quality, Premium,* and *Government Inspected?* Soon enough, the blood is on your hands. It's inescapable.

Aldo Leopold was a hunter who I am sure abjured freeze-dried vegetables and extrusion burgers. His conscience was clean because his hunting was part of a larger husbandry in which the life of the country was enhanced by his own work. He knew that game populations are not bothered by hunting until they are already too precarious and that precarious game populations should not be hunted. Grizzlies should not be hunted, for instance. The enemy of game is clean farming and sinful chemicals, as well as the useless alteration of watersheds by promoter cretins and the insidious dizzards of land development, whose lobbyists teach us the venality of all governments.

A world in which a sacramental portion of food can be taken in an old way—hunting, fishing, farming, and gathering—has as much to do with societal sanity as a day's work for a day's pay.

For a long time, there was no tracking snow. I hunted on horseback for a couple of days in a complicated earthquake fault in the Gallatins. The fault made a maze of narrow canyons with flat floors. The sagebrush grew on woody trunks higher than my head and left sandy paths and game trails where the horse and I could travel.

There were Hungarian partridge that roared out in front of my horse, putting his head suddenly in my lap. And hawks tobogganed on the low air currents, astonished to find me there.

One finger canyon ended in a vertical rock wall from which issued a spring of the kind elsewhere associated with the Virgin Mary, hung with ex-votos and the orthopedic supplications of satisfied miracle customers. Here, instead, were nine identical piles of bear shit, neatly adorned with undigested berries.

One canyon planed up and topped out on an endless grassy rise. There were deer there, does and a young buck. A thousand yards away and staring at me with semaphore ears.

They assembled at a stiff trot from the haphazard array of feeding and strung out in a precise line against the far hill in a dog trot. When I removed my hat, they went into their pogo-stick gait and that was that.

"What did a deer ever do to you?"
   "Nothing."
   "I'm serious. What do you have to go and kill them for?"
   "I can't explain it talking like this."
   "Why should they die for you? Would you die for deer?"
   "If it came to that."

My boy and I went up the North Fork to look for grouse. We had my old pointer Molly, and Thomas's .22 pump. We flushed a number of birds climbing through the wild roses; but they roared away at knee level, leaving me little opportunity for my over-and-under, much less an opening for Thomas to ground-sluice one with his .22. We started out at the meteor hole above the last ranch and went all the way to the national forest. Thomas had his cap on the bridge of his nose and wobbled through the trees until we hit cross fences. We went out into the last open pasture before he got winded. So we sat down and looked across the valley at the Gallatin Range, furiously white and serrated, a bleak edge of the world. We sat in the sun and watched the chickadees make their way through the russet brush.

"Are you having a good time?"

"Sure," he said and curled a small hand around the octagonal barrel of the Winchester. I was not sure what I had meant by my question.

The rear quarters of the antelope came from the smoker so dense and finely grained it should have been sliced as prosciutto. We had edgy, crumbling cheddar from British Columbia and everybody kept an eye on the food and tried to pace themselves. The snow whirled in the window light and puffed the smoke down the chimney around the cedar flames. I had a stretch of enumerating things: my family, hayfields, saddle horses, friends, thirty-ought-six, French and Russian novels. I had a baby girl, colts coming, and a new roof on the barn. I finished a big corral made of railroad ties and 2 x 6s. I was within eighteen months of my father's death, my sister's death, and the collapse of my marriage. Still, the washouts were repairing; and when a few things had been set aside, not excluding paranoia, some features were left standing, not excluding lovers, children, friends, and saddle horses. In time, it would be clear as a bell. I did want venison again that winter and couldn't help but feel some old ridge-runner had my number on him.

I didn't want to read and I didn't want to write or acknowledge the phone with its tendrils into the zombie enclaves. I didn't want the New Rugged; I wanted the Old Rugged and a pot to piss in. Otherwise, it's deteriorata, with mice undermining the wiring in my frame house, sparks jumping in the insulation, the dog turning queer, and a horned owl staring at the baby through the nursery window.

It was pitch black in the bedroom and the windows radiated cold across the blankets. The top of my head felt this side of frost and the stars hung like ice crystals over the chimney. I scrambled out of bed and slipped into my long Johns, put on a heavy shirt and my wool logger pants with the police suspends. I carried the boots down to the kitchen so as not to wake the house and turned the percolator on. I put some cheese and chocolate in my coat, and when the coffee was done I filled a chili bowl and quaffed it against the winter.

When I hit the front steps I heard the hard squeaking of new snow under my boots and the wind moved against my face like a machine for refinishing hardwood floors. I backed the truck up to the horse trailer, the lights wheeling against the ghostly trunks of the bare cottonwoods. I connected the trailer and pulled it forward to a flat spot for loading the horse.

I had figured that when I got to the corral I could tell one horse from another by starlight; but the horses were in the shadow of the barn and I went in feeling my way among their shapes trying to find my hunting horse Rocky, and trying to get the front end of the big sorrel who kicks when surprised. Suddenly Rocky was looking in my face and I reached around his neck with the halter. A 1,200-pound bay quarter horse, his withers angled up like a fighting bull, he wondered where we were going but ambled after me on a slack lead rope as we headed out of the darkened corral.

I have an old trailer made by a Texas horse vet years ago. It has none of the amenities of newer trailers. I wish it had a dome light for loading in the dark; but it doesn't. You ought to check and see if the cat's sleeping in it before you load; and I didn't do that either. Instead, I climbed inside the trailer and the horse followed me. I tied the horse down to a D-ring and started back out, when he blew up. The two of us were confined in the small space and he was ripping and bucking between the walls with such noise and violence that I had a brief disassociated moment of suspension from fear. I jumped up on the manger with my arms around my head while the horse shattered the inside of the trailer and rocked it furiously on its axles. Then he blew the steel rings out of the halter and fell over backward in the snow. The cat darted out and was gone. I slipped down off the manger and looked for the horse; he had gotten up and was sidling down past the granary in the star shadows.

I put two blankets on him, saddled him, played with his feet, and calmed him. I loaded him without incident and headed out.

I went through the aspen line at daybreak, still climbing. The horse ascended steadily toward a high basin, creaking the saddle metronomically. It was getting colder as the sun came up, and the rifle scabbard held my left leg far enough from the horse that I was chilling on that side.

We touched the bottom of the basin and I could see the rock wall denned by a black stripe of evergreens on one side and the remains of an avalanche on the other. I thought how utterly desolate this country can look in winter and how one could hardly think of human travel in it at all, not white horsemen nor Indians dragging travois, just aerial raptors with their rending talons and heads like cameras slicing across the geometry of winter.

Then we stepped into a deep hole and the horse went to his chest in the powder, splashing the snow out before him as he floundered toward the other side. I got my feet out of the stirrups in case we went over. Then we were on wind-scoured rock and I hunted some lee for the two of us. I thought of my son's words after our last cold ride: "Dad, you know in 4-H? Well, I want to switch from Horsemanship to Aviation."

The spot was like this: a crest of snow crowned in a sculpted edge high enough to protect us. There was a tough little juniper to picket the horse to, and a good place to sit out of the cold and noise. Over my head, a long, curling plume of snow poured out, unchanging in shape against the pale blue sky. I ate some of the cheese and rewrapped it. I got the rifle down from the scabbard, loosened the cinch, and undid the flank cinch. I put the stirrup over the horn to remind me my saddle was loose, loaded two cartridges into the blind magazine, and slipped one in the chamber. Then I started toward the rock wall, staring at the patterned discolorations: old seeps, lichen, cracks, and the madhouse calligraphy of immemorial weather.

There were a lot of tracks where the snow had crusted out of the wind; all deer except for one well-used bobcat trail winding along the edges of a long rocky slot. I moved as carefully as I could, stretching my eyes as far out in front of my detectable movement as I could. I tried to work into the wind, but it turned erratically in the basin as the temperature of the new day changed.

The buck was studying me as soon as I came out on the open slope: he was a long way away and I stopped motionless to wait for him to feed again. He stared straight at me from 500 yards. I waited until I could no longer feel my feet nor finally my legs.

It was nearly an hour before he suddenly ducked his head and began to feed. Every time he fed I moved a few feet, but he was working away from me and I wasn't getting anywhere. Over the next half hour he made his way to a little rim and, in the half hour after that, moved the 20 feet that dropped him over the rim.

I went as fast as I could move quietly. I now had the rim to cover me and the buck should be less than 100 yards from me when I looked over. It was all browse for a half mile, wild roses, buck brush, and young quakies where there was any runoff.

When I reached the rim, I took off my hat and set it in the snow with my gloves inside. I wanted to be looking in the right direction when I cleared the rim, rise a half step and be looking straight at the buck, not scanning for the buck with him running 60, a degree or two out of my periphery. And I didn't want to gum it up with thinking or trajectory guessing. People are always trajectory guessing their way into gut shots and clean misses. So, before I took the last step, all there was to do was lower the rim with my feet, lower the buck into my vision, and isolate the path of the bullet.

As I took that step, I knew he was running. He wasn't in the browse at all, but angling into invisibility at the rock wall, racing straight into the elevation, bounding toward zero gravity, taking his longest arc into the bullet and the finality and terror of all you have made of the world, the finality you know that you share even with your babies with their inherited and ambiguous dentition, the finality that any minute now you will meet as well.

He slid 100 yards in a rush of snow. I dressed him and skidded him by one antler to the horse. I made a slit behind the last ribs, pulled him over the saddle and put the horn through the slit, lashed the feet to the cinch dees, and led the horse downhill. The horse had bells of clear ice around his hoofs, and when he slipped, I chipped them out from under his feet with the point of a bullet.

I hung the buck in the open woodshed with a lariat over a rafter. He turned slowly against the cooling air. I could see the intermittent blue light of the television against the bedroom ceiling from where I stood. I stopped the twirling of the buck, my hands deep in the sage-scented fur, and thought: This is either the beginning or the end of everything.

THE SOLACE OF OPEN SPACES

Gretel Ehrlich

It's May and I've just awakened from a nap, curled against sagebrush the way my dog taught me to sleep—sheltered from wind. A front is pulling the huge sky over me, and from the dark a hailstone has hit me on the head. I'm trailing a band of two thousand sheep across a stretch of Wyoming badlands, a fifty-mile trip that takes five days because sheep shade up in hot sun and won't budge until it's cool. Bunched together now, and excited into a run by the storm, they drift across dry land, tumbling into draws like water and surge out again onto the rugged, choppy plateaus that are the building blocks of this state.

The name Wyoming comes from an Indian word meaning "at the great plains," but the plains are really valleys, great arid valleys, sixteen hundred square miles, with the horizon bending up on all sides into mountain ranges. This gives the vastness a sheltering look.

Winter lasts six months here. Prevailing winds spill snowdrifts to the east, and new storms from the northwest replenish them. This white bulk is sometimes dizzying, even nauseating, to look at. At twenty, thirty, and forty degrees below zero, not only does your car not work, but neither do your mind and body. The landscape hardens into a dungeon of space. During the winter, while I was riding to find a new calf, my jeans froze to the saddle, and in the silence that such cold creates I felt like the first person on earth, or the last.

Today the sun is out—only a few clouds billowing. In the east, where the sheep have started off without me, the bench-land tilts up in a series of eroded red-earthed mesas, planed flat on top by a million years of water; behind them, a bold line of muscular scarps rears up ten thousand feet to become the Big Horn Mountains. A tidal pattern is engraved into the ground, as if left by the sea that once covered this state. Canyons curve down like galaxies to meet the oncoming rush of flat land.

To live and work in this kind of open country, with its hundred-mile views, is to lose the distinction between background and foreground. When I asked an older ranch hand to describe Wyoming's openness, he said, "It's all a bunch of nothing—wind and rattlesnakes—and so much of it you can't tell where you're going or where you've been and it don't make much difference." John, a sheepman I know, is tall and handsome and has an explosive temperament. He has a perfect intuition about people and sheep. They call him "Highpockets," because he's so long-legged; his graceful stride matches the distances he has to cover. He says, "Open space hasn't affected me at all. It's all the people moving in on it." The huge ranch he was born on takes up much of one county and spreads into another state; to put 100,000 miles on his pickup in three years and never leave home is not unusual. A friend of mine has an aunt who ranched on Powder River and didn't go off her place for eleven years. When her husband died, she quickly moved to town, bought a car, and drove around the States to see what she'd been missing.

Most people tell me they've simply driven through Wyoming, as if there were nothing to stop for. Or else they've skied in Jackson Hole, a place Wyomingites acknowledge uncomfortably because its green beauty and chic affluence are mismatched with the rest of the state. Most of Wyoming has a "lean-to" look. Instead of big, roomy barns and Victorian houses, there are dugouts, low sheds, log cabins, sheep camps, and fence lines that look like driftwood blown haphazardly into place. People here still feel pride because they live in such a harsh place, part of the glamorous cowboy past, and they are determined not to be the victims of a mining-dominated future.

Most characteristic of the state's landscape is what a developer euphemistically describes as "indigenous growth right up to your front door"—a reference to waterless stands of salt sage, snakes, jack rabbits, deerflies, red dust, a brief respite of wildflowers, dry washes, and no trees. In the Great Plains the vistas look like music, like Kyries of grass, but Wyoming seems to be the doing of a mad architect—tumbled and twisted, ribboned with faded, deathbed colors, thrust up and pulled down as if the place had been startled out of a deep sleep and thrown into a pure light.

I came here four years ago. I had not planned to stay, but I couldn't make myself leave. John, the sheepman, put me to work immediately. It was spring, and shearing time. For fourteen days of fourteen hours each, we moved thousands of sheep through sorting corrals to be sheared, branded, and deloused. I suspect that my original motive for coming here was to "lose myself" in new and unpopulated territory. Instead of producing the numbness I thought I wanted, life on the sheep ranch woke me up. The vitality of the people I was working with flushed out what had become a hallucinatory rawness inside me. I threw away my clothes and bought new ones; I cut my hair. The arid country was a clean slate. Its absolute indifference steadied me.

Sagebrush covers 58,000 square miles of Wyoming. The biggest city has a population of fifty thousand, and there are only five settlements that could be called cities in the whole state. The rest are towns, scattered across the expanse with as much as sixty miles between them, their populations two thousand, fifty, or ten. They are fugitive-looking, perched on a barren, windblown bench, or tagged onto a river or a railroad, or laid out straight in a farming valley with implement stores and a block-long Mormon church. In the eastern part of the state, which slides down into the Great Plains, the new mining settlements are boomtowns, trailer cities, metal knots on flat land.

Despite the desolate look, there's a coziness to living in this state. There are so few people (only 470,000) that ranchers who buy and sell cattle know one another statewide; the kids who choose to go to college usually go to the state's one university, in Laramie; hired hands work their way around Wyoming in a lifetime of hirings and firings. And despite the physical separation, people stay in touch, often driving two or three hours to another ranch for dinner.

Seventy-five years ago, when travel was by buckboard or horseback, cowboys who were temporarily out of work rode the grub line—drifting from ranch to ranch, mending fences or milking cows, and receiving in exchange a bed and meals. Gossip and messages traveled this slow circuit with them, creating an intimacy between ranchers who were three and four weeks' ride apart. One old-time couple I know, whose turn-of-the-century homestead was used by an outlaw gang as a relay station for stolen horses, recall that if you were traveling, desperado or not, any lighted ranch house was a welcome sign. Even now, for someone who lives in a remote spot, arriving at a ranch or coming to town for supplies is cause for celebration. To emerge from isolation can be disorienting. Everything looks bright, new, vivid. After I had been herding sheep for only three days, the sound of the camp tender's pickup flustered me. Longing for human company, I felt a foolish grin take over my face; yet I had to resist an urgent temptation to run and hide.

Things happen suddenly in Wyoming, the change of seasons and weather; for people, the violent swings in and out of isolation. But good-naturedness is concomitant with severity. Friendliness is a tradition. Strangers passing on the road wave hello. A common sight is two pickups stopped side by side far out on a range, on a dirt track winding through the sage. The drivers will share a cigarette, uncap their thermos bottles, and pass a battered cup, steaming with coffee, between windows. These meetings summon up the details of several generations, because, in Wyoming, private histories are largely public knowledge.

Because ranch work is a physical and, these days, economic strain, being "at home on the range" is a matter of vigor, self-reliance, and common sense. A person's life is not a series of dramatic events for which he or she is applauded or exiled but a slow accumulation of days, seasons, years, fleshed out by the generational weight of one's family and anchored by a land-bound sense of place.

In most parts of Wyoming, the human population is visibly out-numbered by the animal. Not far from my town of fifty, I rode into a narrow valley and startled a herd of two hundred elk. Eagles look like small people as they eat car-killed deer by the road. Antelope, moving in small, graceful bands, travel at sixty miles an hour, their mouths open as if drinking in the space.

The solitude in which westerners live makes them quiet. They telegraph thoughts and feelings by the way they tilt their heads and listen; pulling their Stetsons into a steep dive over their eyes, or pigeon-toeing one boot over the other, they lean against a fence with a fat wedge of Copenhagen beneath their lower lips and take in the whole scene. These detached looks of quiet amusement are sometimes cynical, but they can also come from a dry-eyed humility as lucid as the air is clear.

Conversation goes on in what sounds like a private code; a few phrases imply a complex of meanings. Asking directions, you get a curious list of details. While trailing sheep I was told to "ride up to that kinda upturned rock, follow the pink wash, turn left at the dump, and then you'll see the water hole." One friend told his wife on roundup to "turn at the salt lick and the dead cow," which turned out to be a scattering of bones and no salt lick at all.

Sentence structure is shortened to the skin and bones of a thought. Descriptive words are dropped, even verbs; a cowboy looking over a corral full of horses will say to a wrangler, "Which one needs rode?" People hold back their thoughts in what seems to be a dumbfounded silence, then erupt with an excoriating perceptive remark. Language, so compressed, becomes metaphorical. A rancher ended a relationship with one remark: "You're a bad check," meaning bouncing in and out was intolerable, and even coming back would be no good.

What's behind this laconic style is shyness. There is no vocabulary for the subject of feelings. It's not a hangdog shyness, or anything coy—always there's a robust spirit in evidence behind the restraint, as if the earth-dredging wind that pulls across Wyoming had carried its people's voices away but everything else in them had shouldered confidently into the breeze.

I've spent hours riding to sheep camp at dawn in a pickup when nothing was said; eaten meals in the cookhouse when the only words spoken were a mumbled "Thank you, ma'am" at the end of dinner. The silence is profound. Instead of talking, we seem to share one eye. Keenly observed, the world is transformed. The landscape is engorged with detail, every movement on it chillingly sharp. The air between people is charged. Days unfold, bathed in their own music. Nights become hallucinatory; dreams, prescient.

Spring weather is capricious and mean. It snows, then blisters with heat. There have been tornadoes. They lay their elephant trunks out in the sage until they find houses, then slurp everything up and leave. I've noticed that melting snowbanks hiss and rot, viperous, then drip into calm pools where ducklings hatch and livestock, being trailed to summer range, drink. With the ice cover gone, rivers churn a milkshake brown, taking culverts and small bridges with them. Water in such an arid place (the average annual rainfall where I live is less than eight inches) is like blood. It festoons drab land with green veins; a line of cottonwoods following a stream; a strip of alfalfa; and, on ditch banks, wild asparagus growing.

I've moved to a small cattle ranch owned by friends. It's at the foot of the Big Horn Mountains. A few weeks ago, I helped them deliver a calf who was stuck halfway out of his mother's body. By the time he was freed, we could see a heartbeat, but he was straining against a swollen tongue for air. Mary and I held him upside down by his back feet, while Stan, on his hands and knees in the blood, gave the calf mouth-to-mouth resuscitation. I have a vague memory of being pneumonia-choked as a child, my mother giving me her air, which may account for my romance with this windswept state.

If anything is endemic to Wyoming, it is wind. This big room of space is swept out daily, leaving a bone yard of fossils, agates, and carcasses in every stage of decay. Though it was water that initially shaped the state, wind is the meticulous gardener, raising dust and pruning the sage.

I try to imagine a world in which I could ride my horse across uncharted land. There is no wilderness left; wildness, yes, but true wilderness has been gone on this continent since the time of Lewis and Clark's overland journey.

Two hundred years ago, the Crow, Shoshone, Arapaho, Cheyenne, and Sioux roamed the intermountain West, orchestrating their movements according to hunger, season, and warfare. Once they acquired horses, they traversed the spines of all the big Wyoming ranges—the Absarokas, the Wind Rivers, the Tetons, the Big Horns—and wintered on the unprotected plains that fan out from them. Space was life. The world was their home.

What was life-giving to Native Americans was often night-marish to sodbusters who had arrived encumbered with families and ethnic pasts to be transplanted in nearly uninhabitable land. The great distances, the shortage of water and trees, and the loneliness created unexpected hardships for them. In her book *O Pioneers!,* Willa Cather gives a settler's version of the bleak landscape:

> *The little town behind them had vanished as if it had never been, had fallen behind the swell of the prairie, and the stern frozen country received them into its bosom. The homesteads were few and far apart; here and there a windmill gaunt against the sky, a sod house crouching in a hollow.*

The emptiness of the West was for others a geography of possibility. Men and women who amassed great chunks of land and struggled to preserve unfenced empires were, despite their self-serving motives, unwitting geographers. They understood the lay of the land. But by the 1850s the Oregon and Mormon trails sported bumper-to-bumper traffic. Wealthy landowners, many of them aristocratic absentee landlords, known as remittance men because they were paid to come West and get out of their families' hair, overstocked the range with more than a million head of cattle. By 1885 the feed and water were desperately short, and the winter of 1886 laid out the gaunt bodies of dead animals so closely together that when the thaw came, one rancher from Kaycee claimed to have walked on cowhide all the way to Crazy Woman Creek, twenty miles away.

Territorial Wyoming was a boy's world. The land was generous with everything but water. At first there was room enough, food enough, for everyone. And, as with all beginnings, an expansive mood set in. The young cowboys, drifters, shopkeepers, schoolteachers, were heroic, lawless, generous, rowdy, and tenacious. The individualism and optimism generated during those times have endured.

John Tisdale rode north with the trail herds from Texas. He was a college-educated man with enough money to buy a small outfit near the Powder River. While driving home from the town of Buffalo with a buckboard full of Christmas toys for his family and a winter's supply of food, he was shot in the back by an agent of the cattle barons who resented the encroachment of small-time stockmen like him. The wealthy cattlemen tried to control all the public grazing land by restricting membership in the Wyoming Stock Growers Association, as if it were a country club. They ostracized from roundups and brandings cowboys and ranchers who were not members, then denounced them as rustlers. Tisdale's death, the second such cold-blooded murder, kicked off the Johnson County cattle war, which was no simple good-guy-bad-guy shoot-out but a complicated class struggle between landed gentry and less affluent settlers—a shocking reminder that the West was not an egalitarian sanctuary after all.

Fencing ultimately enforced boundaries, but barbed wire abrogated space. It was stretched across the beautiful valleys, into the mountains, over desert badlands, through buffalo grass. The "anything is possible" fever—the lure of any new place—was constricted. The integrity of the land as a geographical body, and the freedom to ride anywhere on it, were lost.

I punched cows with a young man named Martin, who is the great-grandson of John Tisdale. His inheritance is not the open land that Tisdale knew and prematurely lost but a rage against restraint.

Wyoming tips down as you head northeast; the highest ground —the Laramie Plains—is on the Colorado border. Up where I live, the Big Horn River leaks into difficult, arid terrain. In the basin where it's dammed, sandhill cranes gather and, with delicate legwork, slice through the stilled water. I was driving by with a rancher one morning when he commented that cranes are "old-fashioned." When I asked why, he said, "Because they mate for life." Then he looked at me with a twinkle in his eyes, as if to say he really did believe in such things but also understood why we break our own rules.

In all this open space, values crystalize quickly. People are strong on scruples but tenderhearted about quirky behavior. A friend and I found one ranch hand, who's "not quite right in the head," sitting in front of the badly decayed carcass of a cow, shaking his finger and saying, "Now, I don't want you to do this ever again!" When I asked what was wrong with him, I was told, "He's goofier than hell, just like the rest of us." Perhaps because the West is historically new, conventional morality is still felt to be less important than rock-bottom truths. Though there's always a lot of teasing and sparring, people are blunt with one another, sometimes even cruel, believing honesty is stronger medicine than sympathy, which may console but often conceals.

The formality that goes hand in hand with the rowdiness is known as the Western Code. It's a list of practical do's and don'ts, faithfully observed. A friend, Cliff, who runs a trap-line in the winter, cut off half his foot while chopping a hole in the ice. Alone, he dragged himself to his pickup and headed for town, stopping to open the ranch gate as he left, and getting out to close it again, thus losing, in his observance of rules, precious time and blood. Later, he commented, "How would it look, them having to come to the hospital to tell me their cows had gotten out?"

Accustomed to emergencies, my friends doctor each other from the vet's bag with relish. When one old-timer suffered a heart attack in hunting camp, his partner quickly stirred up a brew of red horse liniment and hot water and made the half-conscious victim drink it, then tied him onto a horse and led him twenty miles to town. He regained consciousness and lived.

The roominess of the state has affected political attitudes as well. Ranchers keep up with world politics and the convulsions of the economy but are basically isolationists. Being used to running their own small empires of land and livestock, they're suspicious of big government. It's a "don't fence me in" holdover from a century ago. They still want the elbow room their grandfathers had, so they're strongly conservative, but with a populist twist.

Summer is the season when we get our "cowboy tans"—on the lower parts of our faces and on three fourths of our arms. Excessive heat, in the nineties and higher, sends us outside with the mosquitoes. In winter we're tucked inside our houses, and the white wasteland outside appears to be expanding, but in summer all the greenery abridges space. Summer is a go-ahead season. Every living thing is off the block and in the race: battalions of bugs in flight and biting; bats swinging around my log cabin as if the bases were loaded and someone had hit a home run. Some of summer's high-speed growth is ominous: lark-spur, death camas, and green greasewood can kill sheep—an ironic idea, dying in this desert from eating what is too verdant. With sixteen hours of daylight, farmers and ranchers irrigate feverishly. There are first, second, and third cuttings of hay, some crews averaging only four hours of sleep a night for weeks. And, like the cowboys who in summer ride the night rodeo circuit, night-hawks make daredevil dives at dusk with an eerie whirring sound like a plane going down on the shimmering horizon.

In the town where I live, they've had to board up the dance-hall windows because there have been so many fights. There's so little to do except work that people wind up in a state of idle agitation that becomes fatalistic, as if there were nothing to be done about all this untapped energy. So the dark side to the grandeur of these spaces is the small-mindedness that seals people in. Men become hermits; women go mad. Cabin fever explodes into suicides, or into grudges and lifelong family feuds. Two sisters in my area inherited a ranch but found they couldn't get along. They fenced the place in half. When one's cows got out and mixed with the other's, the women went at each other with shovels. They ended up in the same hospital room but never spoke a word to each other for the rest of their lives.

After the brief lushness of summer, the sun moves south. The range grass is brown. Livestock is trailed back down from the mountains. Water holes begin to frost over at night. Last fall Martin asked me to accompany him on a pack trip. With five horses, we followed a river into the mountains behind the tiny Wyoming town of Meeteetse. Groves of aspen, red and orange, gave off a light that made us look toasted. Our hunting camp was so high that clouds skidded across our foreheads, then slowed to sail out across the warm valleys. Except for a bull moose who wandered into our camp and mistook our black gelding for a rival, we shot at nothing.

One of our evening entertainments was to watch the night sky. My dog, a dingo bred to herd sheep, also came on the trip. He is so used to the silence and empty skies that when an airplane flies over he always looks up and eyes the distant intruder quizzically. The sky, lately, seems to be much more crowded than it used to be. Satellites make their silent passes in the dark with great regularity. We counted eighteen in one hour's viewing. How odd to think that while they circumnavigated the planet, Martin and I had moved only six miles into our local wilderness and had seen no other human for the two weeks we stayed there.

At night, by moonlight, the land is whittled to slivers—a ridge, a river, a strip of grassland stretching to the mountains, then the huge sky. One morning a full moon was setting in the west just as the sun was rising. I felt precariously balanced between the two as I loped across a meadow. For a moment, I could believe that the stars, which were still visible, work like cooper's bands, holding together everything above Wyoming.

Space has a spiritual equivalent and can heal what is divided and burdensome in us. My grandchildren will probably use space shuttles for a honeymoon trip or to recover from heart attacks, but closer to home we might also learn how to carry space inside ourselves in the effortless way we carry our skins. Space represents sanity, not a life purified, dull, or "spaced out" but one that might accommodate intelligently any idea or situation.

From the clayey soil of northern Wyoming is mined bentonite, which is used as a filler in candy, gum, and lipstick. We Americans are great on fillers, as if what we have, what we are, is not enough. We have a cultural tendency toward denial, but, being affluent, we strangle ourselves with what we can buy. We have only to look at the houses we build to see how we build *against* space, the way we drink against pain and loneliness. We fill up space as if it were a pie shell, with things whose opacity further obstructs our ability to see what is already there.

VARIATIONS ON A THEME BY CRÈVECOEUR

Wallace Stegner

There are many kinds of wildernesses, Aldo Leopold wrote in *A Sand County Almanac,* and each kind forces on people a different set of adaptations and creates a different pattern of life, custom, and belief. These patterns we call cultures.

By that criterion, the West should have a different cultural look from other American regions, and within the regional culture there should be discernible a half dozen subcultures stemming from our adaptations to shortgrass plains, alpine mountains, slickrock canyons, volcanic scablands, and both high and low deserts.

But cultural differentiation takes a long time, and happens most completely in isolation and to homogeneous peoples, as it happened to the Paiutes. The West has had neither time nor isolation nor homogeneity of race and occupation. Change, both homegrown and imported, has overtaken time, time and again. We have to adapt not only to our changed physical environment but to our own adaptations, and sometimes we have to backtrack from our own mistakes.

Cultures evolving within heterogeneous populations do not grow steadily from definable quality to definable quality. Not only is their development complicated by class, caste, and social mobility, but they undergo simultaneous processes of erosion and deposition. They start from something, not from nothing. Habits and attitudes that have come to us embedded in our inherited culture, especially our inherited language, come incorporated in everything from nursery rhymes to laws and prayers, and they often have the durability of flint pebbles in puddingstone. No matter how completely their old matrix is dissolved, they remain intact, and are deposited almost unchanged in the strata of the new culture.

The population that for the eleven public-lands states and territories was four million in 1900 was forty-five million in 1984, with at least a couple of million more, and perhaps twice that many, who weren't counted and didn't want to be. Many of those forty-five or forty-seven or forty-nine million came yesterday, since the end of World War II. They have not adapted, in the cultural sense, very completely. Some of them are living anonymously in the Spanish-speaking barrios of San Diego, El Paso, Los Angeles, San Jose, where the Immigration Service can't find them. Some are experimenting with quick-change life-styles in the cultural confusion of western cities. Some are reading *Sunset Magazine* to find out what they should try to become. Some think they already know, from the movies and TV.

Being a Westerner is not simple. If you live, say, in Los Angeles, you live in the second-largest city in the nation, urban as far as the eye can see in every direction except west. There is, or was in 1980—the chances would be somewhat greater now—a 6.6 percent chance that you are Asian, a 16.7 percent chance that you are black, and a 27 percent chance that you are Hispanic. You have only a 48 percent chance of being a non-Hispanic white.

This means that instead of being suitable for casting in the cowboy and pioneer roles familiar from the mythic and movie West, you may be one of those "Chinks" or "Spics" or "Greasers" for whom the legendary West had a violent contempt. You'd like to be a hero, and you may adopt the costume and attitudes you admire, but your color or language or the slant of your eyes tells you that you are one of the kind once scheduled to be a villain or a victim, and your current status as second-class citizen confirms that view. You're part of a subculture envious of or hostile to the dominant one.

This ethnic and cultural confusion exists not only in Los Angeles but in varying proportions in every western city and many western towns. Much of the adaptation that is going on is adaptation to an uncertain reality or to a reality whose past and present do not match. The western culture and western character with which it is easiest to identify exist largely in the West of make-believe, where they can be kept simple.

As invaders, we were rarely, or only temporarily, dependent on the materials, foods, or ideas of the regions we pioneered. The champagne and oysters that cheered midnight suppers during San Francisco's Gold Rush period were not local, nor was the taste that demanded them. The dominant white culture was always aware of its origins; it brought its origins with it across the plains or around the Horn, and it kept in touch with them.

The Spanish of New Mexico, who also brought their origins with them, are in other ways an exception. Settled at the end of the sixteenth century, before Jamestown and Quebec and well before the Massachusetts Bay Colony, New Mexico existed in isolation, dependent largely on itself, until the newer Americans forcibly took it over in 1846; and during those two and a half centuries it had a high Indian culture close at hand to teach it how to live with the country. Culturally, the Spanish Southwest is an island, adapted in its own ways, in many ways alien.

By contrast, the Anglo-American West, barely breached until the middle of the nineteenth century, was opened during a time of rapid communication. It was linked with the world by ship, rail, and telegraph before the end of the 1860s, and the isolation of even its brief, explosive outposts, its Alder Gulches and Cripple Creeks, was anything but total. Excited travelers reported the West in words to match its mountains; it was viewed in Currier and Ives prints drawn by enthusiasts who had never been there except in imagination. The outside never got over its heightened and romantic notion of the West. The West never got over its heightened and romantic notion of itself.

The pronounced differences that some people see between the West and other parts of America need to be examined. Except as they involve Spanish or Indian cultures, they could be mainly illusory, the result of the tendency to see the West in its mythic enlargement rather than as it is, and of the corollary tendency to take our cues from myths in the effort to enhance our lives. Life does sometimes copy art. Not only drugstore cowboys and street-corner Kit Carsons succumb. Plenty of authentic ranch hands have read pulp Westerns in the shade of the bunkhouse and got up walking, talking, and thinking like Buck Duane or Hopalong Cassidy.

• • •

No matter what kind of wilderness it developed in, every part of the real West was a melting-pot mixture of people from everywhere, operating under the standard American drives of restlessness, aggressiveness, and great expectations, and with the standard American freedom that often crossed the line into violence. It was supposed to be a democracy, and at least in the sense that it was often every man for himself, it was. Though some of its phases—the fur trade, the gold rushes, the open-range cattle industry—lasted hardly longer than the blink of an eye, other phases—logging, irrigation farming, the stock farm with cattle or sheep—have lasted by now for a century or more, and have formed the basis for a number of relatively stable communities with some of the attributes of place, some identity as subcultures of the prevailing postfrontier culture of America. If Turner's thesis is applicable beyond the 98th meridian, then the West ought to be, with minor local variations, America only more so.

Actually it is and it isn't. It would take fast footwork to dance the society based on big reclamation projects into a democracy. Even the cattle kingdom from which we derive our most individualistic and independent folk hero was never a democracy as the Middle West, say, was a democracy. The real-life cattle baron was and is about as democratic as a feudal baron. The cowboy in practice was and is an overworked, underpaid hireling, almost as homeless and dispossessed as a modern crop worker, and his fabled independence was and is chiefly the privilege of quitting his job in order to go looking for another just as bad. Some went outside the law. There is a discrepancy between the real conditions of the West, which even among outlaws enforced cooperation and group effort, and the folklore of the West, which celebrated the dissidence of dissent, the most outrageous independence.

The dynamics of contemporary adaptation work ambiguously. The best imitators of frontier individualism these days are probably Silicon Valley and conglomerate executives, whose entrepreneurial attributes are not greatly different from those of an old-time cattle baron. Little people must salve with daydreams and fantasy the wounds of living. Some may imagine themselves becoming captains of industry, garage inventors whose inventions grow into Fortune 500 companies overnight; but I think that more of them are likely to cuddle up to a culture hero independent of the system and even opposed to it— a culture hero given them by Owen Wister, an eastern snob who saw in the common cowherd the lineaments of Lancelot. Chivalry, or the daydream of it, is at least as common among day dreamers as among entrepreneurs.

Physically, the West could only be itself. Its scale, its colors, its landforms, its plants and animals, tell a traveler what country he is in, and a native that he is at home. Even western cities owe most of their distinctiveness to their physical setting. Albuquerque with its mud-colored houses spreading like clay banks along the valley of the Rio Grande could only be New Mexico. Denver's ringworm suburbs on the apron of the Front Range could only be boom-time Colorado. Salt Lake City bracing back against the Wasatch and looking out toward the dead sea and the barren ranges could only be the Great Basin.

But is anything except their setting distinctive? The people in them live on streets named Main and State, Elm and Poplar, First and Second, like Americans elsewhere. They eat the same

Wheaties and Wonder Bread and Big Macs, watch the same ball games and soaps and sitcoms on TV, work at the same industrial or service jobs, suffer from the same domestic crises and industrial blights, join the same health clubs and neighborhood protective associations, and in general behave and misbehave much as they would in Omaha or Chicago or East Orange. The homogenizing media have certainly been at work on them, perhaps with more effect than the arid spaciousness of the region itself, and while making them more like everybody else have also given them misleading clues about who they are.

"Who is the American, this new man?" Crèvecoeur asked rhetorically in his *Letters from an American Farmer* more than two hundred years ago, and went on to idealize him as the American farmer—industrious, optimistic, upwardly mobile, family-oriented, socially responsible, a new man given new hope in the new world, a lover of both hearth and earth, a builder of communities. He defined him in the terms of a new freedom, emancipated from feudalism, oppression, and poverty, but with no wish to escape society or its responsibilities. Quite the contrary.

Crèvecoeur also sketched, with distaste, another kind of American, a kind he thought would fade away with the raw frontier that had created him. This kind lived alone or with a slattern woman and a litter of kids out in the woods. He had no fixed abode, tilled no ground or tilled it only fitfully, lived by killing, was footloose, uncouth, antisocial, impatient of responsibility and law. The eating of wild meat, Crèvecoeur said, made him ferocious and gloomy. Too much freedom promoted in him a coarse selfishness and a readiness to violence.

The pioneer farmer as Crèvecoeur conceived him has a place in western history, and as the Jeffersonian yeoman he had a prominent place in the mistaken effort that oversettled the West, first by homestead and later by reclamation. Traces of him are to be found in western literature, art, and myth. Sculptors have liked his sturdy figure plodding beside the covered wagon on which ride his poke-bonneted wife and his barefoot children. He strides through a lot of WPA murals. The Mormons, farmers in the beginning, idealize him. He has achieved more than life size in such novels of the migration as *The Covered Wagon* and *The Way West*.

But those, as I have already suggested, are novels more of motion than of place, and the emigrants in them are simply farmer-pioneers on their way to new farms. They have not adapted to the West in the slightest degree. They belong where the soil is deep, where the Homestead Act worked, where settlers planted potato peelings in their fireguards and adjourned to build a combination school–church–social hall almost before they had roofs on their shanties. The pioneer farmer is a midwestern, not a western, figure. He is a pedestrian, and in the West, horseman's country even for people who never got on a horse in their lives, pedestrians suffer from the horseman's contempt that seems as old as the Scythians. The farmer's very virtues as responsible husband, father, and home builder are against him as a figure of the imagination. To the fantasizing mind he is dull, the ancestor of the clodhopper, the hayseed, and the hick. I have heard Wyoming ranch hands jeer their relatives from Idaho, not because the relatives were Mormons—so were the ranch hands—but because they were farmers, potato diggers.

It was Crèvecoeur's wild man, the borderer emancipated into total freedom, first in eastern forests and then in the plains and mountains of the West, who really fired our imaginations, and still does. We have sanitized him somewhat, but our principal folk hero, in all his shapes, good and bad, is essentially antisocial.

In real life, as Boone, Bridger, Jed Smith, Kit Carson, he appeals to us as having lived a life of heroic courage, skill, and self-reliance. Some of his manifestations, such as Wild Bill Hickok and Buffalo Bill Cody, are tainted with outlawry or showmanship, but they remain more than life-size. Even psychopathic killers such as Billy the Kid and Tom Horn throw a long shadow, and some outlaws, such as Butch Cassidy and Harry Longabaugh, have all the engaging mutability of Robin Hood. What charms us in them is partly their daring, skill, and invulnerability, partly their chivalry; but not to be overlooked is their impatience with all restraint, their freedom from the social responsibility that Crèvecoeur admired in his citizen-farmer, and that on occasion bows the shoulders of every man born.

Why should I stand up for civilization? Thoreau asked a lecture audience. Any burgher or churchwarden would stand up for that. Thoreau chose instead to stand up for wildness and the savage heart.

We all know that impulse. When youths run away from home, they don't run away to become farmers. They run away to become romantic isolates, lone riders who slit their eyes against steely distance and loosen the carbine in its scabbard when they see law, or obligation, or even company, approaching.

Lawlessness, like wildness, is attractive, and we conceive the last remaining home of both to be the West. In a folklore predominantly masculine and macho, even women take on the look. Calamity Jane is more familiar to us than Dame Shirley, though Dame Shirley had it all over Jane in brains, and could have matched her in courage, and lived in mining camps every bit as rough as the cow towns and camps that Calamity Jane frequented. But then, Jane grew up in the shortgrass West, Dame Shirley in Massachusetts.

The attraction of lawlessness did not die with the frontier, either. Look at the survivalist Claude Dallas, who a few years ago killed two Idaho game wardens when they caught him poaching—shot them and then finished them off with a bullet in the back of the head. In that act of unchivalrous violence Dallas was expressing more than an unwillingness to pay a little fine. For months, until he was captured early in 1987, he hid out in the deserts of Idaho and Nevada, protected by people all over the area. Why did they protect him? Because his belated frontiersman style, his total self-reliance and physical competence, his repudiation of any control, appealed to them more than murder repelled them or law enlisted their support.

All this may seem remote from the life of the average Westerner, who lives in a city and is more immediately concerned with taxes, schools, his job, drugs, the World Series, or even disarmament, than with archetypal figures out of folklore. But it is not so remote as it seems. Habits persist. The hoodlums who come to San Francisco to beat up gays are vigilantes, enforcing their prejudices with violence, just as surely as were the miners who used to hunt down Indians and hang Chinese in the Mother Lode, or the ranchers who rode out to exterminate the nesters in Wyoming's Johnson County War.

Habits persist. The hard, aggressive, single-minded energy

that according to politicians made America great is demonstrated every day in resource raids and leveraged takeovers by entrepreneurs; and along with that competitive individualism and ruthlessness goes a rejection of any controlling past or tradition. What matters is here, now, the seizable opportunity. "We don't need any history," said one Silicon Valley executive when the Santa Clara County Historical Society tried to bring the electronics industry together with the few remaining farmers to discuss what was happening to the valley that only a decade or two ago was the fruit bowl of the world. "What we need is more attention to our computers and the moves of the competition."

We are not so far from our models, real and fictional, as we think. As on a wild river, the water passes, the waves remain. A high degree of mobility, a degree of ruthlessness, a large component of both self-sufficiency and self-righteousness, mark the historical pioneer, the lone-riding folk hero, and the modern businessman intent on opening new industrial frontiers and getting his own in the process. The same qualities inform the extreme individualists who believe that they belong to nothing except what they choose to belong to, those who try on lifestyles as some try on clothes, whose only communal association is with what Robert Bellah calls "life-style enclaves," casual and temporary groupings of the like-minded. One reason why it is so difficult to isolate any definitely western culture is that so many Westerners, like other Americans only more so, shy away from commitment. Mobility of every sort—physical, familial, social, corporate, occupational, religious, sexual—confirms and reinforces the illusion of independence.

Back to the freedom-loving loner, whom we might call

Leatherstocking's descendant, as Henry Nash Smith taught us to, if all that tribe were not childless as well as orphaned. In the West this figure acquired an irresistible costume—the boots, spurs, chaps, and sombrero bequeathed to him by Mexican vaqueros, plus the copper-riveted canvas pants invented for California miners by a peddler named Levi Strauss—but he remained estranged from real time, real place, and any real society or occupation. In fact, it is often organized society, in the shape of a crooked sheriff and his cronies, that this loner confronts and confounds.

The notion of civilization's corruption, the notion that the conscience of an antisocial savage is less calloused than the conscience of society, is of course a bequest from Jean-Jacques Rousseau. The chivalry of the antisocial one, his protectiveness of the weak and oppressed, especially those whom James Fenimore Cooper customarily referred to as "females," is from Cooper, with reinforcement from two later romantics, Frederic Remington and Owen Wister, collaborators in the creation of the knight-errant in chaps.

The hero of Wister's 1902 novel *The Virginian* is gentle-seeming, easygoing, humorous, but when the wicked force him into action he is the very gun of God, better at violence than the wicked are. He is a daydream of glory made flesh. But note that the Virginian not only defeats Trampas in a gunfight as formalized as a fourteenth-century joust, the first of a thousand literary and movie walk-downs, but he also joins the vigilantes and in the name of law and order acts as jury, judge, and hangman for his friend Shorty, who has gone bad and become a rustler.

The Virginian feels sorry about Shorty, but he never questions that the stealing of a few mavericks should be punished by death, any more than Wister questioned the motives of his Wyoming rancher host who led the Johnson County vigilantes against the homesteaders they despised and called rustlers. This culture hero is himself law. Law is whatever he and his companions (and employers) believe (which means law is his and their self-interest). Whatever action he takes is law enforcement. Compare Larry McMurtry's two former Texas Rangers in *Lonesome Dove.* They kill more people than all the outlaws in that book put together do, but their killings are *right.* Their lawlessness is justified by the lack of any competing socialized law, and by a supreme confidence in themselves, as if every judgment of theirs could be checked back to Coke and Blackstone, if not to Leviticus.

Critics have noted that in *The Virginian* (and for that matter in most of its successors, though not in *Lonesome Dove*) there are no scenes involving cattle. There is no manure, no punching of postholes or stringing of barbed wire, none of the branding, castrating, dehorning, dipping, and horseshoeing that real cowboys, hired men on horseback, spend their laborious and unromantic lives at. The physical universe is simplified like the moral one. Time is stopped.

The Virginian is the standard American orphan, dislocated from family, church, and place of origin, with an uncertain past identified only by his nickname. With his knightly sense of honor and his capacity to outviolence the violent, he remains an irresistible model for romantic adolescents of any age, and he transfers readily from the cowboy setting to more modern ones. It is only a step from his "When you call me that, smile" to the remark made famous by a recent mayor of Carmel and by the fortieth president of the United States: "Go ahead, make my day."

There are thousands more federal employees in the West than there are cowboys—more bookkeepers, aircraft and electronics workers, auto mechanics, printers, fry cooks. There may be more writers. Nevertheless, when most Americans east of the Missouri—most people in the world—hear the word "West" they think "cowboy." Recently a documentary filmmaker asked me to be a consultant on a film that would finally reveal the true West, without romanticizing or adornment. It was to be done by chronicling the life of a single real-life individual. Guess who he was. A cowboy, and a rodeo cowboy at that—a man who had run away from his home in Indiana at the age of seventeen, worked for a year on a Texas ranch, found the work hard, made his way onto the rodeo circuit, and finally retired with a lot of his vertebrae out of line to an Oklahoma town, where he made silver-mounted saddles and bridles suitable for the Sheriff's Posse in a Frontier Days parade and spun yarns for the wide-eyed local young.

Apart from the fantasy involved, which is absolutely authentic, that show-business life is about as typically western as a bullfighter's is typically Spanish. The critics will probably praise the film for its realism.

I spend this much time on a mythic figure who has irritated me all my life because I would obviously like to bury him. But I know I can't. He is a faster gun than I am. He is too attractive to the daydreaming imagination. It gets me nowhere to object to the self-righteous, limited, violent code that governs him, or to disparage the novels of Louis L'Amour because they were mass-produced with interchangeable parts. Mr. L'Amour sells in the millions, and at times has readers in the White House.

But what one can say, and be sure of, is that even while the cowboy myth romanticizes and falsifies western life, it says something true about western, and hence about American, character.

Western culture and character, hard to define in the first place because they are only half-formed and constantly changing, are further clouded by the mythic stereotype. Why hasn't the stereotype faded away as real cowboys became less and less typical of western life? Because we can't or won't do without it, obviously. But also there is the visible, pervasive fact of western space, which acts as a preservative. Space, itself the product of incorrigible aridity and hence more or less permanent, continues to suggest unrestricted freedom, unlimited opportunity for testings and heroisms, a continuing need for self-reliance and physical competence. The untrammeled individualist persists partly as a residue of the real and romantic frontiers, but also partly because runaways from more restricted regions keep reimporting him. The stereotype continues to affect romantic Westerners and non-Westerners in romantic ways, but if I am right it also affects real Westerners in real ways.

In the West it is impossible to be unconscious of or indifferent to space. At every city's edge it confronts us as federal lands kept open by aridity and the custodial bureaus; out in the boondocks it engulfs us. And it does contribute to individualism, if only because in that much emptiness people have the dignity of rareness and must do much of what they do without help, and because self-reliance becomes a social imperative, part of a code. Witness the crudely violent code that governed a young Westerner like Norman Maclean, as he reported it in the stories of *A River Runs Through It.* Witness the way in which space haunts the poetry of such western poets as William Stafford, Richard Hugo, Gary Snyder. Witness the lonely, half-attached childhood of a writer such as Ivan Doig. I feel the childhood reported in his *This House of Sky* because it is so much like my own.

Even in the cities, even among the dispossessed migrants of the factories in the fields, space exerts a diluted influence as illusion and reprieve. Westerners live outdoors more than people elsewhere because outdoors is mainly what they've got. For clerks and students, factory workers and mechanics, the outdoors is freedom, just as surely as it is for the folkloric and mythic figures. They don't have to own the outdoors, or get permission, or cut fences, in order to use it. It is public land, partly theirs, and that space is a continuing influence on their minds and senses. It encourages a fatal carelessness and destructiveness because it seems so limitless and because what is everybody's is nobody's responsibility. It also encourages, in some, an impassioned protectiveness: the battlegrounds of the environmental movement lie in the western public lands. Finally, it promotes certain needs, tastes, attitudes, skills. It is those tastes, attitudes, and skills, as well as the prevailing destructiveness and its corrective, love of the land, that relate real Westerners to the myth.

David Rains Wallace, in *The Wilder Shore,* has traced the effect of the California landscape—the several California landscapes from the Pacific shore to the inner deserts—on California writers. From Dana to Didion, the influence has been varied and powerful. It is there in John Muir ecstatically riding a storm in the top of a two-hundred-foot sugar pine; in Mary

Austin quietly absorbing wisdom from a Paiute basketmaker; in Jack London's Nietzschean supermen pitting themselves not only against society but against the universe; in Frank Morris's atavistic McTeague, shackled to a corpse that he drags through the 130-degree heat of Death Valley; and in Robinson Jeffers on his stone platform between the stars and the sea, falling in love outward toward space. It is also there in the work of western photographers, notably Ansel Adams, whose grand, manless images are full of the awe men feel in the face of majestic nature. Awe is common in that California tradition. Humility is not.

Similar studies could be made, and undoubtedly will be, of the literature of other parts of the West, and of special groups of writers such as Native Americans who are mainly western. The country lives, still holy, in Scott Momaday's *Way to Rainy Mountain.* It is there like a half-forgotten promise in Leslie Marmon Silko's *Ceremony,* and like a homeland lost to invaders in James Welch's *Winter in the Blood* and Louise Erdrich's *Love Medicine.* It is a dominating presence, as I have already said, in the work of Northwest writers.

Western writing turns out, not surprisingly, to be largely about things that happen outdoors. It often involves characters who show a family resemblance of energetic individualism, great physical competence, stoicism, determination, recklessness, endurance, toughness, rebelliousness, resistance to control. It has, that is, residual qualities of the heroic, as the country in which it takes place has residual qualities of the wilderness frontier.

Those characteristics are not the self-conscious creation of regional patriotism, or the result of imitation of older by younger, or greater by lesser, writers. They are inescapable; western life and space generate them; they are what the faithful mirror shows. When I wrote *The Big Rock Candy Mountain* I was ignorant of almost everything except what I myself had lived, and I had no context for that. By the time I wrote *Wolf Willow,* a dozen years later, and dealt with some of the same experience from another stance, I began to realize that my Bo Mason was a character with relatives throughout western fiction. I could see in him resemblance to Ole Rölvaag's Per Hansa, to Mari Sandoz's Old Jules, to A. B. Guthrie's Boone Caudill, even to the hard-jawed and invulnerable heroes of the myth. But I had not been copying other writers. I had been trying to paint a portrait of my father, and it happened that my father, an observed and particular individual, was also a type—a very western type.

Nothing suggests the separateness of western experience so clearly as the response to it of critics nourished in the Europe-oriented, politicized, sophisticated, and antiheroic tradition of between-the-wars and postwar New York. Edmund Wilson, commenting on Hollywood writers, thought of them as wreathed in sunshine and bougainvillea, "spelling cat for the unlettered"; or as sentimental toughs, the boys in the back room; or as Easterners of talent (Scott Fitzgerald was his prime example) lost to significant achievement and drowning in the La Brea tar pits.

Leslie Fiedler, an exponent of the *Partisan Review* subculture, came west to teach in Missoula in the 1950s and discovered "the Montana face"—strong, grave, silent, bland, untroubled by thought, the face of a man playing a role invented for him two centuries earlier and a continent-and-ocean away by a French romantic philosopher.

Bernard Malamud, making a similar pilgrimage to teach at Oregon State University in Corvallis, found the life of that little college town intolerable, and retreated from it to write it up in the novel *New Life.* His Gogolian antihero S. Levin, an intellectual, heir to a thousand years of caution, deviousness, spiritual subtlety, and airless city living, was never at home in Corvallis. The faculty he was thrown among were suspiciously open, overfriendly, overhearty, outdoorish. Instead of a commerce in abstract ideas, Levin found among his colleagues a devotion to fly-fishing that simply bewildered him. Grown men!

If he had waited to write his novel until Norman Maclean had written the stories of *A River Runs Through It,* Malamud would have discovered that fly-fishing is not simply an art but a religion, a code of conduct and a language, a way of telling the real from the phony. And if Ivan Doig had written before Leslie Fiedler shook up Missoula by the ears, Fiedler would have had another view of the Montana face. It looks different, depending on whether you encounter it as a bizarre cultural artifact on a Montana railroad platform, or whether you see it as young Ivan Doig saw the face of his dependable, skilled, likable, rootless sheepherder father. Whether, that is, you see it from outside the culture or from inside.

In spite of the testimony of Fiedler and Malamud, if I were advising a documentary filmmaker where he might get the most quintessential West in a fifty-six-minute can, I would steer him away from broken-down rodeo riders, away from the towns of the energy boom, away from the cities, and send him to just such a little city as Missoula or Corvallis, some settlement that has managed against difficulty to make itself into a place and is likely to remain one. It wouldn't hurt at all if this little city had a university in it to keep it in touch with its cultural origins and conscious of its changing cultural present. It would do no harm if an occasional Leslie Fiedler came through to stir up its provincialism and set it to some self-questioning. It wouldn't hurt if some native-born writer, some Doig or Hugo or Maclean or Welch or Kittredge or Raymond Carver, was around to serve as culture hero—the individual who transcends his culture without abandoning it, who leaves for a while in search of opportunity and enlargement but never forgets where he left his heart.

It is in places like these, and through individuals like these, that the West will realize itself, if it ever does: these towns and cities still close to the earth, intimate and interdependent in their shared community, shared optimism, and shared memory. These are the seedbeds of an emergent western culture. They are likely to be there when the agribusiness fields have turned to alkali flats and the dams have silted up, when the waves of overpopulation that have been destroying the West have receded, leaving the stickers to get on with the business of adaptation.

ILLEGAL ALIENS

Sharman Apt Russell

Every year, for the past many years, over a million illegal aliens are arrested as they cross the sometimes invisible line that defines and encloses the United States of America. In the El Paso sector—a pastel-colored desert stretching from Van Horn, Texas to the western end of New Mexico—hundreds of thousands of "undocumented men and women" are caught annually by the Border Patrol, with an estimated twice that number passing through undeterred. A small percentage of this traffic will come through the Mexican town of Palomas, which in English means dove and which lies a mile south of Columbus, New Mexico and its desultory border checkpoint. Most Mexicans crossing through Palomas are seasonal workers who expect to return via the same route. Over the years, what has come to pass for industry in Palomas is a strip of adobe storefronts, brothels, and hotels used by such men coming home with their new-won wages shoved deep in pockets or sewn into the hems of clothing. From nearby ranching and mining communities, Anglos have helped build up this trade in sex and recreation. Although Mexicans entering the States are not likely to partake of the town's luxuries, this is not to say they don't plan to on their return.

From Palomas, an even smaller percentage of *mojados* or "wet ones" will choose to walk up through the sparse creosote of the Chihuahuan Desert, past the town of Deming on Interstate 10, past—walking steadily on, in their fifth day by now—the thrust of Cooke's Peak with its barrel cactus and hidden shelves of pictographs. Under the shadow of this mountain, these men will gravitate to the green-lined Mimbres River and follow its cottonwoods up a narrow valley of irrigated fields and apple orchards. Here, sometimes alone, sometimes in groups of two or three, they might begin to look for work. By the time they reach my house, at the northern end of the valley, the memory of Palomas belongs to another life, another country, and they will have walked nearly a hundred miles.

When I first came to the Mimbres, I often saw illegal aliens traveling purposefully at the edge of the road and my peripheral vision. I did not recognize them as such, although in definable and undefinable ways they seemed out of place on the blacktopped highway. As I drove, silver mailboxes flashed by with the inevitable dirt road, adobe home, or trailer attached. Cattle and horses grazed on the brown hills of grama grass. Fields blazed green along the banks of the river. Against this setting, there was something odd about the isolation of these men dressed in polyester pants and carrying a paper sack, small bag, or bundle of clothing. Miles from any town, they did not hitchhike and did not seem to be walking to or from a car.

Strangely detached, they kept their gaze directed ahead, on a focus which resolved not on the road but at someone's door. The door opened, and the man or woman inside had something for them to do: adobes to make, walls to lay up, fences to fix, or—less satisfactorily—a garden to weed.

In my late twenties and by all standards an adult, I had never thought of myself as an employer, much less one who hired people who hid when a police car passed. So when the men began to appear at my door with their diffident smiles and gestures, I felt uneasy. I did not know how to respond to their questions, how to supply food or even water. Not speaking Spanish was my excuse. But the truth lay more in the way they looked. They looked different. They looked poor. And they were, after all, men. I imagine that in the 1930s other women shared my feelings when the hobos first began to appear on porch steps. Like these women, I adapted, in surprisingly little time, to the stranger at the door.

As the crow flies, the Mimbres Valley lies over a hundred miles north of the nearest metropolis (El Paso), thirty miles east of the nearest town (population 12,000), and directly south of the Gila National Forest. It is hard to make a living here and we miss the proximity of bookstores and corner cafes. In this rural area, our neighbors divide neatly into those who live here because it is familiar and those who came here because it is not. Most of my friends fall in the latter category, and for us the subject of illegal aliens was new and interesting. One friend, who speaks French and Spanish and who has tried unsuccessfully to serve his workers borsht, described the knock at the door as an "informal cultural exchange program." He wrote down the addresses of men he liked and assumed that one day he would visit and be welcomed. Another friend argued that hiring aliens takes jobs from Americans who would work for less if the welfare system were suitably altered. To this, a third friend responded that Mexicans need to work as much as anyone and that she hires for humanness, not nationality.

Some of us theorized that the flow of unemployed and ambitious out of Mexico gave that country a necessary release valve and prevented turmoil, i.e., revolution. This idea, too, divided into two camps: those who thought it was good to prevent revolution and those who thought it was not. From a different viewpoint, many of us believed the current system—in which "aliens" were illegal but hiring an alien was not—wrong because it permitted too much abuse. We all knew of the rancher who turned his workers into the Immigration Service the day before payday. Other employers withheld pay until the job was completed and, in the meantime, fed their workers poorly. It was easy to see how inequity could flourish when the employed had no avenue of complaint or redress. At the same time, we also all knew scores of perfectly decent people—a Hispanic farmer in Deming or a chile grower in Hatch—whose small business depended on alien labor.

More to the point was the Mexican couple who had dinner with us one winter night, a week before Christmas. She was eight months pregnant. He was desperately seeking work. We told them that with the layoffs at the copper mine, unemployment in our county had reached 40 percent. He replied it was 80 percent where he came from. They had just walked nine days in the cold and rain. We did not suggest they turn around and go back.

Increasingly, it seemed that the problem of undocumented

men and women could only be examined one focal length at a time. There was the big picture, and there was a man with a bundle of clothes. As one came into focus, the other blurred.

In any event, for my husband and me, the discussions were academic. We learned to give food. We pointed directions. We sometimes chatted. But when asked about work, we spoke without thinking, without hesitation. *"No trabajo."* No work here.

Then we began to build.

In southwestern New Mexico, building an adobe home is an intense rite of passage which requires, in its purest form, no previous construction experience. For financial reasons, we started with one large room. After the kind of research that involves a lot of driving and staring at other people's houses, we decided to make a traditional mountain adobe altered by passive-solar, south-facing windows. As teachers, we had the summer to make the bricks, lay up the walls, and put on the sloping hipped tin roof. This was traditional "wetback" work, but we never gave a thought to hiring someone else. We would do it together, alone.

It began well. Although a good adobero can talk at interminable length about R values and thermal efficiency, he or she knows that transformation is the truer miracle. A patch of soil becomes a bedroom. Solid ground is transmogrified into a windowsill. An unsightly hole will be a wall nine feet high. For us, such miracles depended upon a borrowed and ancient cement mixer whose idiosyncrasies were my bane as I shoveled dirt and sprayed water into its maw. The mud was then wheelbarrowed away by my husband and poured into a wooden form for three bricks fourteen-by-ten-by-four inches.

Adobe is a cunning mixture of clay and sand. Too much clay and the brick cracks while drying, too little and it lacks strength. We tested the proportions of our soil by throwing handfuls of dirt into a jar of water, shaking vigorously, and watching the layers settle. Amazingly, our land appeared to be a huge dehydrated adobe mix—add water, stir, and pour. This we did, every day, ten hours a day, for three weeks. It was hard work, but not unpleasant. Transformation! The ground formed into squares that we set on their sides to dry and then gingerly stacked. On one good day, eighty wet-looking bricks lay in soldierly rows before us. On most days, there were only sixty or fifty. We ended up with thirteen hundred adobes: a hundred less than we thought we should have, a hundred more than we would actually need.

While we waited two weeks for the bricks to dry, we began to dig the foundation footings, which had to be large to sup-port the heavy walls. In a matter of days, etched deep in the ground, our room became defined. Into these holes, we inserted stakes of metal to which we fastened, at a ninety-degree angle, the longer slim poles of steel rebar. There was something elegant about these complex layers, running in their rectangle of fifteen-by-twenty feet. I almost hated to cover them with cement. I hated it even more as we began to do it, for cement is nothing at all like adobe. The magic was gone, or rather, reversed. It had become bad magic. At the mixer, I glumly shoveled in heavy gravel and two buckets of cement. Moistened with water, the backbreaking load was then dumped into the wheelbarrow which my husband man-fully directed in tottering form to the foundation's edge. The stuff slopped out to disappear into the earth. Again, the process was repeated and another load swallowed. Again, another load, and another, as our muscles strained and our skin split from the alkaline lime.

At this point, things went downhill. There is a Mimbres Valley saying that the couple who builds together divorces together. As our visions of the house altered, diverged, and then collided, as our bodies reminded us that that we were only getting older, we moved from bad temper to the kind of free-floating anger rooted in childhood. Through a haze of misunderstandings, we peeled pine logs for *vigas,* built forms for the next step of the foundation, and eternally mixed more cement. At night, we talked about the house rather than sensibly talking about other things. One day, I left for a brief respite in town. On another day, so did my husband.

When the dust settled, we began again.

Down the road, our neighbor has a small trailer where he once housed illegal Mexican workers who came every year and built what seemed to us a dizzying array of fences. That summer, two young men were busy digging holes on his land, erecting posts, and nailing up expensive-looking wire. They began each day at eight and when they stopped at five the afternoon stretched before them, light and long and empty of things to do. One evening, in the cooling hours of midsummer, they wandered over to watch us lay our sixth course of adobe. With finicky slowness we placed each brick flush to the outside string that served as our level. At intervals, we also put wooden blocks where we estimated heavy pictures or cupboards would go. At that time we agreed, quite incorrectly, that it would be easy enough to install the electrical wires later.

My husband, who speaks Spanish, offered our visitors a beer

and conversation. He inquired as to what part of Mexico they came from. Chihuahua? A nice city. He had been there. He wanted to know the latest exchange rate for pesos. He asked how many adobes they could make in a day. Four hundred? We looked at each other. He asked the Spanish word for hammer. He told them he was a high school teacher.

At five the next afternoon, they showed up again. This time, they clamored into the room like a crew just hired. One took over my task of lifting up the forty-pound brick; another elbowed my husband aside and demonstrated the proper way of setting the adobe in its mortar of mud. They stayed until the sun tipped over the ridge of our western hills. They had taken pity on us.

Although we offered, neither Manuel nor Gabriel wanted money. They liked the cold slide of our beer at the end of the day. But more, they liked the companionship of working with equals. This was their free time, their gift. For two more weeks, they came uncalled when their own day was through—and we, who also had been working since eight and who would work on until dark, were in their debt. The relationship between American and "wetback" turned on its head, and some tension in us relaxed. That next summer, when we started building again, we understood well that we had plenty of work for a skilled adobero. So we began our career of hiring illegal aliens.

Effrem and Jesus sat rather stiffly on the edge of the couch while Shirley Grijalva—rodeo rider and mother of three—spoke swiftly to them in Spanish and then as swiftly to us in English. Shirley knew Effrem well; he was an "old friend" and we were letting her handle the negotiations with our first employees. At that time, in 1983, the going rate was eight dollars a day, plus food and board. (In the next four years, the price would rise to ten or twelve dollars, with strenuous work on a farm or ranch paying fifteen and more. At that time, most wage earners in Mexico were getting the equivalent of three dollars a day.) We offered a dollar above the norm and consulted with Shirley as to what was board. Beans, she said. Beans, meat, tortillas, eggs, potatoes, coffee, and canned food. Effrem, she noted, preferred white bread to tortillas. Employers also had the option of providing cigarettes, beer, and the occasional pair of socks. We would do that, we agreed quickly. We believed in keeping Mexican wages, nine dollars a day, intact for the trip home to Mexico.

I was never to know Effrem or Jesus very well or, for that matter, any of the men who eventually worked for us. Each morning, my husband and they conferred, gathered tools, and went off together making more adobes, stuccoing walls, or digging ditches. I went inside our now completed room to my own projects and, later, child-rearing duties. At lunchtime I cooked a hot meal of beans, eggs, and tortillas which the three men ate outside in the shade of the patio. Then I washed the dishes. In the late afternoon, I prepared a bag of dinner and breakfast food for the workers to take and cook in our neighbor's trailer. My husband and I assumed these segregated roles because we believed that the men would be more comfortable if we did so. Certainly, I felt a need to appear "traditional" and did not, for example, publicly contradict my husband's building ideas (something I did in private) or wear short skirts while hanging up the laundry. My job, as I saw it, was to oil these days, in which we were getting a great deal of work done, with a flow of domesticity.

What I learned, I learned in the evening, second hand. Effrem, my husband told me, had six children and four hundred acres in Chihuahua. Most of his land was scrub desert. The rest was a small but viable apple orchard. Early in the summer, before his harvest, he fell short of cash and came up to the States. In his late forties, his dark hair touched by gray, Effrem proved to be slow, reliable, and meticulous in his work. His gentle manners and soft voice made him seem a very serious man, a family man, sensitive and thoughtful.

Jesus provided a contrast. While Effrem looked broad and solid, Jesus had a tall skinny frame that alternated between nervous energy and an indolent loll. With the dapper moustache and groomed hair appropriate to a twenty-two-year-old, Jesus was full of plans, the owner of a future in which the strokes were broad and the details still vague. Already, he boasted, he had traveled as far south as Nicaragua and as far north as Washington. He was out to see the world, on a young man's lark that required financing along the way. More voluble than Effrem, Jesus came up with a running series of deals. Would we contract to lay the tiles instead of paying a daily wage? Would we sell his cousin in El Paso our old car? Would we hire another worker, a good friend of his, who could do the finish work we so clearly needed? When it came time for Jesus to go, he asked us for a pair of Converse tennis shoes. No matter the cost, he said with largesse, he would pay. We shopped around and came up with a better price, not a Converse, but a good shoe. No, Jesus said. The brand name was important.

Effrem and Jesus promised to return the next summer.

Effrem did and first went to work for one of our neighbors, whom he didn't much like. After a week he moved on and settled further north as a ranch hand. From another young man who stopped at our house, we were shocked to learn that Jesus had been shot to death in a Palomas bar. The young man added that Jesus had been a *coyote,* a descriptive term for those who take money from aliens—usually refugees fleeing Central America —in exchange for transporting them across the border.

The same grapevine that spread the news of Jesus's death also put us on the circuit as a place to stop for information, food, and a day or two of work. By now, we knew that although we could hire aliens and transport them in a southerly direction, there were serious penalties for driving an alien north: possible fines, imprisonment, and an impounded car. We knew that, on their way home, some men liked to be picked up by the green trucks bearing the Immigration's seal—*la Migra,* as we called them. Depending on where they lived, this could save them a walk and usually meant they wound up in an American cell overnight where their money might be safer than on the road. On the other hand, it could also mean being turned over for a shakedown to the Mexican authorities. For this reason, some workers liked their pay put in a postal order they could send home. Others didn't.

That was the summer Ernesto and his "son Luis" came to help us put on an adobe floor for our second room. Ernesto would continue to help us at various tasks for the next three years. He was a small man, possibly in his sixties, with gray stubble and ropy muscles. Each season he came accompanied by a male relative whom he always referred to as his son Luis. Sometimes it was his son. As likely, it could have been a grandson, cousin, or son-in-law. Once the man's name was actually Luis. For the others, their real names only emerged gradually in conversation. This simplification of relationships and names was, I think, Ernesto's version of making the Anglos comfortable.

Ernesto's forte was stonework, and although we didn't plan on terracing our back yard with dry stone walls, his expertise convinced us. Like Effrem, he worked slowly and steadily. The younger relative played the role of helper, fetching the stones in a wheelbarrow and lounging, bored, while Ernesto made his selections. If necessary, Ernesto would trim the stone with a sharp blow of his hammer before fitting it carefully into its arranged niche. The result was a layered work of art, which Ernesto would always want to cap with cement—a practical touch we always vetoed.

In our longer relationship with Ernesto, we learned more about familial patterns and life in Mexico. We watched the pecking order quickly established between relatives, the respect given Ernesto as a skilled worker, and the way in which he jealously guarded his skills. No hands but his placed the stone, for he did not jeopardize his livelihood by teaching it—at least, not yet. We knew that by extending our house into three rooms, 1,000 square feet, we were doubling the size of Ernesto's home. By the fourth year, too, we had worked twice with the son-in-law whose name was really Luis. A genial but restless man with five children, he was widowed when we first met him and newly married the second summer. His first wife, Ernesto's daughter, had died in childbirth and the son-in-law was still coming to the States to pay off the doctor's bill. "I was a screwball for marrying again," he said in Spanish to my husband, and Ernesto agreed.

Because of our growing sense of familiarity, even friendship, it remained a shock when the morning came that we did not see Ernesto and his relative walking up the hill to our house. By nine o'clock we knew they were not coming, and we realized that once again they had left suddenly without telling us. We understood now, but did not condone, why some employers paid at the end of the job. It was to ensure that the job get done, that the adobe bricks were not left unfinished in the rain or a wall half-stuccoed or a floor half-laid. Here, at least, unreliability was the alien's trademark and privilege. His abrupt departures illustrated how tenuous the relationship really was and how unbound by social rules. Sometimes the explanation got back to us: a brother had fallen ill or a child was born. Sometimes the men left because they had an argument in the trailer, or because they were tired of working, or because they were homesick. Since Ernesto didn't trust the postal system, he would be carrying all his money in a handkerchief wadded tightly in his pocket. If he had worked as long as two weeks, that would be $120 in savings—equal in Mexico to two months work. If he was lucky, Ernesto would avoid *La Migra*'s green trucks. If he was lucky, he would catch a ride on the highway and spend the night, not on the road, but in a Palomas hotel.

In June of 1988 a new immigration law began to impose penalties on the employers of illegal aliens. The law requires any employer to ask for documentation—a birth certificate, passport, or driver's license—before hiring. If the employer does not and hires an illegal alien, he or she is liable to a civil fine ranging from $250 to $2,000. For a second offense, the penalty can rise to $5,000 per worker. A third offense may mean six months in jail. (There are, however, many exceptions and workers in certain crops are exempt.) The law also provided amnesty and American citizenship for aliens who had been living in the country since January 1982. Amnesty, of course, did not affect the men we knew since they did not want American citizenship; they wanted to work here seasonally and return to their own country. How the act did affect them is unclear. In some parts of the country, studies seem to show that the 1988 Immigration Law has not significantly stopped the flow of illegal workers. But here in the Mimbres Valley, Ernesto and his relatives do not come anymore. I rarely see men like them along the edge of the highway. And no one drops by our house to ask for food or work.

In truth, we could not say that we would hire any alien who did come. Now that we too risk being illegal, we would have to think that through all over again. We never really knew what we were doing. We never found an answer, right or wrong, but in the end responded to personal needs, ours and theirs. We let the big picture blur and focused on the small. It seemed to work for a time.

THE CLAN OF ONE-BREASTED WOMEN

Terry Tempest Williams

I belong to a Clan of One-Breasted Women. My mother, my grandmothers, and six aunts have all had mastectomies. Seven are dead. The two who survive have just completed rounds of chemotherapy and radiation.

I've had my own problems: two biopsies for breast cancer and a small tumor between my ribs diagnosed as a "borderline malignancy."

This is my family history.

Most statistics tell us breast cancer is genetic, hereditary, with rising percentages attached to fatty diets, childlessness, or becoming pregnant after thirty. What they don't say is living in Utah may be the greatest hazard of all.

We are a Mormon family with roots in Utah since 1847. The "word of wisdom" in my family aligned us with good foods—no coffee, no tea, tobacco, or alcohol. For the most part, our women were finished having their babies by the time they were thirty. And only one faced breast cancer prior to 1960. Tradition-ally, as a group of people, Mormons have a low rate of cancer.

Is our family a cultural anomaly? The truth is, we didn't think about it. Those who did, usually the men, simply said, "bad genes." The women's attitude was stoic. Cancer was part of life. On February 16, 1971, the eve of my mother's surgery, I accidentally picked up the telephone and overheard her ask my grandmother what she could expect.

"Diane, it is one of the most spiritual experiences you will ever encounter."

I quietly put down the receiver.

Two days later, my father took my brothers and me to the hospital to visit her. She met us in the lobby in a wheelchair. No bandages were visible. I'll never forget her radiance, the way she held herself in a purple velvet robe, and how she gathered us around her.

"Children, I am fine. I want you to know I felt the arms of God around me."

We believed her. My father cried. Our mother, his wife, was thirty-eight years old.

A little over a year after Mother's death, Dad and I were having dinner together. He had just returned from St. George, where the Tempest Company was completing the gas lines that would service southern Utah. He spoke of his love for the country, the sandstoned landscape, bare-boned and beautiful. He had just finished hiking the Kolob trail in Zion National Park. We got caught up in reminiscing, recalling with fondness our walk up Angel's Landing on his fiftieth birthday and the years our family had vacationed there.

Over dessert, I shared a recurring dream of mine. I told my

father that for years, as long as I could remember, I saw this flash of light in the night in the desert—that this image had so permeated my being that I could not venture south without seeing it again, on the horizon, illuminating buttes and mesas.

"You did see it," he said.

"Saw what?"

"The bomb. The cloud. We were driving home from Riverside, California. You were sitting on Diane's lap. She was pregnant. In fact, I remember the day, September 7, 1957. We had just gotten out of the Service. We were driving north, past Las Vegas. It was an hour or so before dawn, when this explosion went off. We not only heard it, but felt it. I thought the oil tanker in front of us had blown up. We pulled over and suddenly, rising from the desert floor, we saw it, clearly, this golden-stemmed cloud, the mushroom. The sky seemed to vibrate with an eerie pink glow. Within a few minutes, a light ash was raining on the car."

I stared at my father.

"I thought you knew that," he said. "It was a common occurrence in the fifties."

It was at this moment that I realized the deceit I had been living under. Children growing up in the American Southwest, drinking contaminated milk from contaminated cows, even from the contaminated breasts of their mothers, my mother—members, years later, of the Clan of One-Breasted Women.

It is a well-known story in the Desert West, "The Day We Bombed Utah," or more accurately, the years we bombed Utah: above ground atomic testing in Nevada took place from January 27, 1951 through July 11, 1962. Not only were the winds blowing north covering "low-use segments of the population" with fallout and leaving sheep dead in their tracks, but the climate was right. The United States of the 1950s was red, white, and blue. The Korean War was raging. McCarthyism was rampant. Ike was it, and the cold war was hot. If you were against nuclear testing, you were for a communist regime.

Much has been written about this "American nuclear tragedy." Public health was secondary to national security. The Atomic Energy Commissioner, Thomas Murray, said, "Gentlemen, we must not let anything interfere with this series of tests, nothing."

Again and again, the American public was told by its government, in spite of burns, blisters, and nausea, "It has been found that the tests may be conducted with adequate assurance of safety under conditions prevailing at the bombing reservations." Assuaging public fears was simply a matter of public relations. "Your best action," an Atomic Energy Commission booklet read, "is not to be worried about fallout." A news release typical of the times stated, "We find no basis for concluding that harm to any individual has resulted from radioactive fallout."

On August 30, 1979, during Jimmy Carter's presidency, a suit was filed, *Irene Allen v. The United States of America.* Mrs. Allen's case was the first on an alphabetical list of twenty-four test cases, representative of nearly twelve hundred plaintiffs seeking compensation from the United States government for cancers caused by nuclear testing in Nevada.

Irene Allen lived in Hurricane, Utah. She was the mother of five children and had been widowed twice. Her first husband, with their two oldest boys, had watched the tests from the roof of the local high school. He died of leukemia in 1956. Her second husband died of pancreatic cancer in 1978.

In a town meeting conducted by Utah Senator Orrin Hatch, shortly before the suit was filed, Mrs. Allen said, "I am not blaming the government, I want you to know that, Senator Hatch. But I thought if my testimony could help in any way so this wouldn't happen again to any of the generations coming up after us . . . I am happy to be here this day to bear testimony of this."

God-fearing people. This is just one story in an anthology of thousands.

On May 10, 1984, Judge Bruce S. Jenkins handed down his opinion. Ten of the plaintiffs were awarded damages. It was the first time a federal court had determined that nuclear tests had been the cause of cancers. For the remaining fourteen test cases, the proof of causation was not sufficient. In spite of the split decision, it was considered a landmark ruling. It was not to remain so for long.

In April 1987, the Tenth Circuit Court of Appeals overturned Judge Jenkins's ruling on the ground that the United States was protected from suit by the legal doctrine of sovereign immunity, a centuries-old idea from England in the days of absolute monarchs.

In January 1988, the Supreme Court refused to review the Appeals Court decision. To our court system it does not matter whether the United States government was irresponsible, whether it lied to its citizens, or even that citizens died from the fallout of nuclear testing. What matters is that our government is immune: "The King can do no wrong."

In Mormon culture, authority is respected, obedience is

revered, and independent thinking is not. I was taught as a young girl not to "make waves" or "rock the boat."

"Just let it go," Mother would say. "You know how you feel, that's what counts."

For many years, I have done just that—listened, observed, and quietly formed my own opinions, in a culture that rarely asks questions because it has all the answers. But one by one, I have watched the women in my family die common, heroic deaths. We sat in waiting rooms hoping for good news, but always receiving the bad. I cared for them, bathed their scarred bodies, and kept their secrets. I watched beautiful women become bald as Cytoxan, cisplatin, and Adriamycin were injected into their veins. I held their foreheads as they vomited green-black bile, and I shot them with morphine when the pain became inhuman. In the end, I witnessed their last peaceful breaths, becoming a midwife to the rebirth of their souls.

The price of obedience has become too high.

The fear and inability to question authority that ultimately killed rural communities in Utah during atmospheric testing of atomic weapons is the same fear I saw in my mother's body. Sheep. Dead sheep. The evidence is buried.

I cannot prove that my mother, Diane Dixon Tempest, or my grandmothers, Lettie Romney Dixon and Kathryn Blackett Tempest, along with my aunts developed cancer from nuclear fallout in Utah. But I can't prove they didn't.

My father's memory was correct. The September blast we drove through in 1957 was part of Operation Plumbbob, one of the most intensive series of bomb tests to be initiated. The flash of light in the night in the desert, which I had always thought was a dream, developed into a family nightmare. It took fourteen years, from 1957 to 1971, for cancer to manifest in my mother—the same time, Howard L. Andrews, an authority in radioactive fallout at the National Institutes of Health, says radiation cancer requires to become evident. The more I learn about what it means to be a "downwinder," the more questions I drown in.

What I do know, however, is that as a Mormon woman of the fifth generation of Latter-day Saints, I must question everything, even if it means losing my faith, even if it means becoming a member of a border tribe among my own people. Tolerating blind obedience in the name of patriotism or religion ultimately takes our lives.

When the Atomic Energy Commission described the country north of the Nevada Test Site as "virtually uninhabited desert terrain," my family and the birds at Great Salt Lake were some of the "virtual uninhabitants."

One night, I dreamed women from all over the world circled a blazing fire in the desert. They spoke of change, how they hold the moon in their bellies and wax and wane with its phases. They mocked the presumption of even-tempered beings and made promises that they would never fear the witch inside themselves. The women danced wildly as sparks broke away from the flames and entered the night sky as stars.

And they sang a song given to them by Shoshone grandmothers:

Ah ne nah, nah	*Consider the rabbits*
nin nah nah—	*How gently they walk on the earth—*
ah ne nah, nah	*Consider the rabbits*
nin nah nah—	*How gently they walk on the earth—*

Nyaga mutzi	*We remember them*
oh ne nay—	*We can walk gently also*—
Nyaga mutzi	*We remember them*
oh ne nay—	*We can walk gently also*—

The women danced and drummed and sang for weeks, preparing themselves for what was to come. They would reclaim the desert for the sake of their children, for the sake of the land.

A few miles downwind from the fire circle, bombs were being tested. Rabbits felt the tremors. Their soft leather pads on paws and feet recognized the shaking sands, while the roots of mesquite and sage were smoldering. Rocks were hot from the inside out and dust devils hummed unnaturally. And each time there was another nuclear test, ravens watched the desert heave. Stretch marks appeared. The land was losing its muscle.

The women couldn't bear it any longer. They were mothers. They had suffered labor pains but always under the promise of birth. The red hot pains beneath the desert promised death only, as each bomb became a stillborn. A contract had been made and broken between human beings and the land. A new contract was being drawn by the women, who understood the fate of the earth as their own.

Under the cover of darkness, ten women slipped under a barbed-wire fence and entered the contaminated country. They were trespassing. They walked toward the town of Mercury, in moonlight, taking their cues from coyote, kit fox, antelope squirrel, and quail. They moved quietly and deliberately through the maze of Joshua trees. When a hint of daylight appeared they rested, drinking tea and sharing their rations of food. The women closed their eyes. The time had come to protest with the heart, that to deny one's genealogy with the earth was to commit treason against one's soul.

At dawn, the women draped themselves in mylar, wrapping long streamers of silver plastic around their arms to blow in the breeze. They wore clear masks, that became the faces of humanity. And when they arrived at the edge of Mercury, they carried all the butterflies of a summer day in their wombs. They paused to allow their courage to settle.

The town that forbids pregnant women and children to enter because of radiation risks was asleep. The women moved through the streets as winged messengers, twirling around each other in slow motion, peeking inside homes and watching the easy sleep of men and women. They were astonished by such stillness and periodically would utter a shrill note or low cry just to verify life.

The residents finally awoke to these strange apparitions. Some simply stared. Others called authorities, and in time, the women were apprehended by wary soldiers dressed in desert fatigues. They were taken to a white, square building on the other edge of Mercury. When asked who they were and why they were there, the women replied, "We are mothers and we have come to reclaim the desert for our children."

The soldiers arrested them. As the ten women were blind-folded and handcuffed, they began singing:

> *You can't forbid us everything*
> *You can't forbid us to think—*
> *You can't forbid our tears to flow*
> *And you can't stop the songs that we sing.*

The women continued to sing louder and louder, until they heard the voices of their sisters moving across the mesa:

> *Ah ne nah, nah*
> *nin nah nah—*
> *Ah ne nah, nah*
> *nin nah nah—*
> *Nyaga mutzi*
> *oh ne nay—*
> *Nyaga mutzi*
> *oh ne nay—*

"Call for reinforcements," one soldier said.

"We have," interrupted one woman, "we have—and you have no idea of our numbers."

I crossed the line at the Nevada Test Site and was arrested with nine other Utahns for trespassing on military lands. They are still conducting nuclear tests in the desert. Ours was an act of civil disobedience. But as I walked toward the town of Mercury, it was more than a gesture of peace. It was a gesture on behalf of the Clan of One-Breasted Women.

As one officer cinched the handcuffs around my wrists, another frisked my body. She found a pen and a pad of paper tucked inside my left boot.

"And these?" she asked sternly.

"Weapons," I replied.

Our eyes met. I smiled. She pulled the leg of my trousers back over my boot.

"Step forward, please," she said as she took my arm.

We were booked under an afternoon sun and bused to Tonopah, Nevada. It was a two-hour ride. This was familiar country. The Joshua trees standing their ground had been named by my ancestors, who believed they looked like prophets pointing west to the Promised Land. These were the same trees that bloomed each spring, flowers appearing like white flames in the Mojave. And I recalled a full moon in May, when Mother and I had walked among them, flushing out mourning doves and owls.

The bus stopped short of town. We were released.

The officials thought it was a cruel joke to leave us stranded in the desert with no way to get home. What they didn't realize was that we were home, soul-centered and strong, women who recognized the sweet smell of sage as fuel for our spirits.

ALL BUT THE WALTZ

Mary Clearman Blew

uring the long summer of 1982, I could forget for weeks at a time what was wrong with my husband. Those mornings dawned, one after another, in the transparent blue that foretold hundred-degree heat by noon, and he slept while I woke slowly in the pattern of light cast through the birch leaves outside our window, and he slept while I showered and pulled on a cotton dress and sandals for the office. I was expecting a baby in September, and my every exertion, heaving myself out of a chair, carrying the breakfast plates to the sink, letting myself out the back door and down the steps to my car in the already sweltering morning, cost me a deeper investment in my cocoon of self-absorption.

I had never supposed I would be pregnant again, not after twenty years. As my body swelled and my pace slowed in a sensation of suspended time, I remembered the pregnant teenager I had been as I might have remembered another woman, a passing acquaintance turned up again after more than twenty years. I drove to work already panting for breath in what passed for morning cool, along the residential streets of Havre where sprinklers plied the lawns for their allotted hours in the drought, and at five o'clock, arching my back against the ache, I drove home through the haze of dust that had filtered in from the fields. My feet and hands had swollen from the heat until I could not wear my shoes or wedding ring. I felt as though I would always be pregnant.

Except for occasional shortness of breath, Bob was still himself. Earlier in the spring he had driven out to the farm every day at first light for the brief frenetic weeks of spring seeding, but now, in the midsummer space between seeding and harvest, he had little to do but worry about the drought. He got up at noon, had breakfast downtown, drank coffee, and talked about rain with the other farmers.

By the beginning of the 1980s, Havre no longer rocked all night long as it had in the glory days of oil and gas exploration on the highline. The big poker games downtown had closed when the mudmen and the landmen and the drillers and toolpushers and roughnecks went broke or moved to Wyoming in search of new oil developments or, like Bob, went into soberer lines of work. But there were little poker games around town, at the Oxford Bar or PJ's Lounge, for a man looking for a distraction from the weather. At two or three in the morning I would hear the familiar sound of his Wagoneer in the driveway and rouse as Bob slipped into bed beside me, his arm raised to encompass mine as I turned, heavy-bellied, into the curve of his back. He had not yet, not perceptibly, begun to lose muscle tone.

In January he had had the flu, and it seemed to hang on.

Sometimes, heading down the three back steps toward his Wagoneer, he had to stop and double over, gasping to get his breath in great racking heaves that left him exhausted. There seemed to be no reason for his lack of breath; he had no other symptoms.

"You ought to see a doctor," I said.

"Oh hell, I'm all right."

As the winter wore on he admitted that the boys down at the coffee shop were urging him to get in and see the doc. Hell, maybe it was mono.

I made an appointment with the doctor for him, but he didn't show up for it.

I had plenty else to think about. Bob and I had been married four years, had been together seven years, and my pregnancy seemed too good to be true. I was undergoing amniocentesis and furnishing a nursery and dreaming about this baby as I had not had the time or inclination when, in my teens, my other children had been born.

Besides, it didn't seem possible that Bob could be sick. He was too crazy, too lucky, too full of the zest of living.

The son of a Kansas cattleman, Bob had left the ranch early for the glamour of the oil patch. Starting out as a roughneck, he went on to sell tools and oil field supplies, then to operate a fleet of water trucks, then to his own drilling rigs. He rode the roller coaster of oil and gas exploration and production, addicted like a gambler to the upward swoops and the adrenaline rushes, landing on his feet when he hit bottom, starting over on another of his nine lives. He came to Havre in the early 1970s, broke, to make a new start drilling gas wells into the shallow Judith River and Eagle formations. He went broke again and lost his rigs, but then he hit a lucky streak, scalping oil field pipe. When I met him, he was rolling in money.

"Hell, I'm the luckiest son of a bitch I know," he told me.

He bought himself an airplane and a new Wagoneer, and he bought electric guitars for his sons in Kansas. When he began spending money on my children, buying them new cowboy boots and saddles, I was transfixed; I'd never seen money flow like . . . well, like water. Born in a drought myself, brought up in the hard-luck tradition of the depression, I could no more have spent money the way Bob did than I could have let water run, wasted, out of a tap. And yet, God, I liked to watch him spend it.

Bob had a jester's license to pull off every audacious stunt I might have longed to try but been afraid to all my life. Under his tutelage I learned to pilot a plane. I let him initiate me into the mile-high club in sweet daylight at ten thousand feet, with the plane on automatic pilot through pillows of cumulus; I flew with him to Calgary, to Houston; and I drank with him in petroleum clubs in the blue haze of the Marlboros he chain-smoked. Through him I met the ragtag and bobtail, newly rich and newly busted exotics of the oil patch, and I listened to their boasting, fatalistic stories of success and disaster. After living twenty years of my life in diligence on college campuses, Bob's exuberance, his grasshopper's delight in the sunlit present, flowed through me like an elixir. I loved his soft Kansas voice, just touched with the flat twang of the Oklahoma border, and I loved his blond hair and diamond-blue eyes and his grin, and I loved his loving me.

After he had spent most of his money, he bought farmland north of Havre and gambled all over again on the weather. I married him in 1978. I wasn't worried; I had a good enough job to pay the bills.

The trees that used to arch over the streets in the heart of Great Falls have been cut down. Ancient cottonwoods with their upper branches lopped against the rot still cast shade over the rambling old residences in the central district, but the Great Falls Clinic abuts the pavement and seems to levitate in the sun. In June of 1982 I used to sit in one of its windowless waiting rooms, stabbing away at a piece of needlepoint and listening to the air-conditioning until I could listen no longer and would heave myself out of the chair and limp through the doors and into the scorching heat.

Across from the clinic was a sandwich shop called the Graham Cracker. I would limp across the street and sit at a tiny Formica table where I sipped bitter coffee and listened to the vibrations of another air conditioner and watched the heat shimmer off the cement on the other side of the plate glass until that, too, became intolerable. As I limped back across the street to the clinic my feet felt like hot sponges. I imagined a tiny squirt of fluid out of my sandals with every step I took.

A week earlier I had gone to a state humanities committee meeting at Big Sky Resort, south of Bozeman, Montana, and Bob had thrown his golf clubs in the back of my car and gone along. It was a chance for us to have a few days away together, and I looked forward to it. Surely, once he got away from the dust of the highline and his fields of shriveled crops, Bob would be himself again.

But as we turned off the interstate and left the plains,

climbing along a highway that follows the Gallatin River where it plunges and dashes from its source, twisting through crags and pines and extravagant outcroppings, Bob grew moody. When we reached the resort and checked into our room, he dropped on the bed and closed his eyes.

"You go ahead," he finally muttered. "I don't want anything to eat."

"Where's Bob?" friends asked when I went down to dinner alone, and I answered, "He isn't feeling well."

I felt more annoyed than alarmed. He had no symptoms that I could see but his inexplicable fatigue. I knew he had fought secret bouts with depression for years, but what was he depressed about?

His crops? But every farmer was a gambler, every farmer faced the perils of drought, blight, rain at the wrong time. When had Bob ever backed away from a gamble?

The baby?

No, I couldn't believe that. But there had always been about Bob a hidden sadness, a deep private well into which the jester sometimes retreated while the face went on smiling.

By lunch the next day he pulled himself together and came downstairs to sit on the terrace under the firs with everyone else, but he had little to say, and when one of my friends made an off-hand remark, Bob snarled a retort that briefly stopped all conversation. That evening he would not leave the room at all.

"You need to eat something," I argued. "You missed dinner last night, and again tonight—no wonder you're exhausted."

"I don't want a thing," he said. He lay on the bed with his eyes closed, breathing in short gasps. "What's wrong?"

"Nothing. I just feel like hell. I'm tired."

"Could you eat if I carried you some soup on a tray?"

"Just let me alone!"

I went downstairs alone. I was angry and frightened. What I had hoped would be a tiny vacation with my husband had turned ugly, and I didn't know why.

The next morning was Saturday. The committee concluded its business and adjourned. Everyone was hurrying back and forth with luggage to check out of the resort by eleven. I went upstairs and let myself into the room with my key. The windows were darkened, and Bob slept, naked, on the bed. His clothing and shaving gear were scattered where he had dropped them.

"Just—lemme rest," he muttered.

I sat down on the bed. "We have to check out."

He opened his eyes, closed them and sighed.

"Do you want me to try to find a doctor?" I asked. We were thirty miles from Bozeman and the nearest medical facilities.

He raised his head off the pillow, let it drop. "Hell no, just— lemme rest a minute."

I sat on the bed a moment longer, trying to decide what to do. I couldn't lift him. He still had, at that time, the frame and weight of the college halfback he once had been, and all 185 pounds of him was inert on the bed. The unreality of it all was defeating me. Call an ambulance? All the way from Bozeman? Surely not. After all, I had seen Bob sink into spells of lassitude before, go into strange fugues of enervation when he seemed incapable of getting out of bed—was this one any different? *Well, yes, it was.* But how?

At last I gathered up the folds of my dress, got up from the bed, and moved slowly around the room, picking up his clothing and packing his shaving kit. Then I made two trips to carry two suitcases down to the lobby, putting my feet care-fully down in front of me on stairs I could not see. I brought the car around and parked it in the no-parking zone, as close to the main doors of the resort as I could get it.

"Can you get dressed?" I asked him, back in the darkened room once more.

He roused and nodded. He swung his legs off the bed and then doubled over, his head between his knees.

"Shall I try to find a doctor?" I asked again.

The word *doctor* irritated him into effort. "Don't need a god-damned doctor," he growled, and he sat up and eased his arm into the shirtsleeve I held. Shirt, pants, loafers, and then he stood up, white-faced. Leaning on me, he managed the corridor and the stairs. Once in the lobby, in the sight of other people, he made the effort to straighten and walk by himself out to the car.

I drove down the twisting highway along the Gallatin River while Bob lay back in the passenger seat with his eyes closed. *I'll drive to the emergency room in Bozeman,* I thought. But when I reached the Bozeman exit, I glanced at his face and saw that his color had come back and his breathing was slow and relaxed.

"Hell, keep driving," he said without opening his eyes, and I kept driving.

With the mountains behind us, we drove down through the Gallatin Valley and into the plains. Another thirty miles and we had descended eight thousand feet and come to the little river town of Townsend, halfway between Bozeman and Helena. As I watched the blue outline of the mountains recede in the rearview mirror I thought about Big Sky Resort and the thin cool air at eleven thousand feet above sea level. Bob opened his eyes and sat up in the seat.

"I'm hungry," he said.

I pulled over at a café on Townsend's main street and came around to help him out of the car. His legs were shaky, but he made it into the café and wolfed down a couple of hamburgers.

"Nothing's wrong with me. I just felt like I was worn out," he said.

When we reached Helena, he asked me to pull over and let him drive the rest of the way home.

"You've got to see a doctor."

"Hell, nothing's wrong! I been tired."

"You've got to see a doctor!"

"I'll see how I feel after harvest."

"You aren't going to make it through harvest at this rate! Here's the specialist's number. Will you call him, or shall I?"

"Jesus Christ!" he exploded, finally. "If that's what it takes to shut you up——"

Our doctor in Havre had sounded shaken. "The X rays show a film over the lungs," he said. "I don't know what it is."

The pulmonary specialist in Great Falls did a series of blood oxygen tests and recommended a lung biopsy.

"Hell no, I ain't letting him go down my throat and snip out a piece of my lungs!"

"But we have to find out what's wrong——"

"Nothing's wrong!"

I raged, begged, pleaded with him until he fled the house for the peace and quiet of the all-night coffee shop. Nothing was the matter with him, just a little fatigue, and he could not understand why I was getting so worked up about nothing. The night I threw myself on the kitchen floor and accused him of deliberately intending to leave me a widow with an unborn child, he was shaken by the state I was in. To quiet me, and not because he believed he was sick, he agreed to the biopsy.

After all those hours of waiting in the Great Falls Clinic came the verdict. Refusing to make eye contact, forcing out his words as though each one came with a price tag, the young specialist explained to us that the film that had shown up on the X rays was pulmonary fibrosis, the incurable, progressive spread of fibrous connective tissues that gradually would choke the capacity of the lungs to take in oxygen and supply it to the body. Bob's blood oxygen level was already about 45 percent, compared with a normal level of 98 percent.

While the growth of the fibroids could not be halted or reversed, the specialist said, it could sometimes be slowed. He recommended a massive therapy of steroids and warned us that mood swings could be among the side effects. Bob should be careful and exact in taking his doses.

"And quit smoking," he told him.

Smoking didn't cause pulmonary fibrosis, although it would exacerbate it. A likely cause was contact with asbestos.

Bob shook his head. Didn't believe he'd ever handled the stuff, he said.

"We may never know where it started," said the specialist, and I wondered why it mattered. He wrote out prescriptions for prednisone and scheduled another appointment in a month's time.

The world must be full of battered souls who stayed on the track because the idea of being run over by a train was more preposterous than the evidence of their own eyes.

For me, the sun rises and another day begins to burn without hope of rain. I pull on a fresh cotton tent dress over my enormous self and cram my feet into sandals and drive to the office for another day of the trivia that pester a college campus in the summer. I cannot believe in September and the end of this pregnancy any more than I can believe in the finality of breath. Bob seems himself these days. More than himself. The steroids have infused him with energy.

"Yeah, I'm runnin' on Prestone," he tells his friends at first.

But he does not like the idea of his body being altered in ways he cannot control by these opaque white pills. When he begins to tinker with his dosage, he drives me nearly crazy with apprehension. Feeling better one day, he takes half his pills. Worse the next, he takes double.

"But the doctor warned us about exact dosages!" I scream. "Hell, that doc doesn't know a goddamned thing about the way I feel."

"What about the cigarettes?"

"I'll quit after harvest."

In my own way I am as certain as Bob that I can control the invisible menace growing in his lungs. Take the medication, follow the doctor's instructions to the letter, and the menace will be slowed, perhaps for years, and meanwhile we can live as we always have, going our separate ways by day and holding each other by night, delighting in each other's pulse and breath, looking forward to the baby.

Bob's denial, on the other hand, is less complex.

"I don't know why, but the prednisone has stopped working," says the specialist on our next visit to the Great Falls Clinic. "I'm going to start you on interferon. It's a drug used in transplant cases to break down the body's natural immune system, and it must be monitored with extreme care."

I listen, panicky, to his instructions. Was Bob's tinkering with his prednisone dosage the reason for its failure to slow the growth of his fibrosis? What will he do with this potential dynamite? What can I do about it?

On the way home, I find out.

"Hell," he says flatly. "I ain't gonna touch that shit. I'm going to wait until after harvest, and then"—he takes his eyes off the road, looks squarely at me—"then I'm going find out what the hell it is I'm allergic to."

Rachel was born at the end of September, and Bob drove us home from the hospital through the last blaze of autumnal color. I carried her into the nursery I had furnished and laid her, sleeping, in her crib. Bob dropped down in a chair beside the crib without taking off his coat or gloves. He watched as she slept: the transparent eyelids of the newborn, the little fists thrown back on either side of her head, the rise and fall of her tiny chest. When I looked in an hour later, neither Rachel nor Bob had moved.

But he had begun to lose weight. Down to 175, then 165 pounds. He bruised easily. Once, while he was holding Rachel, her little fist flailed out and nicked his face with a fingernail, and blood seeped down his cheek for an hour.

He refused to see the specialist again, or any other doctor, but I gleaned information about the progress of his disease where I could find it. "It's the fibrosis that causes the weight loss," explained Rachel's pediatrician when I took her in for her six weeks' checkup. "His body can't maintain itself."

But what caused the mood swings? Was it last summer's dosage of prednisone, still wreaking its roller-coaster damage on his reactions? Was he depressed over an illness he insisted he'd been misdiagnosed with? Or had the dark impulse run within Bob from the beginning, hidden until the combination of drugs and debilitation broke down his defenses? Which was the real Bob?

How much financial havoc can a man cause when he sets a farming operation into motion and then watches as through a haze of detachment while fields go uncultivated, obligations unmet, notes unrenewed? How many additional difficulties can he bring down around his shoulders as well as his family's when he fails to file his corporation reports? His PICA and W-4 forms? What if he fails to file his income taxes? Answer: more difficulties than I ever dreamed possible.

I lay awake at two, three, four o'clock in the morning while birch twigs brushed against the bedroom window and cast a maze of shadows as complex and random as the maze my life had become. Hundreds of thousands of dollars whirred through my brain on a squirrel-wheel frequency, organizing themselves into columns and disintegrating to form new totals at rising interest rates. What was I to do? What to do, what to do? Every hope for a way out of the maze was as treacherous as false dawn. The bank would foreclose on the farm in lieu of the $450,000 note? Very well, but the bank would report the transaction to the IRS as a forgiven debt. What, I wondered, did the IRS do with people like me who owed income tax on $450,000? Did they have jails with squirrel wheels in them?

By this time I lay awake alone, usually, in the bed in the

shadows of birch twigs. In the mornings I rose and dressed, drove Rachel to her sitter, and hammered away at the solutions that had eluded me in the small hours. By confronting every debt and filing every delinquent report, I could still cling to my illusions. *Face it! Fight it! If we can once deal with the finances, we can still live comfortably on my salary, and surely the disease can be slowed, maybe for years—if you don't believe in the diagnosis, we'll find another specialist. We'll go to Seattle or San Francisco and find another course of treatment, and surely, surely we can buy time, we can have years together. You'll see Rachel grow up—*

But Bob was away from home most of the time now, driven by my frantic tirades and his own denial of the disease that was slowly strangling him. Fired with the idea of getting back into the oil business, of another chance of striking it lucky, he went back to his native Kansas for weeks and then months at a stretch, coming home only to try to raise money for the leases he was buying.

"I found another oil well!"

He looks up from the logbook he has unfolded on the dining room table. Another thirty or forty logbooks are stacked around him or strewn on the floor. Cigarette smoke hangs blue over his head.

"See here? Where the line wavers? I don't see how they could have overlooked it. When they perforated, they missed the zone entirely. I can go in there, unplug it and reperforate, maybe run acid, get the well on stream for fifty, sixty barrels a day, initially—"

Sometimes he finds two or three oil wells in an evening.

"—cost?"

His eyes go opaque for an instant, as though my question has traveled on some dim transmission from outer space.

"What? The cost to rework one well? Hell, I don't know, honey, it'd be just one part of my program—twelve wells, say, at fifteen or twenty thousand—Hell, the cost of one well don't make no nevermind. I'll be talking to my old buddy the banker when I go back to Kansas next week. Now, can you see this? This jiggle on the graph? That's another oil-producing zone they missed when they finished this well—"

"Honey, I realize you don't know a goddamn thing about the oil business, but I don't understand why you can't *see* it! Hell, it's right there on the log! And fifty, sixty barrels a day, even at thirteen dollars a barrel—"

He's down to 150 pounds now. His skin has shrunken over his cheekbones, and his nails are cyanosed. Still, he's drawing on some invisible source of energy; his eyes are huge, his voice urgent as he stabs out one cigarette, lights another, and uses it to gesture at his logbook. All he needs to get on his feet again is a few thousand dollars I have in a savings account. Listening to his fevered chatter, I feel drawn into his dream, his certainty that out there somewhere, in the next fold of the graph, the next thousand feet of well pipe, is the ultimate fountainhead of wealth and health. I could drift with him, believe in him . . . *It was the drought, it was the farm crisis that bankrupted us, it wasn't his fault—and he knows the oil business, knows what he's talking about, it's just a matter of giving him his chance—*

But no.

He flies into a rage at my refusal. "You make me want to puke! *Puke! Puke! Puke! Puke! Puke!*"

A week of verbal bludgeoning is more than enough. I hand

over the money, and he sets off for Kansas, serene in his knowledge that the next throw of the dice is his.

A month later he calls home, jabbering, ecstatic. His old buddy the banker believes in him.

"It's growing on trees down here! The money's growing on trees!"

We don't hear from him after that. Another spring deepens into another hot summer, and the lawns and evergreens in Havre suffer the stress from curtailed watering. After work I pick Rachel up from her sitter's and play with her in the swing I have hung in the backyard willow. Rachel has seen so little rain in her life that when a brief deceptive shower fits its way overhead and a few raindrops lash the willow leaves, she asks, "What's that, Mom?"

Swing, swing, every day a bead on a string. Take Rachel to the sitter's and go to work in the mornings, pick her up and come home at night, swing her in the swing and bathe her and feed her and put her to bed. A whiskey and a book and Emmylou Harris for me. Swing, swing, the phone doesn't ring.

"Why don't you divorce him?" one of the attorneys had asked last summer.

This summer I file for divorce.

"Honey, *why?*"

In the hum of the long-distance line between Montana and Kansas, I try to think why.

"I'm coming home," he says after the silence. "I don't really have the time, I got a well just coming into production, but I can see you ain't left me no other choice."

Rachel and I drive to Great Falls to meet him at the airport. I recognize the man who appears on the ramp by his fair hair. He walks a step or two, gasps for breath. A ghost's eyes glow at us.

"Sure missed my two honeys," says the ghost. "Sure hated being away."

One of the disembarking flight attendants touches my arm. "Something's really wrong with this man," she says. "He's having terrible trouble breathing."

I nod.

She hesitates, glancing over our small sick circle. "Well— just so somebody knows," she says finally, and hurries off with her flight bag rolling behind her on its little wheels.

Rachel cuddles up to him. "My honey," he says, teary-eyed.

When we reach the car, he gets in the driver's seat and lights a cigarette. "We'll get rid of this pig," he says, "and buy you a new Lincoln as soon as the well comes on stream. They got new dealers' models in Kansas for under twenty thou. Helluva deal. There's a house down there I want you to see. It's an estate, actually."

"Let me drive."

"Hell, I feel fine! Long as I stay on my medication, I'm fine."

"Medication?"

"My Primatene Mist."

"The banker here in Havre don't want to make me a loan. He says he heard you've filed for divorce. But I told him you're dropping the action. You are dropping the action, aren't you?"

Hell, we got no problems, honey!

If only I could suspend my disbelief, accept the invitation to waltz with this rattling skeleton. But I hear him shouting into the phone at someone in Kansas: *It's still pumping water? Guess we'll have to go down further and shoot the second zone! What? Hell, I don't know! I'm planning to come back down to Kansas by the end of the week! At least by Monday! Hell yes, you'll get paid!*

"I'm having to sue my old buddy the banker for that sixty thousand he still owes me," he explains. "Sonovabitch got cold feet. Hell, can't blame him, in a sense. He don't know a god-damn thing about the oil patch."

No, I won't descend any further with him into his shadow world. I'll murder him instead with disbelief. From the light's edge I will watch as he walks under dead trees where dreams hang like leaves, as he fades into transparency and gibbers at me from the dim reaches: *It sure makes me feel good to know how much confidence my wife's got in me, Mary!*

"You've got to get him out of the house," says the attorney.

You try to divorce me, and you'll never see that little girl again, Mary! Hell no, I'm not talking about custody! I'm just telling you, Mary! You'll never see her again!

"But how can I take him seriously?" I plead.

"We have to take his threats seriously," says the attorney.

The second or third time the police have to come and drag him out of the house, the attorney applies to the judge for a restraining order. So he hides behind a hedge in a borrowed car until a new neighbor comes running across the street: "Quick! A man's trying to coax your little girl into his car with him!"

"We can't put him in jail," says the police lieutenant. "My God, the man's on oxygen."

I don't know why you can't see it, Mary! Hell, that lawyer's just running up his fees. I know I can't tell you a goddamn thing. You think you know it all. But eventually you're going to find out—

I have my phone number changed, and changed again, and still there comes at midnight or one a.m. the single ring. I pick it up to dial tone or to the hesitant whisper: *Honey? Hell, I'll forgive you. I just don't understand how you could throw me out.*

He has hired himself an attorney by now, and the paperwork blizzards back and forth. He demands a division of property, a maintenance allowance, and custody of Rachel. But when it comes to settlement, he backs off; when a hearing date is set, he calls the judge and gets an extension. What he really wants is not to be divorced.

"We could leave it like this," says the attorney finally, wearily. "You have a restraining order and temporary child custody, pending settlement. And you're leaving Montana in a month or two."

So it will never end.

"You don't think he'd try to follow you?" the attorney asks.

"I think he's too sick to follow far."

He lives in a room in the Havre Hotel. Bed, dresser, air-conditioning unit in the window. He can sit in the lobby downstairs and watch TV or watch the traffic on First Street. He can walk around the corner to PJ's Lounge and play a little poker, but he has to carry his portable oxygen supply everywhere he goes. He's a walking skeleton. He has nothing to do, nothing to look forward to——How could she have done it to him?

No, it will never end. Not with the ringing of a telephone, three Octobers later in the golden Palouse. Not when I agree with his sister that yes, we should lay him beside his parents; yes, I will want to bring Rachel. And it will not end with the late-night flight into Wichita, and not with the familiar faces of my kind brother-in-law and his wife waiting to drive us through the murky country roads to the small-town parlor where he waits. Rachel goes wild in the car, kicking, struggling; but when we get to Little River, she calms down and walks up the porch steps and through the door with its oval of Victorian glass.

"Why are his eyes shut?"

It is the first time I have seen him in the flesh since that day three years ago, just before I left Montana for good, when he cornered me in public and ranted, raged, finally slapped my face with all the feeble fury he could muster at my refusal to his waltz. For a moment I fight off the irrational feeling that, sensing my presence, he will sit up in his coffin, chattering, his ghost's eyes glowing: *Why, Mary? Why?*

"How old are you?" the Methodist minister asks Rachel.

"Seven," she whispers.

The Little River cemetery holds the only high ground for miles, and the grass is as stiff and sere as it would be in Montana in October. The wind snarls at the grass and roars in the canopy they have pitched over the open grave, and I remember another cemetery ridge a long time ago, and another dry-eyed woman named Mary.

At the end they fold the flag and hand it to me, the technical widow; and I turn as prearranged and hand it to one of his sons. No, it never ends. Perhaps my grandmother could have told me that. Her shade follows, as does his, through the windswept grass as Rachel and I walk hand in hand down the gravel track from the knoll.

LA VIDA LOCA*

Jimmy Santiago Baca

It's that beautiful Mexican music that understands so well a man's sadness, a man's humility, and a man's love and courage.

In prison, on torpid Saturdays, I would maybe write a letter, or call out or make hand signs to friends in the cellblock. But the pain in the soul, the twisting and slamming in my guts, like a desperate hand beating on a door; because somewhere someone is chasing the stranger and he can only find refuge behind this door, the door that never opens.

In La Pinta, in prison, you don't go anywhere. You breathe the moist rancidness of stone, of body smells, that stain prison air as nicotine stains the fingers of chain smokers, the pungency of hurt and suffering and rage. And this, Mexican music understands. I would tune my radio to a Mexican station and

---

*Literally "crazy life." In this instance, it connotes the indigenous artistic sensibility as it is affected by and expresses barrio life.

somehow the music drained my body of the poison fluid of grief. *Camaradas* in the cellblock would nod as I danced in my cell, writing poems in my head, bursting with images of flowery balconies and the potency of bulls in heat.

As a child, I used to go to bars with the men. There's a photograph of me in diapers, sitting on the wood floor of a *cantina* in Mexico, spinning empty miniatures of whiskey. And all around me old men with sweat-hardened dusty sombreros were talking and dancing. I would stare at their buckles embossed with bucking horses, bulls, or rodeo riders. They wore their jeans low, hanging from their hips, their pant cuffs crumpled on their boots; their shirts were blue or red or white, plain, simple colors. Most of them had crude, heavy rings and hefty watchbands, and crosses hung from their sun-scorched necks. Their skin was coarse from a lifetime's exposure to wind and rain, dust and heat and blowing grit.

I remember the Mexican voices that came from the jukeboxes in those places, slurred, rough, provocative voices that clawed the heart. Those passionate gasping and gripping pleas somehow exorcised my people's fears and urged them to dance and laugh and drink and seize life's pleasures, the bitter graces of their lives. And in those *cantinas* they felt a solidarity, were reassured that they had not betrayed themselves, still sustained their heart's pride.

The men and women I saw there rejected the kind of behavior that compromises dignity and bends to flattery. There was something in the way they spoke, with biblical solemnity and passionate romance, full of meaning in its simplicity, that held me.

And I fell in love with the woman in the dark corner booth, holding up her mirror to darken her luscious lips. The flashing neon sign outside the bar window would illuminate an unshaven face in another corner, and it seemed to me so handsome and exotic, this exquisitely hardened face, like a rose stiff with youth and firm with health, grown out of spring into the full height of its beauty on this one night. Tough *chucos* wearing shades, their collars turned up under snappy fedoras with dark bands and small feathers or gold pins, leaned in towards their listeners as if to conceal what they were saying. And near the bar were men and women in cowboy duds, robustly open, standing erect and tall. On the walls all around, pictures of Mexican rebels wielding pistols and embracing beautiful dark-haired women set the scene.

But of the men and women in those bars, as a child or later, I never saw their whole story, their whole life. Although I think they knew I was a friend, they peered at me as if from jungle leaves, with jaguar eyes, covert and watchful. In their faces you saw the golden-gray glossiness of eagle feathers and their sharp black shoes were eagle talons or jaguar claws that pointed when they walked, always toward Aztlán.

Late at night the gamblers would come in, impeccable in tailored suits, smelling of expensive cologne, and with dazzling women on their arms. They got up poker games, or conned the racing forms, their jeweled hands flashing money.

There were never bright lights in the life of my youth. My life was played out in the subdued lighting of small lamps and light bulbs, dim parking lights, flashlights, cigarette-lighter flames. In parking lots and on roadsides, in fields, outside darkened houses and shadowy bars, I too lived my life like a jaguar ambushed behind the dark filters of leaves. When I came to manhood, I held my woman's hand in alleys, in shadowy rooms musty with earth smells. There the couches were covered with crocheted cloths and religious pictures hung on all the walls. On little tables, good luck candles flickered before figures of Christ and the saints and bowls of hard candies. Through the always open windows, from behind blowing curtains, I would watch the sky redden and darken, studying the stars for answers to my heart's questions. Always there was that sense of being a part of everything in the universe, and always the sense that I could not find my rightful place there; that I was a coward and lost, because I was unable to tell the world who I was.

I had a car for cruising, a woman near me for loving, and Mexican music on the radio—that was my life. And all around me was this strange labyrinth called a city, not built for me. So I burned the map made for others, crumpled it and burned it in the fire, rolled my tortillas and fried me some green chile for comfort, in my room. But in the streets I was an exile looking in past doors left ajar, just a stranger passing through.

Even now, in some ways it's still the same. And puffing on my cigarette, my hands deep in my pockets, my collar up around my neck, my hat atilt—I laugh. Sometimes I warm myself at old photographs of prison friends, or photographs of my mother and father. Or, maybe, I trim my mustache and comb it out in its full scrub-brush glory. And when I walk city streets in the night, the reflection I see in the shop windows may not be me but some Pancho Villa laughing at me as he puffs on his cigar. Maybe El Francisco is with me, in the little fedora hat he always wears and his starched pink shirt, and we loiter on street corners shooting the breeze and waving at friends passing by. And maybe some woman he knows pulls over in her convertible and we have a few laughs together. And maybe we decide to pick up Eppy and Efrin and Gilbert and throw a cruise down *las calles* of our universe, and stop around midnight at Conchas for a little *menudo* or *caldo.* And while we eat we listen to Mexican music on the jukebox. Then I leave them and walk home alone, looking up at the stars from street corner pyramids, like some Mayan charting the future by the stars.

I learned my life in the kiss, in the passionate embrace, in a friend's trust, from the earth. I learned it from those people who took care of me, for a night, or a week, or a year—who taught me love. I took a little bit of each of you, *camaradas,* from your souls at their most blissful and vulnerable: from that deep and secret core that only Mexican music knows.

DUST, OR ERASING THE FUTURE: THE NEVADA TEST SITE

Rebecca Solnit

Dawn was only a faint glow behind the crests of Skull Mountain and the Specter Range when I swung off Highway 95 and arrived, ten hours hard driving away from home. It was still too dark to pitch a tent, so I bundled my sleeping bag around me and curled up on the car seat. An hour later, groggy and aching, sleeping bag strings imprinted upon my cheek, I gave up on sleep and ventured out with my tin cup in hope of coffee. Someone who'd seen my little brother up at the gates of the encampment sent me his way.

In the morning light everything looked familiar again, the hard pale ground paved with rocks and the roads kicked into dust, the evenly spaced tufts of thorny grasses and scrubby bushes—the almost ubiquitous texture of the Great Basin, the plateau between the Sierra and the Rockies. The explorer John C. Fremont named it the Great Basin in the 1840s, when he realized that this vast expanse doesn't drain into either side of the Continental Divide. For one thing, there's hardly anything to drain. The major river in this place, the Humboldt, doesn't go anywhere at all; after flowing most of the way across northern Nevada it fades away into an alkali flat. Range after range of mountains, each separated by a flat expanse like the one the camp was in, rise for hundreds of dry miles across the state of Nevada into Utah, stretching north into Oregon and Idaho, hemmed in on the south by the Colorado River. It was the lowest, hottest, driest southwest corner of the Basin that I woke up in, and across the Funeral Mountains to the west, the Basin ends, and California, Death Valley, and the Mojave Desert begin.

I remembered to be afraid of the dust, the dust that might be radioactive, the dust that over the next few days would powder everything to biscuit color, the dust that might be the dust of the hundreds of nuclear tests conducted somewhere across the highway I'd just driven in on. At first I hadn't been alarmed by the dust here, and later it became second nature to fear dust everywhere, but this dust didn't look like anything special to the naked eye. Most studies suggested that the background radiation at the Peace Camp wasn't any worse than that in Las Vegas, seventy miles to the south, since they were both upwind of most of the nuclear tests—though that wasn't comforting, especially if you lived in Las Vegas. It wasn't the background radiation but the fallout mixed into the fine, pale, silky powder that posed the most threat, however. "I will show you fear in a handful of dust," said a poet.

But to see mortality in the dust by imagining in it the unstable isotopes of radioactive decay took an act of educated faith or perhaps of loss of faith in the government. It looked like ordinary dust, and perhaps it will be, so far as the health of most of those who camped here are concerned. And people were living in this dust I had driven into, in a place called the Peace Camp, the gathering place for thousands who came every spring to prepare to invade the Nevada Test Site. The particular basin we were in is sliced in half by Highway 95, and across the road, along with Skull Mountain and the Specter Range, is the Nevada Test Site, the place where the U.S. and Britain have been setting off nuclear bombs for four decades, more than 900 so far in the hot secret heart of the Arms Race.

The Nevada Test Site (NTS) is big on a scale possible in few parts of the world, and in a way that only the West of the United States is big. The Test Site hewn out of Nellis Air Force Range in 1951 is 1,350 square miles, which makes it bigger than Yosemite National Park or Rhode Island. Nellis is a little over four times as big—5,470 square miles—bigger than Connecticut, a place that approaches one of the world's smaller nations in size—Israel, say, or Belgium. And if an army were to depopulate Belgium for half a century and explode hundreds of nuclear bombs on it, people would probably notice. Yet this has happened in the Great Basin, and few Americans know it has.

Before the bombs had gone underground, the public had been more aware of the goings-on at the NTS. The flashes were many times brighter than the sun, and those who were out before dawn could see the light of atomic fission from as far away as the mountaintops of northern California and southern Idaho. Strangely colored clouds drifted east across Nevada and Utah from the predawn explosions, and pictures of mushroom clouds sometimes appeared in the news. Nearby, the bombs felt like earthquakes. Since 1963, all of the tests here have been underground, but they have still been colossal explosions and they still leak radiation into the atmosphere. Since 1963, even most antinuclear activists haven't paid much heed to the Test Site. Nuclear war, whether you are for or against it, is supposed to be a terrible thing that might happen someday, not something that has been going on all along.

Test is something of a misnomer when it comes to nuclear bombs. A test is controlled and contained, a preliminary to the thing itself, and though these nuclear bombs weren't being dropped on cities or strategic centers, they were full-scale explosions in the real world, with all the attendant effects. I think that rather than tests, the explosions at the Nevada Test Site were rehearsals, for a rehearsal may lack an audience but contains all the actions and actors. The physicists and bureaucrats managing the U.S. side of the Arms Race had been rehearsing the end of the world out here, over and over again.

Even those who didn't question the legitimacy of the Arms Race sometimes questioned the necessity of testing. There were other ways to ensure the efficacy of existing nuclear weapons, and tests were only necessary for developing new weapons. The bombs set off in Nevada seemed instead a way of making war by display and displacement, as some cultures and species do—demonstrating their ability to attack rather than actually doing so. For every bomb set off in Nevada was potentially a bomb dropped on Odessa or Tashkent, and every bomb signified the government's willingness to drop a bomb on such a place, to pursue such a policy. And even if the bombs were invisible to most people in the U.S., the Soviets watched and took warning.

Other nations besides the U.S. and the U.S.S.R. had tested nuclear bombs, but only these two were rehearsing the end of the world, for they alone had developed enough bombs to annihilate not specific targets, but possibly whole continents of people and with them the natural order, the weather, perhaps the genetic codes of most living things. The bomb at Hiroshima was the end of a war, but the bombs on Tashkent and Odessa would have been the beginning of one, and the beginning of the end. The rehearsals were largely invisible, and so was the damage. Radiation is invisible, and the effects of radiation are invisible too. Although many more people are born with defects and die of cancer and other metabolic disorders in places affected by atomic fallout, the effects can only be calibrated statistically, with exhaustive research. There are already atomic epidemics, previews of what would happen to those who didn't die in an atomic war. And genetic damage— the scrambling of the codes—is as invisible as cancer, and as hard to trace to a cause. Radiation can make cells lose their memory, and loss of memory seems to be one of the cultural effects of the bombs too, for Americans forgot that bomb after bomb was being exploded here. Or perhaps people never forgot we were testing bombs, rehearsing the end of the world, but learned it so well and so deeply that the bomb-makers no longer needed to terrorize children with bomb drills, or adults with civil defense scenarios and mushroom clouds on TV. Perhaps the bomb came to affect us all as an invisible mutation in our dreams, a drama we could watch in our sleep instead of the Nevada skies.

The Test Site was a blank on many maps, a forgotten landscape, off limits to the public and swallowed up in a state which itself seemed sometimes to be overlooked by the rest of the country. Even though Nevada is growing rapidly, its population is still not much over a million, half of it in Las Vegas and most of the rest of it in the Reno-Carson City area. There aren't many people living in all that open space, and few artists and writers have celebrated its qualities. Not very many people were displaced when the land that became Nellis was sealed off in 1941, when the population of Nevada was around 110,000, and not many people objected, because this landscape is widely thought to be worthless already.

Space itself isn't an absolute, or at least the spaciousness of landscapes isn't. Up close, aridity means that even the plants grow far apart from each other; for people and animals, this sparseness means that they too have to spread out to make a living off the land. In the East, a cow can live off a few acres of grass; out here the land is often overgrazed at only a few cows per thousand acres, and where they overgraze the soil erodes back to dust and rock. It is rock—geology—that dominates this landscape. In lusher landscapes, it is as though the skin and bones of the earth are dressed in verdure; here the earth is naked, and geological processes are clearly visible. It is geological time and geological scale that dominate this landscape, dwarfing all the biological processes within the uplift of ranges, the accretion of basins. The very rocks on the ground have lain in place so long around the Test Site that their tops and bottoms are different colors, and any disturbance leaves a lasting scar. Every act out here has to be measured against this scale of change and scope. It is this apparent geology, this bare rock, that makes newcomers read the desert as a dead or barren landscape, though if you spend more time in it, you may come

to see the earth itself lives, slowly and grandly, in the meta-
morphoses of geology.

About half a mile down the road to Highway 95, I found my
little brother and eight of his friends piling into a station
wagon, and when they urged me to join them, I crammed in.
They were on their way down 95 to blockade the workers
coming from Las Vegas to Mercury, the industrial town within
the Test Site. They were merry inside the car, burbling incon-
sequentialities, joking, drinking out of water bottles, bota
bags, and canteens, clad in Levis, flannel shirts, T-shirts advertising other actions and causes, in army surplus, bandannas,
shawls, ethnic oddments, tights and thermals. That spring
morning, the desert was cold. We passed the main gate to the
Test Site, the gate on the road into Mercury, and kept going
south. By day Mercury is a faint glimmer of dust-colored buildings five miles into the Test Site, but by night it looks like a quilt
of fallen stars, the only electric light visible anywhere from the
camp. These days most of the Mercury workers live in Las
Vegas, and we were apparently planning on preventing them
from getting to work. If there was a nuclear war going on, then
there was a war against it as well, and this morning of March
30, 1990, these scruffy young people were the people who were
fighting it most directly.

There were times when the conflict between government
and activists became deadly serious, dangerous, even fatal for the
activists, but there were more times when it was a neatly staged
conflict in which both sides played by the rules. The rules on the
activists' side were first and most crucially those of nonviolent
direct action, often called civil disobedience. Nonviolence means

not merely refraining from violence, but of working for change without violence—which means embodying the ideal you work for. Some political theorists call it "the politics of prefiguration," which means that it attempts to realize within the movement what it seeks to bring about on a grander scale. By making such change part of their means rather than simply their end, such activists have already begun to realize their goals, whether their action causes further change or not. Nonviolence also makes a qualitative rather than merely a strategic distinction between sides: To take violent action is to endorse violence as a means. And nonviolence disrespects violence, undermines force and might as arbiters of fate.

The theory of nonviolent direct action, first articulated in Henry David Thoreau's "Civil Disobedience," is a noble one. The practice is far more complicated. Many religious people, notably Catholics and Quakers, commit civil disobedience with quiet fervor; a lot of anarchists and other young radicals commit civil disobedience with an insurrectionary verve that is harder to associate with Gandhi and Martin Luther King. Like civil obedience it requires a tacit cooperation with some form of governmental authority—that's the civility of it. If Thoreau hadn't let himself be hauled off to jail and hadn't stayed there (until his aunt bailed him out), he would have been a tax cheat, not a civil disobedient. Every once in a while, the governmental body in charge gets wise and doesn't show up, neutralizing the civil disobedience and diluting the impact of the demonstration. Sometimes the civil disobedients get crushed—as they were in Tiananmen Square in 1989—and the government then wins the battle, but loses the support of the public. And sometimes the force of unarmed people in public places is enough to topple governments, as it has in Eastern Europe and other parts of the world in recent times.

Here nonviolent direct action most often gets trivialized, by the general population as well as by the media and the courts. At the trials, defense of necessity, prevention of a crime, and Nuremberg principles are almost never allowed to be introduced into court. The Thoreauvians are tried for acts stripped of political meaning—obstructing a public thoroughfare, trespassing, damaging property, although unlike criminals, nonviolent direct activists take action publicly with readiness to deal with the consequences of their acts.

Civil disobedience has a proud directness to it, unlike all the supplicatory lobbying and petitioning that somehow endorse the imbalance of power they seek to redress. People who are shocked by others who break the law and challenge the government seem to regard government as a parent, to which we owe respect and obedience (and they tend to confuse the country, which includes land and people, with the government that regulates them; "I love my country but I fear my government," says a bumper sticker that tries to straighten out this muddle). The government is not a finished work, and it must constantly be re-created, maintained, improved, corrected for the well-being of the land and people, and in this sense it is also a child.

Then, too, those who are shocked conceive of government as an inalienable whole. But the government as an ideal—the law and the source of justice—is often distant from the government as individuals engaged in specific acts, and citizens must often choose between the ideals and the individuals. There have been many illegal government acts in recent decades, and many questionable ones. And then there are higher laws: international laws, human rights, and natural law. The right to protest by speech and public assembly is in the First Amendment. But the need to commit it is often an issue of natural law, of adherence to an idea of justice that transcends lawbooks. And the duty to commit civil disobedience is implicit in the international laws of the Nuremberg Principles, which signal the end of obedience as an adequate form of citizenship. The Nuremberg Principles are abstracted from the Nuremberg trials of Nazi war criminals who justified their acts as following orders, a justification the world refused to accept. "The fact that a person acted pursuant to an order of his government or of a superior does not relieve him of responsibility under international law, provided that a moral choice was in fact possible for him," says the fourth Nuremberg principle. The principles cover crimes against peace, war crimes, and crimes against humanity; the testing of nuclear weapons violates all three. These principles remove us from the shelter of authority—of doing what we do because we are told to do it— and put us in the roofless territory of individual conscience.

There's a nice symmetry between Thoreau's night in Concord jail in 1846 and the activity around the Nevada Test Site. By refusing to pay taxes, Thoreau was protesting the U.S.'s war on Mexico, which was a war for land. The land acquired through that war included Nevada and most of the Southwest, from Texas to California, though no one paid much attention to Nevada at the time; it was until 1861 part of Utah Territory anyway.

The morning after his night in jail, Thoreau took a group of his fellow citizens out huckleberrying.

• • •

About three dozen people took over the two north-bound lanes of Highway 95, which is a divided road as it approaches the Test Site. Luxury cruiser buses full of Test Site workers, pickups, Winnebagos, and four-wheel drives began to back up for blocks, then for half a mile. The arrests that began at seven that morning were rowdy. Activists were expected to wander into the Test Site, but not into oncoming traffic, so the sheriffs, thick and red-faced in tight, shortsleeved uniforms the same color as the dust, were irate. Most of the people sitting in the road used passive resistance—they didn't struggle, but they didn't cooperate with the people arresting them. They had to be carried off the road. Some of them entwined arms with each other and then linked their own hands beneath their knees, making a human chain. This was a surprise action and there was no place to take the blockaders away to until requisitioned buses came, so the handcuffed activists were put down by the side of the highway.

The crowd on the road thinned and the crowd by its shoulder thickened, then everyone suddenly rushed back onto the road and sat down again. Supporters standing on the gravelly freeway divider yelled at the sheriffs to treat the blockaders with care whenever they saw an arm being twisted or a body being dragged instead of carried. Other than these cries of care, it was as silent as a pantomime. Only rarely did a stopped car honk, a protester or sheriff speak. There was no way I was going to get arrested until after I had a cup of coffee, so I just watched. All the shadows that filled the hollows of the mountains were gone, chased out by the rising sun, and the landscape already had the flat, stark brightness of midday. As I watched the burly men picking up blockaders by arms and legs stiff with resistance, I saw their frail forms as *bodies,* as potential corpses and as pathetically vulnerable objects to put between the landscape and the military, and my eyes filled with tears.

Finally, the buses came and took all the handcuffed people away, including my little brother. (I fell into calling him that to distinguish him from all the other Davids, and all my other brothers, and I should add that he has been a little over six feet for the last decade or so, though he was smaller than me once.) He is an anarchist, and a key organizer for the antinuclear movement, and though he was initially an anarchist in the sense that innumerable punks were in the '80s, he has read his Bakunin and Kropotkin and is now very seriously an anarchist. Anarchy, I should explain, means not the lack of order but of hierarchy, a direct and absolute democracy. Voting democracy, as anarchists point out, simply allows a majority to impose its will on a minority and is not necessarily participatory or direct. They themselves continue the process of negotiation until all participants achieve consensus, until everyone—not merely a majority—has arrived at a viable decision. Anarchy proper usually works out to mean excruciatingly interminable meetings, rather than the mayhem the word evokes in most American imaginations. The Peace Camp and American Peace Test, which organized the camp and the actions, were run on anarchist lines: Each affinity group—the basic organizing unit of direct action—deliberated over the issues and then sent a spokesperson to represent its decisions at a spokescouncil.

During the Spanish Civil War, the writer Sylvia Townsend Warner once said of anarchy—the prevailing ideology of the Spanish antifascists—that "the world was not yet worthy of it, but it ought to be the politics of heaven." During the season that the movie *Reds* came out, my little brother, then still a teenager living at home, was so inspired by John Reed's extravagant Bohemian anarchy in the early part of the century that he imitated him, tacking a sign to our mother's front door that said, "Property is theft; walk right in," an ideal he put on hold when he moved to the city. I myself am not yet worthy of anarchy, or at least I have never found the patience and tolerance necessary to work with group consensus for extended periods. During the several years we both lived in San Francisco, however, my brother and I worked out a beautiful symbiosis: He was much better at going to meetings, and I was much better at spelling, so he organized, and I pitched in on the publication projects he took on and showed up for the demonstrations. Occasionally, like Thoreau's aunt, I paid his bail.

So many Americans seem to think that activism is an aberrant necessity brought on by a unique crisis, and then throw themselves into it with an unsustainable energy brought on by the belief that once they realize some goal or other, they can go home and be apolitical again. I always admired my brother for the steady nonchalance with which he approached his work, recognizing that political engagement was a normal and permanent state, and because however much he idealized direct action and populism, he never lost his ability to see the ludicrous aspects of the movement. He was the force that got me to Nevada the first time, though it was the desert and the bomb that kept me coming back again and again.

After the bus pulled away, I went back to camp and pitched my tent beside three yuccas and crawled inside. Around noon I stuck my head out and looked up into the sky, which had filled with clouds while I slept. Rain fell straight into my eyes, a few light drops in a shower that lasted only a minute or so, and left the landscape as dry as before. I took out my water bottle and stove and made coffee, sitting in the door of my tent, bemused by the reduction of my domesticity to a bagful of gear, my privacy to a tube of ripstop nylon, to find myself drinking coffee in solitude in the middle of all the bustle of the camp surrounded by all the silence of the desert. That utter abstraction the Arms Race and its sister the Cold War only became believable for me when they acquired a location, a landscape: this landscape. This was the place where the end of the world had been rehearsed since 1951, and this was my third spring at the camp. We were living closer to nuclear war than anyone but its technicians and its victims, which should have been devastating, but we were doing something about it, which was heartening.

The present large-scale actions had begun in earnest a few years earlier. An annual Lenten vigil had been held out here since 1977—a remarkable Franciscan nun named Sister Rosemary had initiated it—and the spring actions had grown over the years, bringing together Quakers and other religious denominations with the Franciscans, then nonreligious activists (and pagans). Around the equinoxes was the only time most people could bear to live out in the desert at all, because the heat of summer and cold of winter were both fierce. Even in spring, the nights could be freezing and the days could climb into the nineties. Secular antinuclear activists decided that it was time to turn to the very heart of the Arms Race and held a thirty-day protest out here in 1985, organized by the direct-action task force of the national nuclear freeze movement.

When the movement decided to quit sponsoring direct action, the task force split off into American Peace Test, the central organization in coordinating the mass actions since. This year, 1990, attendance was down a little, probably because so many Americans took the peaceful changes in the Eastern Bloc countries as a sign that everything would turn out all right without their participation. The Cold War, popular wisdom had it, was thawing. France had said it would stop testing if the U.S. and the U.S.S.R. did, and forty-one nations were clamoring for a comprehensive test ban treaty at the 1991 U.N. conference. And the U.S. was testing, despite the moratoriums of the U.S.S.R., and so we were here.

On a few occasions, people actually stopped nuclear tests. Most people hadn't the stamina or conviction to do more than a ritual act of civil disobedience, a symbolic interference with the Arms Race, but some had walked to Ground Zero and prevented tests from taking place. Walking to Ground Zero meant carrying seventy-pound packs with gallons of water, walking by night and sleeping in gullies and mesa shadows by day, for three days or so. In 1986 a Greenpeace team showed up at Ground Zero and disrupted a scheduled test, but the team's announcement and photograph hardly made the news when it rushed them out over the wire services. In 1988, a woman walked to an observation tower at Ground Zero and locked her neck to a steel pole there. The precautionary guidelines American Peace Test published for such actions were terrifying in themselves: "The Nevada Test Site is a highly radioactive place with many hot spots, dumps, and storage areas. . . . There is little that can be done to protect your body from beta and gamma rays which are unseen and penetrate your body. Alpha particles, however, may have more longterm effects. They are found on dust particles that can be breathed in or ingested. Cover your face when walking in the wind. Do not eat food dropped on the ground. Don't use bare, dirty hands for eating. . . . A large test can throw someone three meters into the air at Ground Zero and kill them. There is a rippling of ground motion that goes out from this center. Detonations create limited earthquakes. The Nellis Air Force Base surrounds the Test Site on the east, west and north. Depending on which part you venture through, you will have to deal with ammunition strafing, falling bombs, unexploded bombs on the ground, maneuvering around targets, and Stealth bomber security. At the time of arrest, it is vital that team members make no sudden moves that might be considered threatening to the security forces. They are very well armed and quite capable of shooting if they feel threatened."

A lot of people hadn't gone all the way to Ground Zero, but had reached surprisingly far into the Test Site. Some Western Shoshone people had simply disregarded the fences and signs and continued to walk across the land, visit traditional sites, and hunt and gather on it during the decades after its withdrawal from the public domain in 1941, and Pauline Esteves, an elder from the Timbisha Shoshone community in Death Valley, remembers her uncle going deer hunting there in the 1940s. Presumably the place where all our nuclear weapons are tested should be a major national security area, but the government has always counted on the remoteness of the place and indifference of the people to shield its actions. In practice this place was liable to be overrun at any time, was an area without much security at all, even against a bunch of loosely organized pacifists.

The night that I first got arrested at the Test Site, something else happened there. I didn't hear the real story until years later, when I was driving one of the participants back from Nevada to San Francisco—another all-night drive on the route that had become a roster of familiar landmarks. On the last leg of the journey, past the white windmills of Altamont Pass and down through Livermore, California, where nuclear bombs are designed and the H-bomb was conceived, as daybreak came like a postcard in my rearview mirror, Rachel told me about the Princesses of Plutonium. The year before, at the Mother's Day 1987 action, two of the future Princesses had succeeded in reaching Mercury and had been cited and released with everyone else, and somehow going to Mercury became their goal. They talked about what they could do when they got there. Rachel came up with the mask she had been using for another project, so they all acquired expressionless silvery robotic masks and white paper coveralls that looked like radiation suits.

At night, after the big arrest action in 1988, the Princesses of Plutonium took off for Mercury. "And we really were princesses. We travelled in comfort, with thermoses of coffee and tea and chocolate-covered espresso beans, and every time we had to hide, we had a little snack," Rachel recalled. They took a leisurely approach to the forbidden city, hiding and refreshing themselves frequently during the night. The last time they thought they were seen, they hid in a ditch, and during that halt they donned their rad suits and masks and waited, then climbed a fence at the eastern side of Mercury and began to walk around. "And we were there for a long time, ten of us, in the early morning on a Sunday, we stuck together and we put up stickers and things: We were really visible and we couldn't believe we were just free to walk around. Finally a Wackenhut came up, a red-faced senior guy I see at the cattle-guard all the time now, and I'll never forget how shocked and scared he looked. He couldn't tell by looking if we were men or women or what.

"And they took us into custody and interviewed each of us alone for a long time. They were pretty cool; we all gave our name as Priscilla, after a particularly dirty balloon-dropped nuclear test in 1957, and the interviewer was saying that it certainly was a coincidence that there were so many of us with that name. Then they took us to Beatty, and we started to have problems. Some of the people who had never been arrested before were really scared, and got upset at others for leading them into this. They took us to jail and kept us till Tuesday [from Saturday]. We had to give our real names then; they took away our possessions and clothes, gave us jail uniforms, the works. But the peace camp was great. They came and did support actions outside the jail and some men went to Mercury in solidarity with us, and we could yell and sing at them in the jail. I tried to drink as little water as possible because the water there's really radioactive. When we got home, things started to fall apart with the Princesses. There was disagree-ment on how to handle the case and things. We worked on it for months, and then they dropped the charges."

Priscilla exploded on June 24, 1957, fifth in the Plumbbob series of twenty-four large bombs. Unlike most Test Site bombs, this one was set off in the southeast corner of the Test Site, at Frenchman Flat, a few miles north of Mercury. Near Ground Zero were live pigs dressed in specially tailored military uniforms to test the fabrics' abilities to protect against thermal radiation. The explosion was bigger than expected, and the remote-control camera captured the pigs writhing and squealing as they died in what proved to be a pointlessly cruel exercise. Slightly further away were soldiers in trenches, one of whom wrote an account of Priscilla. Marine Lieutenant Thomas Saffer wrote, "A thundrous rumble like the sound of thousands of stampeding cattle passed directly overhead, pounding the trench line. Accompanying the roar was an intense pressure that pushed me downward. The shock wave was traveling at nearly four hundred miles per hour, pushed toward us by the immense energy of the explosion. The earth began to gyrate violently, and I could not control my body. Overcome by fear, I opened my eyes. I saw that I was being showered with dust, dirt, rocks, and debris so thick that I could not see four feet in front of me. . . . A light many times brighter than the sun penetrated the thick dust, and I imagined that some evil force was attempting to swallow my body and soul. . . . The metallic taste in my mouth was foul and would not go away." The Plumbbob tests dropped fallout from Oregon to New England.

I came to the Test Site four springs in a row, and the third spring, the spring of 1990, the place began to make sense to me. The first year, the afternoon before the Princesses set out, I walked with friends into the arms of the waiting guards. We had simply climbed through the fence a short distance away from the road entrance to the place, and they had come to get us. The boundary of the site is marked by a barbed-wire fence, and the point at which one is trespassing on the road is the far side of the cattleguard (cattleguard, easterners and urbanites: a set of thick bars running the length of a trench across the road, easy for human feet to cross by stepping on the bars but impossibly treacherous for hooves). It seems typically Western that all the Test Site boundaries are designed to obstruct livestock rather than people, for no serious walker is halted by a cattleguard in the road or a fence across the land.

My second year at the Test Site I went in with a bunch of anarchist women from San Francisco and Seattle. Two of the northerners became friends of mine later, but I didn't know any of them well at the time. We'd agreed that we would pair off so that no one got abandoned or left at the guards' mercy without a witness, and then we'd hiked northwest up 95 about a mile north of the main gate, so that we'd have time to cover some ground before we were interfered with. I'm not sure what our purpose was—curiosity?—but my own desire was always to walk as long as possible across the land that was off limits. "Reclaim the Test Site," the big American Peace Test action of spring 1988 had been called. Walking claims land not by circumscribing it and fencing it off as property but by moving across it in a line that however long or short connects it to the larger journey of one's life, the surrounding roads and trails, that makes it part of the web of experience, confirmed by every foot that touches the earth.

Actually, that spring afternoon in 1989 the dozen other women and I only got about a quarter mile in, walking in a gully that made it hard to see us from the land, before the helicopters found us, swooping low overhead with men in paramilitary uniforms leaning out ready to jump. If we were conducting our war as a picnic meander, they were conducting their job as a military maneuver. But when the hovering copter got low enough to pelt us with gravel spat from the ground by its gust of air, we ran, and the men leapt out and ran after us. I ran madly in the bad footing of the desert, with its soft patches of sand and crusted-over dust, cobbled stretches, boulders, loose rocks, and low bushes, only slowing down enough to keep pace with the woman with whom I'd paired off. The anarchists were all wearing vivid colors, and I in my dusty khaki regretted that we were so visible. I wondered this time, as I did so many others, whether I could disappear from view if I walked by myself, but solitude was discouraged here—it could be dangerous.

I ran for a ways without looking back, and then I turned my head a little and saw a man in camouflage all but close enough to grab me, far closer than I expected. He must have decided to join another chase, because it seems unlikely that I actually outran him. And running was one of the things that we usually agreed not to do, as it wasn't in keeping with the spirit of nonviolent direct action. Urgent, unpredictable, quick actions threw the security forces into a panic, made it possible for things to go astray.

I gave up easily, letting them handcuff my hands behind my back, but my companion resisted, letting the two guards know why she was here and by what laws she had the right to be here. She cited the fact that the land was stolen from the Western Shoshone in the first place, and that we had permission from them to be here, that she was following the

Nuremberg Principles they were violating. Now I can't even remember which of the women she was, only the unwavering conviction with which she refused to cooperate. She refused to walk, too, and so they herded the two of us into another gully and handcuffed us ankle to ankle. One stood guard over us while the other went for reinforcements. The other women were no longer visible. Picture an immensity of flatness populated only by two immobilized women and two men in camouflage, one of whom was rapidly disappearing. There was nothing to say. The Test Site looked exactly like the landscape outside, though we were now unable to stand up in it because of our shackles.

The second guard came back with a third man. While one guard walked behind me to make sure that I didn't attempt to flee, the other two picked her up, each taking one arm and one leg, and carried her. We progressed a couple of hundred yards in this way, when an older, red-faced guard joined our group of five. He snarled at the guards not to indulge her by carrying her. First he got them to drag her by her arms, then he got them to stop going around the obstacles. They began to drag her through thornbushes and over cacti.

He had convinced them to engage in a mild form of torture, and it didn't seem to have occurred to any of them that they could refuse his orders, though it was this kind of mindless obedience that the Nuremberg Principles she cited were made to combat. Finally she gave up and, near tears, asked them to stop. She began to walk, so she wouldn't be dragged. We walked to the dirt road that ran parallel to the Test Site periphery, where a big van was waiting for us, along with several of the other women in our group. The van was there to take us to the huge holding pens the Department of Energy had built a year or so before, next to the main gate. The guards cut off the plastic handcuffs we were bound with and rehandcuffed us with our hands in front, letting the cut pairs lie where they fell. My companion offered me a drink of water from the bota bag they hadn't confiscated, then she took off her hiking boot with awkward double-handed gestures and took out her Swiss army knife. I pulled out as many of the thorns in her foot as I could with the knife's tweezers. Some of them were huge, and one long one broke off deep in her foot.

I have trouble with the abstract and the concrete. In the abstract we were committing civil disobedience in the cause of peace and justice, making a gesture that echoed the gestures of Thoreau in Concord in 1846 and the trials in Nuremberg in 1946, the resistance of the Shoshone and of pacifists in many places and times. In the concrete we were scrabbling around in the scrub, playing tag with a bunch of mercenaries who thought that we were completely demented. My faith wavers. I always had trouble seeing the guards as representatives of U.S. military policy rather than as rednecks with limited career options, though I think many of the activists at the Test Site had the opposite problem, that perhaps the concrete didn't complicate their abstract ideals. The invisible background to all this, to our plastic handcuffs, to the thorn that broke off in her foot, to the helicopter pelting gravel and the men making a living by wearing camouflage and chasing pacifists, to the whole ramshackle peace camp and direct action, the background we would never see, was even harder to keep in mind: huge nuclear weapons detonations in preparation for international wars and as part of a local nuclear war nearing the forty-year mark.

There is a theory about lines of energy that traverse the earth, running through sacred sites, called "ley lines." The people who have developed this theory demonstrate it by showing the alignment of important sites along straight lines. I'm not sure about ley lines, but I believe in lines of convergence. These lines are no more visible in the landscape than ley lines, and I am not even proposing that they have any existence at all outside our imaginations—which are themselves crucial territories. These lines of convergence are the lines of biography and history and ecology that come together at a site, as the history of nuclear physics, the Arms Race, anti-Communism, civil disobedience, Native American land-rights struggles, the environmental movement, and the mysticism and fanaticism deserts seem to inspire in Judeo-Christians all come together to make the Nevada Test Site, not as a piece of physical geography, but of cultural geography, not merely in the concrete, but in the abstract. Such places bring together histories which may seem unrelated—and when they come together it becomes possible to see new connections in our personal and public histories and stories, collisions even. A spiderweb of stories spreads out from any place, but it takes time to follow the strands.

There's a strangely popular subject of speculation for hikers and explorers: whether they were the first people ever to tread on a piece of land. It comes out of the American obsession with virgin wilderness, which is itself a deeply problematic idea, and it speculates about the possibility of the utterly new, of an experience without predecessors. It is usually mistaken in its premises. There are few places in North America that were not first walked upon by the indigenous inhabitants of the continent, and even if one were to take out one's mountaineering gear and reach a peak literally untouched before by human beings, one is making a gesture that depends for its meaning and motives on a long history of such gestures. Though you may be the first to climb a peak in the Sierra and your foot may touch a place no human foot has touched, you are covering cultural territory covered by great mountaineers from Clarence King and John Muir onward. And the actual act of climbing a mountain depends for its meaning on the romantic cult of mountains, and so even if you have never read Shelley's "Mont Blanc," you have inherited it, and when you step on that piece of ground, you step where Shelley went, and where a wide road of meaning has been worn since. You may not know that the Italian poet Petrarch was the first modern man who climbed a mountain for the pleasure of the view, but you are treading in his six-hundred-year-old footsteps. New or old, it seems you should know where you came from to understand where you are, and only a true and absolute amnesiac could come from nowhere in arriving somewhere. We all carry the burden of history and desire; sometimes it's good to sit down and open the suitcases.

I want to be able to see the history of gestures behind even a voyage into the new, and I want more to be able to remember the lines of convergence that lead to a place like the Nevada Test Site. This is the abstract whose weight I have tried to feel behind every concrete gesture at the Test Site, a place that however few may see it, however invisible it may be, is the hub of so many crucial lines of our history. But it was hard to remember all this while pulling thorns out of someone's sweaty foot with my hands cuffed together.

• • •

However foolish and futile this antinuclear activism seemed close up, at a distance it commanded respect. Maybe it was an accident that we helped inspire an extraordinarily successful movement on the other side of the globe, and maybe it wasn't. The fact remains that on February 12 and 17, 1989, underground nuclear tests vented radiation into the atmosphere in Kazakhstan, the central Asian republic where the Soviets tested most of their nuclear weapons and where the environment and human health had suffered terribly from radiation over the decades. And on February 27, the Kazakh poet Olzhas Suleimenov appeared live on television and instead of reading his poetry as scheduled, he read a statement condemning nuclear testing and calling for a public meeting. The next day 5,000 people came to the Hall of the Writers Union in Alma Ata, the Kazakh capital, and named themselves the Nevada-Semipalatinsk Antinuclear Movement, in solidarity with the antinuclear and indigenous activists of Nevada—an extraordinary line of convergence running from test site to test site halfway round the globe.

Local officials were members of this movement, along with distinguished professionals and many, many writers. On the confident assumption that the Test Site activists had the same kind of entrenchment in local institutions, the Nevada-Semipalatinsk Antinuclear Movement sent statements of solidarity to Nevada government officials, who must have been bemused to find that Communists thought they had a lot in common. In October, two huge Soviet tests triggered demonstrations of tens of thousands of Kazakhs, the republic's miners threatened to go on strike, and more than a million people signed the Nevada-

Semipalatinsk statement opposing nuclear testing. However bleak the political situation, the culture was enviable, one in which a poet had such power and the public could join together so effectively. By October 21, 1989, the Soviets had stopped testing, begun a unilateral moratorium, and agreed to close the sites down altogether by the mid-'90s.

The people of the Nevada-Semipalatinsk Movement had timing on their side, of course. They began in the midst of the reforms sweeping the Soviet Union, when the nation was in fragile condition, when all things nuclear still recalled the meltdown at Chernobyl for most Soviet citizens, when civil disobedience and public demonstration had become a powerful new tool for them and for Eastern Europeans. Kazakhs would say, "We realized nuclear testing was bad, and so we demanded that our government stop it, and so they did. We don't understand why you don't do the same thing." Then the U.S. activists would try to explain the military-industrial complex, the sabotage of democracy by money politics, and the way that the U.S. government has successfully ignored popular protest, realizing that trivialization and obliviousness are its most effective weapons, the way the media overlooked us and everything else that took place in the state of Nevada.

That year, 1989, the year of the cactus thorns and of Suleimenov's statement, law-enforcement officials arrested 1,090 people for trespassing in one fell swoop, unloaded us into the special cattle pen they'd built for us, left us there with a canister of water and a portable toilet for the afternoon, then loaded us onto buses. They used the same buses for us that they used to transport the workers from their homes in Las Vegas to Mercury, air-conditioned coaches with tinted windows, reclinable seats, even toilets. It was a peculiar experience, sitting on the soft upholstery provided by the Department of Energy, watching the scenery roll by at sixty or seventy miles an hour on the way up 95. My first year there, 1988, they'd taken all 1,200 of us nearly 200 miles north to the remote town of Tonopah, and I had worried that they wouldn't take us that far unless they planned on hanging onto us for a while. It was a long enough ride, on that strange road as the sun set, to imagine many things. But every year they just hauled us north to inconvenience us, unloaded us a few buses at a time, snipped off our cuffs, and told us to go away and not come back. (Usually we were dumped in Beatty—"gateway to Death Valley"—a former mining boomtown that had restaurants with fingerbowls and tuxedoed waiters in 1906, but was more of a corn-dog kind of place by my time, and was the town where the Princesses had been held.) By the end of the ten-day event in 1988, 2,000 people had been arrested from among the 5,000 participants—and no charges were pressed in the vast majority of the cases. It was one of the biggest civil disobedience arrests in U.S. history, and it barely made the local news.

In 1988, the nuclear bombs exploded at the Test Site were named Kernville, Abeline, Schellbourne, Laredo, Comstock, Rhyolite, Nightingale, Alamo, Kearsage, Bullfrog, Dahlhart, and Misty Echo. Most of them ranged from 20 to 150 kilotons (Hiroshima was laid waste with 15 kilotons, Nagasaki with 21), as did 1989's bombs: Texarkana, Kawich, Ingot, Palisade, Tulia, Contact, Amarillo, Disko Elm, Hornitos, Muleshoe, Barnwell, and Whiteface. They didn't make the news either.

The reasons why we didn't get more severe treatment had to do with money and land. The land of the Nevada Test Site is itself under considerable dispute. The U.S. Department of Energy (DOE), which operates the Test Site, has an agreement whereby the Nye County authorities are responsible for legal aspects of the security of the site. It's supposed to have been a tradeoff for the economic benefits of having a major employer in the county. But Nye, the second largest county in the U.S., has a population in the low ten thousands, and though the DOE subsidizes Nye County sheriffs arresting activists, it doesn't pay the county to put activists through the legal system. So every year they've rounded us up and hauled us away and tossed us out with a reprimand or two: As long as they don't prosecute us, we serve as an additional light seasonal income for the county, rather than a burden on it. It resembles a cattle roundup more than a criminal arrest process, what with the quantity of people, the logistics of large-scale cuffing and bussing, and the general lack of animosity between parties. Some people said that Nye was trying to annoy the DOE into patrolling its own premises by letting us off so lightly.

The land shouldn't really be controlled by any of these authorities, however—local, state, or federal—because legally the Nevada Test Site is part of a much larger expanse that never really became part of the United States. U.S. claim to the land is based on the Treaty of Guadalupe Hidalgo, the 1848 treaty by which the U.S. concluded its war with Mexico, the war Thoreau went to jail to protest. It was that treaty, and a $15 million sweetener, which transformed northwestern Mexico into the southwestern states of the United States, from western Texas and New Mexico to California. What was then called Utah Territory was of little concern to either side at the time. Utah was named after the Utes, a linguistic and cultural subgroup of one of the continent's major indigenous groups, the Shoshonean people. From the Wyoming Rockies to the Sierra, and from Idaho to California's Mojave, tribes including the Western and Mountain Shoshone, Bannock, Utes, and Northern and Southern Paiutes lived for centuries before the first Mormons and mountain men wandered in. It was a Wind River Shoshone woman, Sacajawea, who with her newborn baby in her arms led Lewis and Clark on their journey across the continent in 1805–1806 to find a way to the Pacific and to begin the national imagining of a sea-to-sea United States. And it was Shoshonean peoples who learned how to live within the severe limits and delicate balances of the Great Basin, who made it a home and named its places long before Fremont and the Death Valley Forty-Niners applied the morbid appellations of their eastern imaginations to the place.

Nevada means snowy, a sign that Nevada was settled from the western, Sierran side, and it only became a separate territory, and a territory settled by non-Mormon whites, when it turned out that Nevada was full of gold and silver. Much of Nevada still belongs to the Western Shoshone. The Western Shoshone do not believe that land can be sold, and they have never sold their land. Nor have they given it away, or leased it, or been conquered as a nation by the nation of the United States; for all intents and purposes, they have never ceded their land, and nothing has superseded the treaty they signed with the U.S. in 1863 (and the Treaty of Guadalupe Hidalgo also asserts that prior land ownership would be respected by the new government). Called the Treaty of Ruby Valley, for the lush region in northeastern Nevada where it was signed, it describes the vast expanse of the Western Shoshone Nation and states the terms by which the Shoshone might cede their land and become reservation Indians. The reservations and other treaty terms were never met, however, and the Shoshone never ceded their land, and they are still fighting for their right to it today. The federal government has admitted their legal ownership of the land to the extent of trying to force the Shoshone to accept payment for it, but the paltry sum allocated still sits in a Department of the Interior bank account, where it has more than doubled since the government granted itself permission to purchase the land in the 1970s. And the Nevada Test Site is in the southwestern corner of the 43,000 square miles of the nation the Western Shoshone call *Newe Sogobia,* and nuclear testing, along with many other military and industrial assaults on the environment, violates Shoshone religious beliefs. So the Shoshone have become active in the international struggle against nuclear testing, and they issue permits to be on their land, and one of the pleasant things that can be said to one's arresting officer is that he, in fact, is the one who is trespassing.

There's something profoundly American about getting arrested at the Nevada Test Site: The very issues are, not cowboys and Indians, but land, war technology, apocalypse, Thoreauvian civil disobedience, bureaucratic obscurity, and Indians, part of the great gory mess of how we will occupy this country, whose questions are as unsettling as its land is unsettled. Then, of course, after being un-handcuffed and thrown out, the obvious thing to do is to celebrate, which in Beatty means going to one of the diner-cum-casinos for drinks and American food. To start the day in the deadly cold of a desert morning, sitting on rocks and drinking coffee, to fill one's water bottle and mill around with friends and acquaintances as the day gradually creeps toward hotness, to sit through a sometimes stirring and often dull rally of speeches and music (folk to punk and back again), to commit the fairly abstract act of climbing under a wire fence that separates the rocky expanse of cactus and creosote bushes from the rocky expanse of creosote bushes and cactus, to be confronted by hired help in the wrong-colored camouflage (as though they, not we, had a use for stealth), to go through numerous pairs of disposable plastic handcuffs as we captives are rearranged, to idle in a sort of cattle pen built just for us, to be escorted after many hours in the sun into a special luxury bus and be given a tour of scenic Highway 95, to be interrogated by hard-faced sheriffettes with piles of teased hair who are irritated by anyone who wants to give a more complicated name than Jane Doe or Shoshone Guest, to be tossed out into a small town, to catch up on one's friends' well-being and head for fast food and ice cream in the middle of the night, to plunk quarters into slot machines while waiting for the food to come, winning the occasional handful of change, to retrace the pointless route as the liberated activists get driven back to the camp, to wander back through the rocks and thorns in the dark to a sleeping bag on hard, uneven ground under a sky more full of stars than almost anyplace else in the world—could anything be more redolent of life, liberty, and the pursuit of happiness?

THE MAZE AND AURA

Jack Turner

. . . a work of art opens a void, a moment of silence, a question without answer, provokes a breach without reconciliation where the world is forced to question itself.

—Michel Foucault

I

Just before dawn sometime in April 1964, I shoved my Kelty behind the seat of a small Piper Cub, climbed into the passenger seat, and fastened my safety belt as we motored onto the airport runway at Moab, Utah. Since it was empty, we kept going into the take-off without stopping and then climbed slowly, the little plane grinding for altitude. Soon we banked west, and as we cleared the cliffs bordering the Spanish Valley, a vast array of mesas spread before us, glowing faintly in the morning light.

We turned again, southwest, and set a course for Junction Butte, a landmark tower at the confluence of the Green and

Colorado Rivers. Beyond the confluence was the Maze, a terra incognita some people wanted preserved as part of the newly proposed Canyonlands National Park. *National Geographic* magazine believed the Maze might harbor something to persuade Congress to include it in the new park. My friend Huntley Ingalls and I were to explore the area for three days and photograph what we found. The plane would drop us as close to the Maze as possible. In the darkness of the runway we had flipped a coin to see who would go in first, and I won.

The pilot—Bud—was silent. Since he knew the country below from landing at remote sites for uranium and oil companies, I tried to question him about features in the landscape. But the noise of the motor made conversation difficult so we lapsed into silence and flew on, bouncing like a boat in rapids off the thermals coming up from the canyons. Below, the Colorado River meandered through swells of slickrock muted by purple shadow, while to the north, miles of fluted red walls led to Grand View Point. By the time we crossed the Green River, the first light had illuminated the grass covering the sandbars, and pools of water in the slickrock gleamed like tiny silver mirrors. There was not a cloud in the sky—a perfect day.

At Junction Butte we had turned west toward Ekker Butte. Beneath it, to the south, was Horse Canyon, an open valley that receded into a labyrinth of slots—the Maze. On a bench between Ekker Butte and the canyon was an airfield that looked like a matchstick. Bud dropped the nose of the Piper Cub and we made a pass several hundred feet above the dirt strip. It had not been used in years, Bud said, and I believed him. It was covered with small plants and netted with arroyos. Worse, the south fork of Horse Canyon was far away, and since it led into the heart of the Maze, I feared that if we landed here, we'd never reach our main objective. So I began to search for options.

Beyond the nearest fork of Horse Canyon—the north fork—a two-track struck south to the edge of the south fork, a point now called the Maze Overlook. It was a perfect place to start from and I wanted to land there. Bud turned south. The road turned out to be old Caterpillar scrape, one blade wide—probably cut by a seismographic survey crew when oil companies explored this basin in the '50s. I asked Bud if he could land on the scrape. He wasn't sure. I wanted him to try. He was silent.

We dropped down for a closer look and banked slightly left above the narrow dirt path, Bud's face pressed against the window. Then we gained altitude and headed back, still in silence. Bud flipped switches and studied the instrument panel. Soon we were sinking toward the road, then slowly we settled in.

Several feet above the ground, a gust of wind blew us to the right and we landed hard in the blackbush flats. The right wheel hit first, and when the wheel strut punctured the floor between my feet, I pitched forward, striking my head against the instrument panel and spewing blood over the cockpit. The plane bounced gracefully into the air and Bud worked the stick, murmuring softly, "Whoa Baby, Whoa Baby." We lost control in slow motion, but we were without panic, a space I've encountered many times. Then the plane hit again, the wheels snagged a shallow arroyo, and we flipped upside down, sliding across the desert with a sickening screech.

When we stopped, we were hanging upside down from our seat belts. The pressure of our body weight made it difficult to release them so we hung there kicking, trying to brace ourselves against the windshield. I smelled my own blood—that strange metallic tang. I tried to smell gas, and all the while I'm thinking, "We're gonna get roasted." Finally Bud released his buckle and crashed into the windshield. He helped me release mine, and we sat together on the roof of the cockpit, trying to open the doors. Unfortunately, the wings were bent up just enough to prevent the doors from opening, so we both kicked hard on one door until something gave. Then we crawled out into the warm silence of a desert morning.

We were ecstatic—laughing, shaking hands, kicking our heels, and praising each other as though we had by sheer intelligence and talent achieved a magnificent goal. I licked the blood off my hands and congratulated myself for surviving my first airplane wreck. I was twenty-two years old.

While Bud searched for the first-aid kit, I got some water from the Kelty. I had six quarts, the standard rock climber's ration: two quarts per person per day, anywhere, under any conditions. We patched the gash in my head. Then, the adrenaline wearing off, we considered our plight. Bud felt he should walk to Anderson Bottom, a grassy stretch along the Green River with a line shack occupied by one of the local ranchers. I thought we should stay put. We had warm clothes, one sleeping bag, gas from the plane, matches for a brush fire, food, and water. Furthermore, we were highly visible—a light green airplane on a red desert. Within hours, Huntley would organize a rescue flight and easily spot us from above the airfield across the north fork. Bud would not stay, however, and after a few minutes he left, walking north with neither water nor supplies. The next day he was picked up near the Green River.

I examined my Kelty for what, typically, was not there: no

compass, no maps, no tent, no stove, no binoculars, no flares, no signal mirror. This probably had something to do with being kicked out of Boy Scouts. There were just two climbing ropes, some rock-climbing gear, a bivouac tarp, a sleeping bag, a Leica M2, the usual climber's food—summer sausage, cheese, gorp—and water.

I walked to the rim of the south fork. It was perhaps five hundred feet to the bottom of Horse Canyon. Across the canyon were spires of shale topped by dollops of White Rim sandstone, a formation now called "the Chocolate Drops." The canyon walls were more eroded than the Navajo and Kayenta sandstone I was familiar with from Glen Canyon, but everywhere were braids of a real labyrinth. The so-called south fork divided into at least three more canyons and everything kept forking. To my delight I saw marshes and a pool of water. It was utterly still. I sat on the rim and asked a question that came up often during the next thirty years: Why, exactly, am I here?

I was there because of Huntley. During the '50s he worked in southern Utah for the Coast and Geodetic Survey, traveling by Jeep and foot throughout the canyonlands conducting magnetic surveys. During those years he photographed spires he thought would make interesting rock climbs and showed his slides to other climbers living in Boulder, Colorado. He had photographs of the Fisher Towers, Totem Pole, Spider Rock, Standing Rock, Castleton Tower, and the Six-Shooter Peaks. By 1964 these spires had been climbed, some by Yosemite climbers, but many by Huntley and Layton Kor. Huntley had published articles on the first ascents of the Fisher Tower and Standing Rock in *National Geographic,* and now they thought he might use his climbing expertise to explore the

Maze. Since I had climbed a lot with Kor and Huntley, was interested in wild places and was Huntley's friend, here I was staring at the labyrinth.

The Utah desert was relatively unknown in the early '60s. In 1960 the road south of Blanding was dirt most of the way to Tuba City; the bridges were often one lane and made of wood. Eliot Porter's *Glen Canyon: The Place No One Knew* was not published until 1963, and Edward Abbey's *Desert Solitaire* did not come out until 1968. There were no guidebooks to these wild lands. Many of the parks and monuments and wilderness areas that now cover the area did not exist, and the country was vast and wild and easy to get lost in; there were no restrictions, and little management. We wandered the desert as we wished, lounged in the pools at Havasu, waded the Zion Narrows, climbed the desert towers, drifted down Glen Canyon, and explored the Escalante enjoying virtually no contact with other people. The Maze was simply another place on Huntley's long list of wild places to see.

Although the Maze was de facto wilderness, I did not then think of wilderness as a separate place needing preservation. The Wilderness Act was not passed until 1964. To the degree I even thought about preservation, I presumed it was conducted by nice old ladies in big cities. It certainly had nothing to do with me. I simply liked climbing big walls and spires and exploring remote places, preferably before anyone else did. Like most rock climbers, I didn't even like to hike. I didn't know the name of a single wildflower, and Huntley had to tell me, "These are cottonwoods" or "These are Utah juniper." My knowledge of animals derived mainly from hunting and killing them. (Years later, when I read Schopenhauer, I recognized myself in those days: "in the mind of a man who is filled with his own aims, the world appears as a beautiful landscape appears on the plan of a battlefield.")

I walked back to the plane and wrote a message on the road with the heel of my boot: "All OK," "Bud"—then an arrow—and "Anderson Bottom." I drank a quart of water, pulled out my foam pad, and settled into the shade beside the fuselage. I had no books, no paints or nature guides. I wasn't worried, I was bored.

Around eleven in the morning I heard a plane, and soon Huntley flew over in a Cessna 180 piloted by George Hubler, the owner of the Moab airport. After several passes to make sure I was ambulatory, they dropped a message saying they would land Huntley on the old airstrip. He would then cross the north fork and meet me at the wreck.

I settled back into the shade, even more bored. I could not get over the silence; it ate at me and I couldn't sit still. I wandered around looking for something interesting to do and found nothing. So I sat in the shade, oblivious to the glory that engulfed my every moment.

The day passed slowly with no sign of Huntley. In the evening I walked to the rim of the north fork of Horse Canyon and searched for him, but to no avail. That night I consumed more of my water supply. I slept fitfully.

The next morning, when there was still no sign of Huntley, I went back and walked the rim searching for him. Finally, in the late afternoon, I found him placing an expansion bolt several feet below the White Rim sandstone cap. He had already done some wild unroped climbing, but the cap was featureless, and that meant bolting. Soon he was up. We shook hands and greeted each other formally by last name, in the best British mountaineering tradition.

Huntley had left most of his gear at the bottom of the canyon while searching for a way through the cliffs. Since Hubler would return to the airfield the following day at noon, we had less than twenty-four hours to explore the Maze. We decided to leave Huntley's gear where it was and go on into the south fork. The plan was simple: we would walk into the Maze until dark, hike back through the night to the north fork, collect Huntley's things, and climb to the airfield to meet Hubler in the morning.

We returned to the wreck, gathered my gear, and after some scrambling and several rappels, reached the bottom of the canyon. After filling the water bottles at the algae-filled pool (we never treated water in those days), we hiked to the main canyon and up the middle of the three forks.

Soon Huntley began moving slowly and muttering about new boots. (Eventually he would lose all his toenails, which for years he kept in a small jar as a reminder.) After awhile he urged me to go on so I could cover as much ground as possible before dark. We dropped our packs in an obvious spot and I hurried up the canyon in fading light, moving rapidly, my eyes sweeping the landscape like radar. I missed the soaring walls and alcoves of the Escalante, the water, the seeps. I was still bored. But mostly from a sense of obligation, I walked on doggedly through the extraordinary silence.

Then, in the last light of day, I was startled by a line of dark torsos and a strange hand on a wall just above the canyon floor. I froze, rigid with fear. My usual mental categories of alive and not-alive became permeable. The painted figures stared at me, transmuted from mere stone as if by magic, and I stared back in terror.

After a few seconds, my body intervened with my mind, pulling it away from a gaze that engulfed me. The torsos became *just* pictures. My mind discovered a comfortable category for the original perception and the confusion passed. But strangely, seeing them as representations did not reduce the emotion I felt. I was chilled, shivering, though the air was warm. I could not override the feeling that the figures were looking at me, and that I was seeing what I wasn't supposed to see.

I can say now this fear resulted from confusion: perhaps from the exhaustion of the past two days, perhaps because of my anxiety for Huntley's situation and the increasing extremity of our position. But in retrospect, I believe it was the inherent power of the figures.

They were pictographs, but not the usual stick figures and crude animals I'd seen before. There were fifteen of them, painted a dark, almost indigo blue. Some were life-size, some smaller. Some were abstract, like mummies with big buggy eyes and horns. Others had feet and hands. One particularly beautiful figure I assumed was female. Among the figures were small animals, insects, snakes, and birds, all painted in remarkable detail. The most unusual figure displayed an enlarged hand with clearly articulated fingers; springing from the end of the middle finger was a fountain of what looked like blood—a spurting wound. Farther left along the wall were more figures. One did not appear abstract at all. It was dressed and masked, had feet, perhaps even moccasins, and held what looked like a spear.

I yelled for Huntley, hoping he would hear me and be able to see the figures before dark. In a few minutes he came hobbling up the canyon. Although he'd seen many examples of rock art throughout the canyon country, he had never seen anything like these figures, and he too was captured by their powerful presence. While photographing them with long time-exposures, we stared in silence. Although spooky and unsettling, they absorbed us, and we did not want to leave.

Reluctantly, we walked down canyon and collected my gear. By the time we headed for the north fork, it was dark, and Huntley kept walking into things and stubbing his painful toes. After a mile or so, we bivouacked, dividing up my clothes and sleeping bag and adopting fetal positions on a sandstone slab in the middle of the wash. Such nights pass slowly, like time in a hospital, where disturbed sleep confuses what is dream and what is real. I dreamed of traps and spears. Huntley talked in his sleep and screamed at nightmares.

At first light we were up and moving, eating gorp and summer sausage as we walked. By now Huntley was beyond cursing. We walked slowly, reaching his equipment by mid-morning. Then we climbed to the rim by way of a chimney that pierced the White Rim sandstone just below the airfield. Hubler arrived on time, hopping his Cessna over the arroyos, and soon we were back at Moab. We tried to drive home to Boulder, but after several hours we stopped to sleep on the bare ground under a cottonwood, my head resting on my folded hands. Then we drove on into the night, talking about the figures and making plans to return. I did not know then that when I returned—and I knew I would—it would be in another context, with expectations and knowledge that would erode their power.

The contrast between that long weekend and my job appalled me. I knew I wanted to have more experiences like that, even if I couldn't explain what "like that" meant. There was the adventure and the wilderness, of course, but what interested me was something more. Two months later we went back.

II

By May it was clear that the Maze would be left out of the new park, so *National Geographic* was no longer interested in our photographs. We were on our own.

Huntley and I had been talking up the Maze, showing pictures, and researching rock art, so numerous people were now interested in seeing the pictographs. There would be five of us on this trip. Besides Huntley and me, there was my wife Anne and our friends Judith and David. Since we wanted to stay for a week, the main problem was getting supplies into the Maze. None of us had four-wheel drive, so we decided on an airdrop.

By June we were back at the Moab airport. Hubler was piloting the Cessna. We removed the passenger door and seat, and I sat on the floor tied in with a climbing sling. It was going to be an airy ride. Huntley was in the back with a pile of Army duffel bags stuffed with camping supplies and canned food packed in crushed newspapers—there was not much freeze-dried food in those days.

The idea, again, was simple. We would drop into the south fork and sort of stall the plane while Huntley handed me duffels, and I would toss them out. Hubler said we would be close to the ground and moving so slowly they'd survive the fall. Having been a fighter pilot in Korea, he had the right spirit for such an enterprise.

An hour later we were above the Maze Overlook. The Piper Cub was gone, disassembled and hauled out to the old Colorado River crossing at Hite—no mean feat. As we dropped into the south fork, Hubler cut the engine back and we soared between the canyon walls, carving turns with the streambed as we lost altitude. When we were about forty feet above the ground, I shoved a duffel out the doorway and Hubler gunned the plane into what seemed like a ninety-degree turn, straight up the rock walls. From my choice view at the door I could almost pick plants as we cleared the cliffs. Hubler was smiling and allowed that this was better than working for the oil companies. We came around and dropped in again, and this time I got several bags out. A third pass finished the task, and after dropping Huntley and me at the Ekker Butte landing strip, Hubler returned to Moab for the others. By midafternoon, we were all hiking into the south fork.

Most periods of bliss in life are forgotten, but our week in that wild canyon is an exception. The weather was flawless, with days of blue skies following one another like waves out of the sea. We explored all the south fork canyons, and David and Huntley descended the steep and isolated Jasper Canyon, which led directly to the Colorado River. Huntley found a perfect arrowhead. We sat in the sun, bathed in slickrock pools, dreamed of other explorations—and studied the pictographs.

The pictographs were still wonderful, but now they were just things we were visiting. I had become a tourist to my own experience. I tried unsuccessfully to recapture the magic of those first moments. I took notes, but they exceeded my power of description. I kept photographing, first in 35 mm, then with my 2 ¼ x 3 ¼ Zeiss. But what I sought could not be captured with photography or language. Indeed, the more we talked, described, and photographed, the more common they seemed. Everyone was appreciative, impressed, but the unmediated, the raw, and the unique was history.

I tried sitting with them alone in the dark, but they neither gazed at nor engulfed me now. The pictographs remained as they had for centuries, preserved by their isolation and the dry desert air, but what I would later learn to call their "aura" seemed to be gone.

When we returned to Boulder, Anne wrote a paper on the pictographs for an anthropology class and used my photographs as illustrations. That fall, Huntley returned with other friends for still another exploration, but then the Maze passed from our lives. I did not return for thirty-one years.

III

In the years that followed, my life diverged along an axis I came to understand as central to my life. Those early visits to the Maze, Glen Canyon, and the Escalante led me to the margins of the modern world, areas wild in the sense Thoreau meant when he said that in wildness is the preservation of the world: places where the land, the flora and fauna, the people, their culture, their language and arts were still ordered by energies and interests fundamentally their own, not by the homogenization and normalization of modern life.

After divorces and attempts at ordinary jobs, Judith, Huntley, and I drifted into Asia, not so much for adventure as for what existed only at the limits of our world: the archaic, wildness, a faintly criminal madness, drugs, passion, art, Eastern religion—the Other.

Huntley was the first to go. In 1965 he cashed in his retirement and with four thousand dollars headed east. He was gone two and a half years. His first letter came from Herat, Afghanistan, where he had spent most of a winter. The next was from India and concerned blue monkeys and a yogi with a master's degree in physics from Oxford who had taken a vow of silence and who spent his time playing classical Indian instruments. A year later an aerogram arrived from a hill town in northern India. Huntley had been traveling in Sri Lanka, India, and Nepal and was now living among a Gurdjieff group in a small bungalow overlooking the Himalayas.

By the time Huntley returned, I was in graduate school studying philosophy. We talked endlessly of his travels, of gurus, temples, Indian music, drugs, neurophysiology, Cantor sets, and Tibetans. I was envious. My life seemed small and I could not imagine how to make it larger.

Years passed. In 1974, Judith left for Asia. I was living on the southern coast of Crete for the summer, so we met in Istanbul and traveled down the western coast of Turkey and around to Side on the southern shore. Then we hugged good-bye. I rode the Orient Express back to Europe and flew home to Chicago to be a professor; she went overland, alone, to Nepal. Except for short periods, she has lived there ever since. She has a guru, she and her second husband were married in a Hindu ceremony, she studies with teachers of Tibetan Buddhism. Her photographs of Nepali craftsmen are in the Smithsonian Institution, and she has written a book on the indigenous crafts of Nepal. Several years ago, to celebrate her fiftieth birthday, she trekked for five weeks across northwestern Nepal with a porter. Then, worrying about his safety, she crossed the border alone and continued into western Tibet. She bathed naked in the sacred lake of Manasarowar and bowed to sacred Mount Kailas, believed by Hindus, Buddhists, and Jains to be the center of the universe. Judith's letters that first year further underlined my misery in Chicago and with academia, and I determined to go myself.

I spent the following summer wandering the Karakoram Himalaya and the Hindu Kush. By autumn I knew I would leave academia to see as much of the old world as I could before it was gone. Like the bear that went over the mountain, all I wanted to see was the other side, again and again. And I saw a lot. For the next eighteen years I traveled part of each year in the mountains of Pakistan, India, Nepal, Bhutan, China, Tibet, and Peru, scouting or guiding treks and easy mountaineering expeditions.

In retrospect, Judith and Huntley and I were part of a modern exodus of hundreds of thousands of Western people who left home and went to Asia. Some were hippies; some were pilgrims who ended up with Rajneesh in Poona, with Vipassana monks in the forests of Thailand, with Tibetan masters in Kathmandu, with Zen teachers in Kamakura; some were the first wave of what would become the adventure travel and ecotourism industries; some went to war in Vietnam; some went into the Peace Corps; some were merely ambassadors of capitalism and consumerism.

This great exodus and its consequences, especially the transformations of subjective experience that were both the end and means of many journeys to the East, remain unstudied and unknown. Some say, cynically, this is because everyone fried their brains with drugs. I think we still lack the language to describe why people went or what we found. This much, however, is clear: we dragged the modern world with us. We left home with a love of difference, but carried within us the seeds of homogeny. By the '80s it was over, and the cultures we loved were forever altered by modernity. We traveled a modern Asia that was no longer very Other.

My understanding of these events, and my own journey, is anchored in that early experience of those strange figures in the Maze—and in Walter Benjamin's justly famous essay, "The Work of Art in the Age of Mechanical Reproduction." It began with a specific event.

I was standing in a meditation room at Hemis Monastery in Ladakh watching a German professor of Tibetology lecture his tour group. German-speaking members of other groups were attempting, with varying degrees of success, to translate his comments to their comrades. Behind him, two Tibetan monks faced a crowd of perhaps eighty Germans, Americans, French, and Japanese armed with cameras, flash units, camcorders, and tape players. The older monk wore a large white Pan Am button on the lapel of his maroon robe. The younger monk looked scared.

After a while it became clear that the high point of the professor's presentation would be the first public viewing of a particularly sacred *thangka,* a scroll painting on linen depicting a powerful Tibetan deity. Until that moment, it had been viewed just once a year in a religious ceremony attended only by the monks at Hemis. With a flourish the professor asked the senior monk to unveil the *thangka.* The senior monk turned to the young monk, and he froze. Then the professor yelled, the senior monk yelled, and the young monk finally removed a soiled silk veil. As the room exploded with flashes, motor drives, and camcorders, the young monk stood paralyzed, waiting for his blasphemy to be justly punished. But, of course, objectively, nothing happened. The professor smiled, everyone (including me) stretched their necks to see, and the earth continued to spin on its axis.

Later I thought of a passage in Benjamin's essay:

> *The elk portrayed by the man of the Stone Age on the walls of his cave was an instrument of magic. He did expose it to his fellow men, but in the main it was meant for the spirits. Today the cult value would seem to demand that the work of art remain hidden. Certain statues of gods are accessible only to the priest in the cella; certain Madonnas remain covered nearly all year round; certain sculptures on medieval cathedrals are invisible to the spectator on ground level. With the emancipation of the various art practices from ritual go increasing opportunities for the exhibition of their products.*

What I observed that day in the Hemis Monastery was the passage of an object from ritual to exhibition. The object remained; I am sure it is still there today. But something changed that is reflected only in human experience, in, for example, the experience of that young monk. Similarly, the Maze and those wonderful pictographs remain, but for me something is lost, a quality of my experience of them, something Benjamin calls the "aura" of art and landscape: "its presence in time and space, its unique existence at the place where it happens to be."

Benjamin's essay examines two of the processes that diminish aura, both "related to the increasing significance of the masses in contemporary life. Namely, the desire of contemporary masses to bring things 'closer' spatially and humanly, which is just as ardent as their bent toward overcoming the uniqueness of every reality by accepting its reproduction." The primary mode of reproduction is photography; the primary means of bringing the natural and cultural worlds closer is mass tourism. The pictographs and the Maze started down this path when I yelled for Huntley, took photographs, researched rock art, and gave slide shows, and when I brought others there. Had we remained silent, others could have, for a while, shared that powerful experience. And what if everyone remained silent?

Benjamin also discusses the many ways that loss of aura affects an art object: it undermines authenticity, jeopardizes the object's authority, shatters tradition, diminishes the importance of ritual, and perhaps most important, "the quality of its presence is always depreciated." This last point is for me the heart of the matter. If I have an interest in preservation, it is in preserving the power of presence—of landscape, art, flora, and fauna. It is more complicated than merely preserving habitat and species, and one might suppose it is something that could be added on later, after we successfully preserve biodiversity, say. But no, it's the other way around: the loss of aura and presence is the main reason we are losing so much of the natural world.

Photographic reproduction and mass tourism are now commonplace and diminish a family of qualities broader than, though including, our experience of art: aura is affected, but so is wildness, spirit, enchantment, the sacred, holiness, magic, and soul. We understand these terms intuitively, but they evade definition, analysis, and measurement because they refer to our experience of the material world rather than the material world itself. Hence they are excluded from the rationalized discourse of preservation, and we are hard pressed to figure out how to keep them in the world of our experience. You will not read much about them in *Art Forum, Sierra,* or *Conservation Biology.*

Unfortunately, these qualities deserve as much, if not more, attention as the decline of wilderness and biodiversity, because the decline of the latter has its root cause in the decline of the former. We treat the natural world according to our experience of it. Without aura, wildness, magic, spirit, holiness, the sacred, and soul, we treat flora, fauna, art, and landscape as resources and amusement. Fun. Their importance is merely a function of current fashions in hobbies. Virtually all of southern Utah is now photographed and exhibited to the public, so much so that looking at photographs of arches or pictographs, reading a guide book, examining maps, receiving instructions on where to go, where to camp, what to expect, how to act—and being watched over the entire time by a cadre of rangers—is now the normal mode of experience. Most people know no other.

IV

In May of 1995 I returned to the Maze. Things had changed. The Maze is now part of Canyonlands National Park, and the pictographs that so moved me are no longer unknown. They have a name—the Harvest Site (or Bird Site)—and they are marked on topographic maps. A small library of books and articles describes, displays, compares, and analyzes each mark and figure, and various theories pigeonhole the paintings into categories created by these theories themselves. This doesn't mean we know much about them, however. Castleton, in the second volume of his encyclopedic *Petroglyphs and Pictographs of Utah,* concludes his discussion of the Barrier Canyon style, which includes the Harvest Site, with admirable candor: "The dearth of extensive archeological study of them makes it impossible to suggest the cultural affiliation or chronology of the style with any certainty" (289). Nonetheless, it is widely assumed that the paintings are the work of an archaic desert people, hunters and gatherers who occupied the Colorado Plateau from approximately 5500 B.C. until the time of Christ. It was their home in a sense we can no longer imagine.

The Maze itself is laced with trails all clearly marked on maps available at the ranger station, and the roads in and around it are described in detail by a series of books. Indeed, there is a hiking guide to virtually every canyon on the Colorado Plateau, a guide to every dirt road, another for every stretch of the Green and Colorado Rivers, and yet another to every river, creek, and stream in the state of Utah. Not to mention, of course, the rock-climbing guides or mountain-biking guides, or slot-canyon guides, or . . . And this is why southern Utah is no longer wild. Maps and guides destroy the wildness of a place just as surely as photography and mass tourism destroy the aura of art and nature. Indeed, the three together—knowledge (speaking generally), photography, and mass tourism—are the unholy trinity that destroys the mysteries of both art and nature.

The Maze is, however, by modern standards, still remote and difficult to reach—the standard approach is an eighty-mile excursion from the nearest paved road. The park describes it as "a rugged and wild area with remoteness and self-reliance the principal elements of the visitor experience." A visit requires a four-wheel-drive vehicle or a mountain bike, and a hard walk. The scrape where we crashed the plane is now the road to the

Maze Overlook. At the end are two designated campsites and a parking lot. There's also a trail now, a difficult one that drops into the canyon and requires a bit of climbing.

To the degree that can be expected, the Maze is preserved and protected. In 1995 the park passed a tough backcountry management plan that limits both four-wheel-drive camping and hiking, and the rangers stationed there clearly love the place and guard it with a fierce devotion all too rare in the National Park Service. The pictographs remain unmarred.

I am thankful for all these things.

Enough history of the Maze is now known to place our little adventure in a historical context. We were not the first modern people to see the pictographs. Dean Brimhall, a journalist from Salt Lake City, photographed the Harvest Site in 1954 and later explored the intricacies of the south fork for other pictographs and petroglyphs. Local ranchers also knew about the site. For-tunately, I did not know any of this. Had I known the location of the paintings and seen Brimhall's photographs, there would have been less adventure, no exploration, and no aura—the "quality of its presence" would have been diminished if not erased. I can only wonder how many other gifts from the gods have been obscured by knowledge.

The man who visited the Maze in the spring of 1995 had also changed. I drove a 4 × 4 and played old Dylan and Emmylou tapes until I reached the infamous drop named the Flint Trail—a lovely so-called road requiring four-wheel drive, compound low, first gear, and lots of attention. For that I switched to Bach and Yo-Yo Ma. Spring had brought unusually heavy rains, and the desert was alive with lupine, globemallow, evening primrose, and little ruby clusters of Indian paintbrush.

When I stopped and turned off the tape player, the silence was still there, but I was no longer bored.

I parked my truck and hiked into the south fork. From my pack hung a tag—my camping permit. I had reserved a spot by phone, paying for it with my Visa card and verifying my existence with lots of numbers. When I arrived at the Harvest Site, a couple was sitting in the shade of a cottonwood across from the pictographs. After we talked a few minutes, they asked if the paintings were the same as they were thirty-one years ago. When I said they were, the woman said she was glad to hear that. And I was glad to say so. To explain otherwise would have been too dark and sad.

After they left, I painted a small watercolor of the wall and figures, ate summer sausage, cheese, and gorp, and waited for dusk. Then I meditated with the figures for an hour, occasionally raising my eyes to study their mysterious visages. In the silence of the evening light, some of their presence returned. I saw the figures as a work of art, a group portrait—the shaman, the goddess, the hunter, the gatherers, an extended family including the birds and snakes and rabbits and insects. Perhaps the little band returned each year to this place and, as animals do, marked their territory. Whoever they were, they knew how to express and present something we have lost. At the end of my meditation I thanked them and bowed to them.

I am pleased the Harvest Site is preserved in the Maze District of Canyonlands National Park. I am happier still that the pictographs remain difficult to visit. I am delighted they remain in such good condition. I support the tough new backcountry management plan. I praise the rangers for their courage, their vision, and their devotion to a place I love.

But I wish we were wise enough to preserve something more. I wish that children seven generations from now could wander into an unknown canyon and receive at dusk the energy captured by a now-forgotten but empowered people. I wish these children could endure their gaze and, if only for a moment, bask in the aura of their gift.

FIFTH WORLD: THE RETURN
OF MA AH SHRA TRUE EE,
THE GIANT SERPENT

Leslie Marmon Silko

The old-time people always told us kids to be patient, to wait, and then finally, after a long time, what you wish to know will become clear. The Pueblos and their paleo-Indian ancestors have lived continuously in the southwest of North America for twelve thousand years. So when the old-time people speak about "time" or "a long time," they're not speaking about a decade, or even a single lifetime; they can mean hundreds of years. And as the elders point out, the Europeans have hardly been on the continents of the Americas five hundred years. Still, they say, the longer Europeans or others live on these continents, the more they will become part of the Americas. The gravity of the continent under their feet begins this connection, which grows slowly in each generation. The process requires not hundreds, but thousands of years.

The prophecies foretelling the arrival of the Europeans to the Americas also say that over this long time, all things European will eventually disappear. The prophecies do not say the European people themselves will disappear, only their customs. The old people say that this has already begun to happen, and that it is a spiritual process that no armies will be able to stop. So the old people laugh when they hear talk about the "desecration" of the earth, because humankind, they know, is nothing in comparison to the earth. Blast it open, dig it up, or cook it with nuclear explosions: the earth remains. Humans desecrate only themselves. The earth is inviolate.

Tse'itsi'nako, Thought Woman,
is sitting in her room
and whatever she thinks about
appears.

She thought of her sisters,
Nau'ts'ity'i and I'tcts'ity'i,
and together they created the Universe
this world
and the four worlds below.

Thought Woman, the spider,
named things and
as she named them
they appeared.

She is sitting in her room
thinking of a story now
I'm telling you the story
she is thinking.

So perhaps it did not seem extraordinary to the old people that a giant stone snake formation was found one morning in the spring of 1980 by two employees of the Jackpile uranium mine. The mine is located near Paguate, one of seven villages in the Laguna Pueblo reservation in New Mexico. The employees, both Laguna Pueblo men, had been making a routine check of the mine when they discovered the biomorphic configuration near the base of mountainous piles of uranium tailings. The head of the snake was pointed west, its jaws open wide. The stone snake seemed to have always been there. The entire formation was more than thirty feet long and twelve inches high, an eccentric outcrop of yellow sandstone mottled and peppered with darker iron ores, like the stone that had once formed the mesas that had been swallowed up by the open-pit mine.

Reports of the snake formation were at first met with skepticism. The miners must be joking. People from Paguate village and other Laguna Pueblo people had hunted rabbits and herded sheep in that area for hundreds of years. Over time, wind and rain might uncover rock, but the process required years, not weeks. In any case, Laguna Pueblo people have a name and a story for every oddly-shaped boulder within two hundred miles—no way could anything like this giant stone snake have escaped notice. The mine employees swore they had walked the same route twice each month for inspections and seen nothing, and then suddenly, one morning the stone snake was there, uncoiling about three hundred yards from a Jackpile Mine truck yard. And soon there was a great deal of excitement among Pueblo religious people because the old stories mention a giant snake who is a messenger for the Mother Creator.

Ma ah shra true ee is the giant serpent
the sacred messenger spirit
from the Fourth World below.
He came to live at the Beautiful Lake, Kawaik,
that was once near Laguna village.
But neighbors got jealous.
They came one night and broke open the lake
so all the water was lost. The giant snake
went away after that. He has never been seen since.
That was the great misfortune for us, the Kawaik 'meh,
at Old Laguna.

Before the days of the mining companies, the people of Paguate village had fields of corn and melons and beans scattered throughout the little flood plains below the yellow sandstone mesas southeast of the village. Apple and apricot orchards flourished there too. It was all dry farming in those days, dependent on prayers and ceremonies to call in the rain clouds. Back then, it was a different world, although ancient stories also recount terrible droughts and famines—times of great devastation. When large uranium deposits were discovered only a few miles southeast of Paguate village in the late 1940s, the Laguna Pueblo elders declared the earth was the sacred mother of all living things, and blasting her wide open to reach deposits of uranium ore was an act almost beyond imagination. But the advent of the Cold War had made the mining a matter of national security, and the ore deposits at the Jackpile Mine were vast and rich. As wards of the federal government, the small Pueblo tribe could not prevent the mining of their land. Now, the orchards and fields of melons are gone. Nearly all the land to the east and south of Paguate village has been swallowed by the mine; its open pit gapes within two hundred yards of the village.

Before world uranium prices fell, the mining companies had proposed relocating the entire village to a new site a few miles away because the richest ore deposits lay directly under the old village. The Paguate people refused to trade their old houses for new all-electric ones; they were bound to refuse, because there is a small mossy spring that bubbles out of the base of a black lava formation on the west side of Paguate village. This spring is the Emergence Place, the entrance humans and animals used when they first climbed into this, the Fifth World. But the mining companies were not to be stopped; when they couldn't move the people, they simply sank shafts under the village.

When the mining began, the village elders and traditionalists maintained that no one of their people should work at the mine and participate in the sacrilege. But the early 1950s were drought years, and the Laguna people, who had struggled to live off their fields and herds, found themselves in trouble. Moreover, World War II and the Korean War had ushered in other changes within the community itself. The men who returned from military service had seen the world outside. They had worked for wages in the army, and when they came home to Laguna, they wanted jobs. Consequently, increasing numbers of Laguna men, and later women, began working the mine. Cranky old traditionalists predicted dire results from this desecration of the earth, but they had never been very specific about the terrible consequences. Meanwhile, Laguna Pueblo became one of the few reservations in the United States to enjoy nearly full employment. Twenty-five years passed, and then something strange and very sad began to happen at Paguate village.

"Tonight we'll see
if you really have magical power," they told him.

So that night
Pa'caya'nyi
came with his mountain lion.
He undressed
he painted his body
the whorls of flesh
the soles of his feet
the palms of his hands
the top of his head.

He wore feathers
on each side of his head.

He made an altar
with cactus spines
and purple locoweed flowers.
He lighted four cactus torches
at each corner.
He made the mountain lion lie
down in front and
then he was ready for his magic.

He struck the middle of the north wall.
He took a piece of flint and
he struck the middle of the north wall
and flowed down
toward the south.
He said, "What does that look like?
Is that magic powers?"
He struck the middle of the west wall
and from the east wall
a bear came out.
"What do you call this?"
he said again.

"Yes, it looks like magic all right,"
Ma'see'wi said.
So it was finished
and Ma'see'wi and Ou'yu'ye'wi
and all the people were fooled by
that Ck'o'yo medicine man,
Pa'caya'nyi.

From that time on
they were
so busy
playing around with that
Ck'o'yo magic
they neglected the Mother Corn altar.

They thought they didn't have to worry
about anything.

Pueblo communal systems value cooperation and nonaggression above all else. All problems, including the most serious, are resolved through negotiation by the families or clans of the aggrieved parties. Perhaps the harshness of the high desert plateau with its freezing winters and fierce summer droughts has had something to do with the supreme value the old people place upon cooperation and conciliation. For where margin for error is slender—even during the wet years—a seemingly trivial feud might hinder the mobilization and organization necessary to protect crops threatened by dramatic conditions of nature. Moreover, this system of cooperation extends to all living things, even plants and insects, which Laguna Pueblo elders refer to as sisters and brothers, because none can survive unless all survive.

Given this emphasis on balance and harmony, it was especially painful and confusing when, in 1973, Paguate became one of the first American communities to cope with the unexpected tragedy of a teenage suicide pact. The boys and girls all had attended Laguna–Acoma High School, and all but one of the suicides lived at Paguate. Some left suicide notes that made reference to an agreement the young people had made secretly. "Cherylyn did it Saturday so now it's my turn," for example, was the way the suicide notes read.

The Laguna people had already suffered suicides by army veterans sick with alcohol. But the suicide victims at Paguate had been the brightest and most promising students at the school. The usual psychological explanations—unstable family environment, absence of one parent, alienation—don't seem to apply here, as not one of the students had come from a poor or troubled family, and in fact, most had grown up in the house inhabited by their families for hundreds of years and were surrounded by supportive groups of relatives. While teachers and families tried in vain to learn more about the suicide club, it eventually claimed seven lives.

While suicide took its toll, the Pueblo community was disrupted by another horror, an apparently motiveless murder. A Saturday night party in Paguate turned into a slaughter. Two young men were hacked to death at the kitchen table by their friend, who had invited them to stop by the party after they got off swing shift at the mine. The killer then bullied another friend to drive a car they "borrowed," and while the friend drove around the reservation, the killer randomly dumped body parts in the weeds along the way. The impulse to pick up the shiny new axe had been irresistible, the killer later said. He could not explain the murder of his two friends.

But the old people have their own explanation. According to the elders, destruction of any part of the earth does immediate harm to all living things. Teachers at Indian School would ridicule these ideas; they would laugh and say, "How stupid you Indians are! How can the death of one tree in the jungle possibly affect a person in New York City!" But isn't it far more obvious these days *how* important that single tree in the rain forest of Brazil really is to the Manhattanite? And in the same way, the mesas of sandstone seemingly devoured by the uranium mine are as important, as essential. If it has taken environmental catastrophe to reveal to us why we need the rain forest, perhaps we might spare ourselves some tragedy by listening to the message of sand and stone in the form of a giant snake. Perhaps comprehension need not come from obvious catastrophes, like the destruction of the ozone layer, but more through subtle indications, like a stone snake come to remind us that violence in the Americas—against ourselves and against one another—can run as deep, but only as deep, as the deepest shafts with which humankind has pierced the earth.

When I saw the stone snake in June of 1980, I could hear the clanking and creaking of giant earthmovers on the other side of the mounds of tailings. The Jackpile Mine generators roared continuously night and day, seven days a week. At noon, when Jackpile did the blasting, everyone made sure to be indoors because potato-size rocks frequently landed on Paguate doorsteps. (These were the normal, day-to-day living conditions of the Laguna Pueblos in and around Paguate for many years.) Old barbed wire had been loosely strung along a few makeshift juniper posts until someone provided a sagging barrier of chain-link fencing, intended to protect the stone snake from livestock and photographers. Corn meal and pollen, bits of red coral and turquoise had been sprinkled over the snake's head as offerings of spirit food. Holy people from tribes as far away as Canada and Mexico had come to see the giant snake.

There have been attempts to confine the meaning of the snake to an official story suitable for general consumption. But the Laguna Pueblos go on producing their own rich and continuously developing body of oral and occasionally written stories that reject any decisive conclusion in favor of ever-increasing possibilities. This production of multiple meaning is in keeping with Pueblo cosmology in general. For the old people, no one person or thing is better than another; hierarchies presuming superiority and inferiority are considered absurd. No thing or location on the earth is of greater or lesser value than another. And this means that any location can potentially become a sacred spot.

Thus, outsiders who visit the American southwest are often confused by the places in which they find sacred altars or sites of miraculous appearances of the Blessed Virgin or others (could it be the notion of original sin that causes Europeans to define the sacred as the virginal or pure?). They expect to find the *milagros* of Nuestra Señora de Guadalupe in pristine forest grottoes, *not* on the window glass of a cinder block school building in a Yaqui Indian town; or Jesus' face in a rainbow above Yosemite Falls, not on a poor New Mexican woman's breakfast tortilla. The traditional notion of the wondrous in a splendid setting befitting its claim is subverted here in this landscape where the wondrous can be anywhere and is everywhere. Even in the midst of a strip-mining operation.

Just as the Laguna prophecies say that all things European will eventually pass away, Europeans have, particularly in the last century, predicted the demise of all things Native American. In the late 1960s, anthropologists lugged their tape recorders to the pueblos, so that they might have the elders record stories and songs that would be lost when they passed away. Most of the Laguna elders agreed to make the tape recordings, but a few of the old people took a hard line. They said that what is important to our children and our grandchildren will be remembered; what is forgotten is what is no longer meaningful. What is true will persist. In spite of everything, Ma ah shra true ee, the sacred messenger, will appear again and again. Nothing can stop that. Not even a uranium mine.

The wind stirred the dust.
The people were starving.
"She's angry with us,"
the people said.
"Maybe because of that
Ck'o'yo magic
we were fooling with.
We better send someone
to ask our forgiveness."

They noticed hummingbird
was fat and shiny
he had plenty to eat.
They asked how come he
looked so good.

He said
Down below
Three worlds below this one
everything is
green
all the plants are growing
the flowers are blooming
I go down there
and eat.

BELIEVING IN THE AMERICAN WEST

Patricia Nelson Limerick

Growing Up Post-Mormon

My father and I are not Mormons. This fact is true of many other people in the American West, but it is particularly true of us. My father was raised Mormon in Brigham City, Utah. Although it is common for fallen-away members of the Church of Jesus Christ of Latter-day Saints to become fervent believers in other churches, my father took a different path. When he cut his ties to the Mormon Church and moved to California, he turned away from all organized religion.

My sisters and I thus grew up with a particular opportunity to drive our father batty. Here was our distinctive and very gratifying channel of rebellion: we could insist on our First Amendment right to freedom of religion, get dressed up for church, and demand that Father drive us there. The peak of this soul-satisfying mutiny came in asking him for money to put in the collection plate. And, since Mother was (and is) a non-church-attending Congregationalist and thus nearly as vulnerable as Father to the abrasive powers of our piety, there was also considerable pleasure to be gained from coming home from church, sitting down to Sunday dinner, and delivering an earnest prayer on behalf of our parents' redemption.

Such rebellion, however, came at a cost. For me, the cost was repeated exposure to the misery of the unbaptized heathen. Churched or not, our parents had installed into our thinking a great devotion to justice and fairness. And so the dilemma of the poor souls in Africa and Asia, living and dying and heading off to hell without the opportunity to hear the Christian gospel, weighed heavily on me. If God really had decided to let salvation hinge on the basis of the arbitrary facts of place of birth (a fact that He, in His omnipotence, had determined), then God seemed to be following rather questionable values Himself, showing a tenuous understanding of the concept of fairness.

The pleasures of bugging my father were, therefore, already wearing thin on a memorable day in 1962 at the First Baptist Church in Banning, the day on which my rebellion ended. The membership of the First Baptist Church was entirely white. On this Sunday, a black woman, new in town, came to church. I happened to be behind her in the line, waiting to shake hands with the minister. We had spent some time in Sunday School singing about Jesus's transcendence of racial prejudice:

> *Red and yellow, black and white,*
> *They're all sacred in His sight.*
> *Jesus loves the little children of the world.*

This song was not easy to reconcile with the dilemma of the unbaptized heathen, and our minister had, himself, not gotten very far in reconciling Jesus's sentiments with his own. When the black woman shook hands with him, the minister told her that *her* church was on the other side of town.

Since that Sunday, I have learned more about the ways in which race relations in the American West came to bear an unhappy resemblance to race relations in the rest of the country. In religious terms, it was not simply a matter of segregation in Western churches, it was often a matter of the active use of the church as a social institution to maintain racial separation and inequality. The minister of the First Baptist Church not only gave me a memorable introduction to this topic, he also persuaded me that my rebellion against my father had gone far enough. Since then I have taken the path leading away from organized religion and toward what I will call disorganized religion. My father and I remain post-Mormon and unchurched but nonetheless driven by convictions about right and wrong.

For decades, I thought that Father and I had placed ourselves on the margins of conventional religious behavior. But, like so many other Westerners who treasured a picture of themselves as odd birds, we have turned out to be birds positioned right at the center of the flock. "[P]oor church attendance is characteristic of westerners generally," historian Michael Quinn has written. Here lies the West's principal claim to distinctiveness in religious terms: it is the region with the lowest rates of church participation, in both the nineteenth and the twentieth centuries. In the nation as a whole, "the West as a region has the lowest attendance (36 percent) in church or synagogue." The

West thus holds the status of the nation's "Unchurched Belt." In this region, participants in disorganized religion have held and hold a considerable numerical advantage over participants in organized religion.

My father and I turn out to be not rebels and eccentrics but representative Westerners. Still, without official papers of membership, we and our many disaffiliated comrades are not likely to register in the records of Western religious history. Contemplating the prospect of one's invisibility, one finds good reason to question how much the fact of church membership reveals about a matter as subjective and private as religious belief. Churches are, of course, the places where *records* of official religious performance accumulate. Historians of religion, oriented to written documents, have had good reason to place churches and their members at the center of their inquiry, in the manner of labor historians who, for a time, hinged their history of the working class on the much more narrow topic of membership in unions.

"In comparison with Whites in the United States today," the anthropologist Harold Driver once wrote, "the Indians [of the past] were at least ten times as religious." Of all the improbable proclamations of academics made over the last forty years, this one is my personal favorite, an example of confident, social-scientific thinking at its goofiest. And yet, whatever Harold Driver meant by this memorable assertion, one suspects that he did *not* mean that Indians were ten times as religious because they were ten times more likely to join formally chartered and organized churches. On the contrary, Driver thought (and he shared this conviction with many others) that Indian people were more religious because they unmistakably and consistently demonstrated their faith, observing little separation between the secular and the spiritual. They did not need to join churches and attend formal services, because they lived virtually every moment in a religious way. By contrast, in Driver's equally widely shared but considerably more questionable assumption, modern white American people have been a very secular group, driven primarily by economic motives. For a group of people holding their souls on such a tight leash, religious conviction could only appear in official membership in an institutional church, with even that level of religious commitment often confined to attendance at Sunday services, cresting at Easter and Christmas.

Consider, by contrast, the state of affairs in mid-nineteenth-century rural Oregon. True to the Western pattern, church membership there was very limited. But a low percentage of church attendance, historian Dean May has argued, "does not imply . . . an absence of religious sentiment and feelings." The settlers' religious practice was local, often within households, "involving them rarely, if at all, in any broader community." They had Bibles in their homes, and recorded significant family events in those Bibles. "Blessings on food, prayers, prayer meetings, hymn singing, and exhortation were held in home and schoolhouse for gatherings of families and close neighbors." Preachers sent by home missionary societies found Oregon's "seeming incoherence of religious organization" both puzzling and frustrating. In a curious convergence of opinion, historians would come to share the judgment of the preachers: "religion in any setting other than an established congregation was to them hardly religion at all."

Few of the people of the Oregon settlements were joining

churches, but they gave many other signs of religiousness. The pattern of Oregon may well be the pattern of the Western United States. "[E]xcept in Mormon territory, the majority of far westerners have cared little about traditional religious institutions and practices," the historian Eldon G. Ernst put it. "They form the most secular society in the United States if gauged by church membership statistics, yet when questioned they claim to be religiously concerned and find religion to be important in their personal lives."

We return to the common difficulty faced by anyone exploring this topic: in its subjectivity and privacy, religious belief is very hard to track. A few groups—Indians, missionaries, and Mormons—have made the task easier: for all their differences, these groups were believers who consistently and visibly demonstrated their faith in frequent public rituals, steering by religious principles in everyday activities. Whether the ritual was a dance, a hymn, or a ward house meeting, whether the consecrated activity was hunting, teaching, or irrigated farming, Indians, missionaries, and Mormons placed their faith front and center, where no one could miss it. Thus, Western historians fell into a perfectly logical habit of confining the explicit discussion of religion to topics where it simply could not be avoided. For all the other Westerners—for the sizable numbers who were *not* Indians, *not* missionaries, and *not* Mormons, the most resolutely secular history is all they seemed to deserve and generally all they got.

The fact that American westward expansion was so strongly governed by economic motives reinforced the apparent wisdom of this strategy of reserving religious history for the few and leaving secular history for the majority. The experience of overland travel during the Gold Rush had many of the qualities of a sacred pilgrimage, testing determination and persistence in a thousand ways. But a journey undertaken as a tribute to Mammon surrendered its credentials as pilgrimage. Fervent participation in mineral rushes and land rushes, in timber booms and cattle speculation deepened the impression that the determination of white Americans to develop the West's natural resources left very little room for the development of their souls. Often invoked in support of these expanding commercial enterprises, God's name looked as if it had become little more than another product endorsement.

Consider, as a striking example of this linkage of religion with commerce, the memorable song, "The Cowboy's Prayer":

> Lord, please help me, lend me Thine ear,
> The prayer of a troubled cowman to hear
> No doubt my prayer to you may seem strange,
> But I want you to bless my cattle range. . . .
> As you O Lord my fine herds behold.
> They represent a sack of pure gold.
> I think that at least five cents on the pound
> Would be a good price for beef the year round.

When God was asked to intervene on behalf of rising cattle prices, the theological seemed to have made a full surrender to the secular. But then again, when whites asked God to bless their economic undertakings, was this *entirely* different from an Indian hunter's hope that the right gestures of respect would recruit the spirits as the sponsors of a successful hunt? Didn't both practices serve as examples of a people's refusal to draw a hard line between the spiritual and the worldly? If God wanted the best for His Chosen People, wouldn't He *want* them to prosper in the cattle market?

In 1973, my husband and I were driving west, crossing the country on yet another secular pilgrimage. Through the journey, we had invested a great deal in the services of auto mechanics, purchasing, among other things, an entire replacement engine for our VW Bug. We were not entirely sure that we had enough money left to get to California. On a Sunday morning, we turned on the radio and found an evangelist in the middle of a prayer that spoke directly to our dilemma: "Lord," the evangelist asked, "Heal our families; heal our hearts; and heal our finances." When my father wired us money in Laramie, we felt that prayer had been heard.

Westward the Course of Chaos Takes Its Way

The year after I parted with the First Baptist Church, a remarkable event occurred in the demography of Banning, California. A bunch of kids appeared out of nowhere. Banning was a town of eight or nine thousand people, and I thought I knew most of them; I certainly knew the ones around my own age. But when we left the sixth grade at Central Elementary School and moved on to the seventh grade at Susan B. Coombs Junior High School, some fifteen or twenty strangers joined us. Had a large caravan of families moved to town over the summer? On the contrary, and very mysteriously, the strangers claimed that they had lived in Banning most, sometimes all, of their lives. But where had they been? How had they stayed hidden all those years?

The strangers were, it turned out, Catholics. They had been

hidden in parochial school, but parochial school—whatever that was—ended in sixth grade, and so now they were out of hiding. The term "Mormon," I understood, but "Catholic"? Or, even more puzzling, "Jew"? In the First Baptist Sunday School, our education on that particular topic had been *very* brief. One of the children had said to the Sunday School teacher, "We keep seeing the word 'Jew' in the Bible, but we don't know what it means." The teacher looked unhappy and then seized on her way out. "You all know Jeff," she said, pointing to one member of the class. "Jeff used to be a Jew, but now he's a Baptist."

The extent of my Sunday School teacher's—and my—ignorance in these matters was at a cosmic scale and quite surprising, given the West's great history of religious diversity. This diversity represented the realization of the worst fears of many Protestants in the nineteenth-century West. Protestant clergy in the West confronted a region in which every moment in daily life told them that they were working against a great disadvantage. White American Protestants in the nineteenth-century West knew that they were outnumbered. They knew that they had before them a long struggle to find a permanent place in a society in which neither Episcopalians nor Baptists, Presbyterians nor Congregationalists could be numerically dominant.

In many Western areas, Catholics and Mormons had gotten the jump in timing, as well as in membership, on Protestants of any denomination. Jews were early arrivals in many Western settlements. At the same time, American Indian religions and the Buddhism, Taoism, and Confucianism of Asian immigrants stretched the categories of faith along an extraordinarily wide continuum. In the nineteenth-century West, as historian Ferenc Szasz has written, the mainline Protestant groups "confronted the greatest challenge of their day: dealing with religious diversity." Several decades before their counterparts in the Eastern United States would come to face a comparable challenge, Western Protestant ministers "dealt with pluralism on a daily basis." In religious terms, the West was the American future.

For many of those getting an advance look at this future, religious pluralism proved to be fruitful soil for discomfort and doubt. Where we might see an extraordinary and fascinating mosaic of religious practice, the Protestant ministers were more inclined to see chaos, and dangerous chaos at that. Take the concerns and worries recorded by the Reverend Josiah Strong. After two years' service as a Congregationalist minister in Cheyenne, Wyoming, Reverend Strong came down with a pronounced case of Western Protestant anxiety. The West, he wrote in his book *Our Country* (1886) was "peculiarly exposed" to the principal "dangers" of the times: "Mammonism, materialism, luxuriousness, and the centralization of wealth." The region was particularly burdened, as well, with the threats posed by socialism, the saloon, Mormonism, Catholicism, and foreign immigration. Not only were the dangers greatest in the West, the Protestant churches were at their weakest, ill equipped to respond to any of these challenges.

If this was a region in which all its enemies ganged up on Protestant Christianity, might the good news be that the region's sparse population rendered its religious condition irrelevant to the nation's well-being? On the contrary, in Reverend Josiah Strong's judgment, the West determined the national future. With its vast resources, ready to support an equally sizable population, the West "is to dominate the East"; in the near future, "the West will direct the policy of the Government, and by virtue of her preponderating population and influence will determine our national character and, therefore, destiny."

If Protestant Christianity could not save the West, then nothing could save the nation. And the stakes went considerably beyond the national. In Reverend Strong's vision, the settling of the American West would be only one test of the Anglo-Saxon's "instinct or genius for colonizing," a genius that would finally work its way around the entire planet "in *the final competition of races, for which the Anglo-Saxon is being schooled* [his emphasis]." Through the religious challenge posed by the American West, "God was training the Anglo-Saxon race for an hour sure to come in the world's future."

Full of distrust for European immigrants, for Mormons, and for New Mexican Hispanics, Reverend Strong nonetheless reserved his greatest distrust for the actions and beliefs of his fellow Anglo-Saxons, those "church-members who seem to have left their religion behind when they crossed the Missouri." Of course, Reverend Strong would worry about all those others, but it is, at first, a surprise to see how doubtful he was about the religious reliability of his fellow whites. Given the continued status of the West as the nation's unchurched region, he was right to be worried. My father and I, and our many disaffiliated fellow Westerners, are Reverend Strong's worst nightmare come true.

In the intervening century, few writers have been able to produce texts that can match *Our Country* in its remarkable mixture of confidence and doubt. In the space of a few pages, Reverend Josiah Strong could shift from a cosmic confidence in Anglo-Saxon destiny to rule the world and to install God's kingdom in the process, to a dark vision of a West soon to collapse before the pressures of evil and disorder. How could he be at once so confident and so anxious? The paradox here was a great one. On the ground level the American West had the greatest religious diversity of any part of the nation, and the heightened anxiety of the nineteenth-century Protestant clergy testified to the challenge posed by that diversity. And yet, in the broader sweep of history, expansion into the American West seemed to have shown white American religious belief at its most homogeneous, combining a Christian sense of mission with patriotism to form a virtual state religion. Faith in the United States's Manifest Destiny had long ago melted the division between the sacred and the secular. And yet, by a considerable irony, when Protestant fervor merged into national policy, it ended up producing the region in which Protestant denominations had their weakest hold.

Whites had an indisputable claim on the West, Senator Thomas Hart Benton had said, because they used the land "according to the intentions of the CREATOR." As historian Albert Weinberg observed, "[T]heological literature was scarcely more abundant in reference to Providence than was the literature of expansionism." To one typical expansionist during the Mexican-American War, "war was the religious execution of our country's glorious mission, under the direction of Divine Providence, to civilize and christianize, and raise up from anarchy and degradation a most ignorant, indolent, wicked and unhappy people." And yet one outcome of this enterprise was not the redemption of the Mexican people but the slide into religious "anarchy and degradation" of many of the Americans who were supposed to be the agents of the West's redemption. As William Jennings Bryan put it after the

start of the Philippine insurrection, " 'Destiny' is not as manifest as it was" a while ago.

The *Kiva* in My Soul

In New Mexico, it was never possible to draw a firm border
between the secular and the sacred. For centuries, Indian religious belief erased any line between faith and worldly activity.
In the Spanish colonization of the sixteenth and seventeenth
centuries, missionaries played a role in conquest as important,
if not more important, than the role of soldiers. For the Spanish,
religious motives came interwoven with economic and political
motives; even when governors fought with friars for the control of colonies, those struggles dramatized the central role that
religion played in the whole undertaking. In the nineteenth
century, when white Americans entered the scene, Protestant
disapproval of Catholicism added to the contest over land and
labor and to the frictions of nationality and race. In the history
unrolling in New Mexico, religious belief has been everywhere,
shaping and being shaped by even the most secular elements of
human thought and behavior.

In the summer of 1992, Santa Fe—the town called "Holy
Faith"—permitted me a memorable visit to the blurred border
between the secular and the sacred. I was meeting with a group
of international scholars studying American regionalism. From
Senegal to Thailand, from Belgium to the Philippines, all of my
companions had grown up watching Western movies, and
watching them with feelings that bordered on reverence. No
conventionally religious mission society, one learned from the
testimony of these visitors, has ever come close to matching the

achievements of the Hollywood Western in global proselytizing and conversion.

On our last day of class, the participants were having a competition to see who had been the most influenced or tainted by the Wild West myth. We had heard a number of eloquent statements from men whose childhoods had included frequent visits to "Old West" tourist towns in Germany and Austria, where they had cheerfully fired away at the Indian targets in shooting galleries. Then a woman from Poland suddenly and urgently announced her candidacy as the most mythically influenced. "The first thing I can remember," she told us, "is my father reading to me from Karl May's Western novels. As soon as I could read, I read them for myself. I loved old Shatterhand, and even after I saw a movie with a fat Frenchman playing his part, my love for him did not change. You may tell me they are factually wrong, but Karl May's novels are . . ." Here she paused and searched for the right word, seizing on a term she had learned the day before during a tour of a pueblo. "Karl May's novels," she ended, with the right word firmly in hand, "are the *kiva* in my soul."

Here was yet another piece of testimony from Santa Fe, reminding me of the hopelessness of trying to separate faith from worldly fact in Western America. Once again, Santa Fe offered a reminder that of all the places on the planet where the sacred and the secular meet, the American West is one of the hot spots. One could argue (as indeed one had, and at length) that the vision of the West as a romantic place, where strong and good men went down to Main Street or out to the wilderness to take their courageous stands, held little connection to historical fact. And yet, if Karl May's Western fantasies had provided a spiritual and emotional sanctuary for a young woman growing up in Poland in tough times, then we were clearly talking about a realm of belief out of reach of historical fact checking.

Trained in movie theaters in Senegal or Thailand, New York City or Denver, the human spirit has developed the conditioned response of soaring when it confronts certain images: horses galloping across open spaces, wagon trains moving through a landscape of mesas and mountains, cruel enemies and agents of disorder defeated by handsome white men with nerves of steel and tremendous—and justified—self-esteem. And when the human spirit undertakes to soar, it is not necessarily the obligation of the historian to act as air traffic controller and force the spirit down for a landing. Improbable as it may seem to the prosaic historian, an imagined and factually unsubstantiated version of Western American history has become, for many believers, a sacred story. For those believers, a challenge to that story can count as sacrilege.

In American life today, lots of groups have made a heavy emotional investment in the proposition that history is a sacred, not a secular, tale. The best and clearest example of this comes from the Mormons. In the last few years, historians who are Mormon believers but who try to write searchingly and critically about Mormon history have had a rough time. Some of them have been excommunicated for their failure to write what the church's General Authorities call faith-affirming history.

The pattern seen among the Mormons appears everywhere. Consider, for instance, how similar the Mormon call for faith-affirming history is to the Afrocentric call for a history of African American people that consistently praises their accomplishments and affirms their self-esteem. Or consider the desire, on the part of some American Indian people, for a writing of Indian history that enshrines Indian people as ecological and environmental saints and traces an unbroken line of nobility and solidarity among tribal people. When white politicians condemn "revisionist" or "multicultural" history and call for a narrative of the past that affirms the achievements and virtues of white Americans, those politicians show a striking kinship to the Afrocentric intellectuals and to the General Authorities of the Mormon Church. *Everyone* wants faith-affirming history; the disagreement is just a question of which faith any particular individual wants to see affirmed. Each group wants history to provide guidance, legitimacy, justification, and direction for their particular chosen people.

These contests over history, often focused on the West, resemble and echo more familiar contests over religious faith. Different versions of history have become creation stories or origin stories for the people who treasure them, and, with so much feeling at stake, the clash between these sacred tales grows increasingly bitter. And yet, while these separate and contesting claims on history proliferate, more and more evidence emerges from the historical record to counter these assertions of exclusivity. Explorations of Western American history reveal many examples of unexpected kinship, mixed heritage, cultural trading, syncretism, and borrowing. It is not simply a matter of the blending of the West's people through intermarriage, though this is certainly an enormous part of the region's story. It is also a matter of reciprocal influence and mutual assimilation. The various peoples of the American West have been bumping into each other for an awfully long time, and it cannot be a surprise to discover that their habits and beliefs have rubbed off on each other.

Indian religious movements—from the Ghost Dance to the Native American Church with its use of peyote—show many Christian elements. Perhaps the best example of this complexity in religious identity is the Lakota religious leader Black Elk. Thanks to the writer John G. Neihardt's telling of his life story in *Black Elk Speaks,* Black Elk came to stand for the most traditional practice of Indian religion, a practice brought to a tragic end by conquest. But his daughter, Lucy Black Elk Looks Twice, hoped to correct and deepen the standing image of her father, and, working with the anthropologist Michael Steltencamp, Lucy told the postconquest story of Nicholas Black Elk, who became a leading Catholic convert and cathechist on his reservation. This was not a matter of Black Elk's selling out, or betraying his traditional beliefs; this was a matter of sincere religious conviction responding to new beliefs in new times.

In the nineteenth-century West, white Americans had denounced the religions of the others, labeling other systems of belief as paganism, heathenism, superstition, barbarism, or savagery and struggling to convert American Indians and Asian immigrants to Protestant Christianity. In the late-twentieth-century West, the tide seems to be reversing, as a number of white Americans have developed an enthusiasm for tribal religions, as well as for the varieties of Asian Buddhism. Particularly well represented in the West, New Age religion has appropriated pieces and parts of American Indian religions, with both Indian and white claimants to enlightenment, in the familiar area of overlap between commerce and religion, cashing in on the opportunities so presented. Reverend Josiah Strong and his colleagues were presumably tossing in their graves, but all over the West, the lines dividing the vision quest from communion, the *kiva* from the church, were shifting and wavering.

"Dream Other Dreams, and Better"

To many white Americans in our times, belief in the mythic Old West has come to resemble belief in more conventional religious doctrines. For these believers, the Old Frontier is the nation's creation story, the place where the virtues and values of the nation were formed. And yet, for all the faith now invested in it, the mythic version of the Old West had little room for ministers and pastors, congregations and parishes. In a story full of cowboys, sheriffs, saloon girls, outlaws, gun-fighters, prospectors, and stagecoach drivers, the church was, at best, the place where the frightened townspeople gathered to sing hymns and await rescue by the all-too-worldly hero. The church, after all, was aligned with the forces of respec-tability, the forces that would eventually tame the Wild West and end all the fun and adventure of the glory days. If one went in search of the classic heroes in the mythic turf of the Old West, one would not bother to look among the clergy.

In the quest for Western heroes, there is good reason now to look in unexpected, less-explored places. The old heroes are a pretty battered and discredited lot, with their character flaws on permanent display. The examples they provide often affirm the wrong faith entirely—the faith in guns and violence—or serve solely as individual examples of courage and determination, attached to no particular principle. Driven by the values of con-quest and domination, or purely by the goal of personal fortune seeking, the old heroes are looking pretty tired—depleted, exhausted, and ready for retirement. In truth, they deserve a rest.

And yet, when the critics of academic historians say that we have discredited the old heroes and failed to replace them with any new ones, they are right. But this is not because we lack the resources. We have all the material we need to put forward a better team, people whose examples affirm a faith of considerably greater promise. It is time for a different kind of Western hero: the sustainable hero who can replace the old, exhausted, and depleted Western heroes. As Wallace Stegner said of the old Western myths, "dream other dreams, and better."

Sustainability in a hero means, very concretely, providing inspiration that sustains the spirit and the soul. While inconsistency can disqualify a conventional hero, a degree of inconsistency is one of the essential qualifications of a sustainable hero. Models of sustainable heroism are drawn from the record of people doing the right thing *some of the time*—people practicing heroism at a level that we can actually aspire to match. The fact that these people fell, periodically, off the high ground of heroism but then determinedly climbed back, even if only in order to fall again, is exactly what makes their heroism sustainable. Because it is uneven and broken, this kind of heroism is resilient, credible, possible, reachable. Sustainable heroism comes only in moments and glimpses, but they are moments and glimpses in which the universe lights up.

Assigned in 1867 to preside over the vast district of Montana, Idaho, and Utah, Bishop Daniel Tuttle "traveled more than forty thousand miles" by stagecoach. "Most times I enjoyed that mode of traveling," he remembered, "many times I grimly endured it, a few times I was rendered miserable by it." Think about what it meant to ride with strangers for hours and hours, jammed into an inflexible, jostling container, and the fact that

Bishop Tuttle kept his temper and most of the time enjoyed the ride is its own measure of sustainable heroism.

While misery most often derived from the rough road conditions or the inadequacy of stagecoach shock protection, fellow passengers could sometimes match the bumps in the road in their power to annoy. In one case, a fellow passenger "by manner and act was insulting to a colored woman in the coach." Bishop Tuttle firmly "reproved him." When words proved insufficient and the passenger "repeated the offense," Tuttle reported, "I shook him soundly." If this demonstration of muscular Christianity failed to produce a conversion, it still made for a happier ride. "At the next station," the offender "got out and slunk entirely away from our sight."

Bishop Tuttle was a complicated man, full of self-righteous disapproval in his appraisal of Mormon belief and earnestly committed to the growth of his denomination. But when Bishop Tuttle took his stand on behalf of the right of African American women to travel with dignity, he offered a memorable demonstration of sustainable heroism, an episode in faith-affirming history for those trying to hold onto a belief in an American commitment to justice and fairness.

And then there is the remarkable example of heroism set by Reverend Howard Thurman. An African American man who was the chaplain at Howard University, Reverend Thurman headed west to team up with a white man as copastor of a new and courageous church. As a young child, he had attended his father's funeral and listened to a preacher condemn his father as an example of an unredeemed, unchurched sinner. Ever since then, Thurman had been on a campaign against exclusivity in Christian practice, fighting the exclusivity of the smugly saved as persistently as he fought the exclusivity of race. When he learned of an effort to form a church in San Francisco uniting people of all races and backgrounds, Reverend Thurman felt called. The year was 1943, more than ten years before the Montgomery, Alabama, bus boycott.

The location and the timing were both crucial. "Segregation of the races," Reverend Thurman wrote, "was a part of the mores, and of the social behavior of the country." "San Francisco with its varied nationalities, its rich intercultural heritages, and its face resolutely fixed toward the Orient" was the ideal place to undertake a trial run toward a better future in American race relations. War work had brought a much-increased black population to San Francisco and heightened the prospects of community friction. Responding to these challenges, an interracial group had decided to form the Church for the Fellowship of All Peoples, and Reverend Thurman joined them, following his quest to find out "whether or not it is true that experiences of spiritual unity and fellowship are more compelling than the fears and dogmas and prejudices that separate men." There was considerable risk, financial and otherwise, in the "mission" that brought Reverend Thurman and his family "three thousand miles across the continent." And there were constant tests of the spirit, as the Fellowship Church and Reverend Thurman faced the prospects of sponsoring interracial marriage and other challenges to the social order. Simply visiting a member of the congregation in the hospital could prove to be a test of Reverend Thurman's spirit; hospital staffs repeatedly stumbled over and resisted the notion that a white believer could be in the care of a black pastor.

Fellowship Church under Reverend Thurman's leadership proved to be a great success, navigating its way through the difficult divisions between denominations as well as those between races. In God's presence, Reverend Thurman always insisted, "the worshiper is neither male nor female, black nor white, Protestant nor Catholic nor Buddhist nor Hindu, but a human spirit laid bare." "Religious experience," he believed, and he had lived this gospel, "must unite rather than divide men."

The examples set by heroes like Bishop Tuttle and Reverend Thurman encourage me to believe in the real American West, a place—in the past and in the present—of dazzling human and natural possibility. Believing in the other West, the mythic and imagined West, has never been much of an option for me. Instead, the very notion of investing any faith in a simple, romantic, glorified West always brought to mind the verse that I learned from my father when I was very young:

> *With this bright, believing band,*
> *I have no claim to be.*
> *What seems so true to them,*
> *Seems fantasy to me.*

This verse has kept me on course in the company of those who have fallen head over heels in love with a Western illusion; and yet, in the presence of more traditional religious believers, it gives me much less comfort. The company of people secure in their faith, whether that faith is a tribal religion, Catholicism, Judaism, Mormonism, or a Protestant denomination, can make me melt with envy. But then the verse "With this bright, believing band, I have no claim to be" comes to mind and interrupts the melting. I remain a member of a battered, disorganized, but still pretty bright, believing band of my own, churched and unchurched, composed of all races and backgrounds—people who hold onto a faith that fairness and justice might some day prevail in this region and in this nation. That faith, the faith of my father and my mother, of Bishop Tuttle and Reverend Thurman, is the *kiva* in my soul.

THE UNAUTHORIZED AUTOBIOGRAPHY OF ME

Sherman Alexie

Late summer night on the Spokane Indian Reservation. Ten Indians are playing basketball on a court barely illuminated by the streetlight above them. They will play until the brown, leather ball is invisible in the dark. They will play until an errant pass jams a finger, knocks a pair of glasses off a face, smashes a nose and draws blood. They will play until the ball bounces off the court and disappears into the shadows.

Sometimes, I think this is all you need to know about Native American literature.

Thesis: I have never met a Native American. Thesis reiterated: I have met thousands of Indians.

PEN American panel in Manhattan, November 1994, on Indian Literature. N. Scott Momaday, James Welch, Gloria Miguel, Joy Harjo, and myself. Two or three hundred people in the audience. Mostly non-Indians; an Indian or three. Questions and answers.

"Why do you insist on calling yourselves Indian?" asked a white woman in a nice hat. "It's so demeaning."

"Listen," I said. "The word belongs to us now. We are Indians. That has nothing to do with Indians from India. We are not American Indians. We are Indians, pronounced In-din. It belongs to us. We own it and we're not going to give it back."

So much has been taken from us that we hold on to the smallest things with all the strength we have left.

Winter on the Spokane Indian Reservation, 1976. My two cousins, S and G, have enough money for gloves. They buy them at Irene's Grocery Store. Irene is a white woman who has lived on our reservation since the beginning of time. I have no money for gloves. My hands are bare.

We build snow fortresses on the football field. Since we are Indian boys playing, there must be a war. We stockpile snowballs. S and G build their fortress on the fifty-yard line. I build mine on the thirty-yard line. We begin our little war. My hands are bare.

My cousins are good warriors. They throw snowballs with precision. I am bombarded, under siege, defeated quickly. My cousins bury me in the snow. My grave is shallow. If my cousins knew how to dance, they might have danced on my grave. But they know how to laugh, so they laugh. They are my cousins, meaning we are related in the Indian way. My father drank beers with their father for most of two decades, and that is enough to make us relatives. Indians gather relatives like firewood, protection against the cold. I am buried in the snow, cold, without protection. My hands are bare.

After a short celebration, my cousins exhume me. I am too cold to fight. Shivering, I walk for home, anxious for warmth. I know my mother is home. She is probably sewing a quilt. She is always sewing quilts. If she sells a quilt, we have dinner. If she fails to sell a quilt, we go hungry. My mother has never failed to sell a quilt. But the threat of hunger is always there.

When I step into the house, my mother is sewing yet another quilt. She is singing a song under her breath. You might assume she is singing a highly traditional Spokane Indian song. She is singing Donna Fargo's "The Happiest Girl in the Whole USA." Improbably, this is a highly traditional Spokane Indian song. The living room is dark in the late afternoon. The house is cold. My mother is wearing her coat and shoes.

"Why don't you turn up the heat?" I ask my mother.

"No electricity," she says.

"Power went out?" I ask.

"Didn't pay the bill," she says.

I am colder. I inhale, exhale, my breath visible inside the house. I can hear a car sliding on the icy road outside. My mother is making a quilt. This quilt will pay for the electricity. Her fingers are stiff and painful from the cold. She is sewing as fast as she can.

On the jukebox in the bar: Hank Williams, Patsy Cline, Johnny Cash, Charlie Rich, Freddy Fender, Donna Fargo.

On the radio in the car: Creedence Clearwater Revival, Three Dog Night, Blood, Sweat and Tears, Janis Joplin, early Stones, earlier Beatles.

On the stereo in the house: Glen Campbell, Roy Orbison, Johnny Horton, Loretta Lynn, "The Ballad of the Green Beret."

• • •

The fourth-grade music teacher, Mr. Manley, set a row of musical instruments in front of us. From left to right, a flute, clarinet, French horn, trombone, trumpet, tuba, drum. We had our first chance to play that kind of music.

"Now," he explained, "I want all of you to line up behind the instrument you want to learn how to play."

Dawn, Loretta, and Karen lined up behind the flute. Melissa and Michelle behind the clarinet. Lori and Willette behind the French horn. All ten Indian boys lined up behind the drum.

My sister, Mary, was beautiful. She was fourteen years older than me. She wore short skirts and nylons because she was supposed to wear short skirts and nylons. It was expected. Her black hair combed long and straight. 1970. Often, she sat in her favorite chair, the fake leather lounger we rescued from the dump. Holding a hand mirror, she combed her hair, applied her makeup. Much lipstick and eyeshadow, no foundation. She was always leaving the house. I do not remember where she went. I do remember sitting at her feet, rubbing my cheek against her nyloned calf, while she waited for her ride.

She died in an early morning fire in Montana in 1981. At the time, I was sleeping at a friend's house in Washington. I was not dreaming of my sister.

"Sherman," asks the critic, "how does your work apply to the oral tradition?"

"Well," I say, as I hold my latest book close to me, "it doesn't apply at all because I type this. And I'm really, really quiet when I'm typing it."

• • •

Summer 1977. Steve and I want to attend the KISS concert in Spokane. KISS is very popular on my reservation. Gene Simmons, the bass player. Paul Stanley, lead singer and rhythm guitarist. Ace Frehley, lead guitar. Peter Criss, drummer. All four hide their faces behind elaborate makeup. Simmons the devil, Stanley the lover, Frehley the space man, Criss the cat.

The songs: "Do You Love Me," "Calling Dr. Love," "Love Gun," "Makin' Love," "C'mon and Love Me."

Steve and I are too young to go on our own. His uncle and aunt, born-again Christians, decide to chaperon us. Inside the Spokane Coliseum, the four of us find seats far from the stage and the enormous speakers. Uncle and Aunt wanted to avoid the bulk of the crowd, but have landed us in the unofficial pot smoking section. We are overwhelmed by the sweet smoke. Steve and I cover our mouths and noses with Styrofoam cups and try to breathe normally.

KISS opens their show with staged explosions, flashing red lights, a prolonged guitar solo by Frehley. Simmons spits fire. The crowd rushes the stage. All the pot smokers in our section hold lighters, tiny flames flickering, high above their heads. The songs are so familiar. We know all the words. The audience sings along.

The songs: "Let Me Go, Rock 'n Roll," "Detroit Rock City," "Rock and Roll All Nite."

The decibel level is tremendous. Steve and I can feel the sound waves crashing against the Styrofoam cups we hold over our faces. Aunt and Uncle are panicked, finally assured that the devil plays a mean guitar. This is too much for them. It is too much for Steve and me, but we pretend to be disappointed when Aunt and Uncle drag us out of the coliseum.

During the drive home, Aunt and Uncle play Christian music on the radio. Loudly and badly, they sing along. Steve and I are in the back of the Pacer, looking up through the strangely curved rear window. There is a meteor shower, the largest in a decade. Steve and I smell like pot smoke. We smile at this. Our ears ring. We make wishes on the shooting stars, though both of us know that a shooting star is not a star. It's just a sliver of stone.

I made a very conscious decision to marry an Indian woman, who made a very conscious decision to marry me.

Our hope: to give birth to and raise Indian children who love themselves. That is the most revolutionary act possible.

1982. I am the only Indian student at Reardan High, an all-white school in a small farm town just outside my reservation. I am in the pizza parlor, sharing a deluxe with my white friends. We are talking and laughing. A drunk Indian walks into the parlor. He staggers to the counter and orders a beer. The waiter ignores him. Our table is silent.

At our table, S is shaking her head. She leans toward the table as if to share a secret. We all lean toward her.

"Man," she says, "I hate Indians."

I am curious about the Indian writers who identify themselves as mixed-blood. It must be difficult for them, trying to decide into which container they should place their nouns and verbs. Yet, it must be good to be invisible, as a blond, Aryan-featured Jew might have known in Germany during World War II. Then again, I think of the horror stories that a pale Jew might tell about his life during the Holocaust.

• • •

An Incomplete List of People Whom I Wish Were Indian

1. Martin Luther King, Jr.
2. Robert Johnson
3. Meryl Streep
4. Helen Keller
5. Walt Whitman
6. Emily Dickinson
7. Superman
8. Adam
9. Eve
10. Muhammad Ali
11. Billie Jean King
12. John Lennon
13. Jimmy Carter
14. Rosa Parks
15. Shakespeare
16. John Steinbeck
17. Billy the Kid
18. Voltaire
19. Harriet Tubman
20. Flannery O'Connor
21. Pablo Neruda
22. Amelia Earhart
23. Sappho
24. Mary Magdalene
25. Robert DeNiro
26. Susan B. Anthony
27. Kareem Abdul-Jabbar

28. Wilma Rudolph

29. Isadora Duncan

30. Bruce Springsteen

31. Dian Fossey

32. Patsy Cline

33. Jesus Christ

Summer 1995. Seattle, Washington. I am idling at a red light when a car filled with white boys pulls up beside me. The white boy in the front passenger seat leans out his window.

"I hate you Indian motherfuckers," he screams.

I quietly wait for the green light.

1978. David, Randy, Steve, and I decide to form a reservation doo-wop group, like the Temptations. During recess, we practice behind the old tribal school. Steve, a falsetto, is the best singer. I am the worst singer, but have the deepest voice, and am therefore an asset.

"What songs do you want to sing?" asks David.

" 'Tracks of My Tears,' " says Steve, who always decides these kind of things.

We sing, desperately trying to remember the lyrics to that song. We try to remember other songs. We remember the chorus to most, the first verse of a few, and only one in its entirety. For some unknown reason, we all know the lyrics of "Monster Mash," a novelty hit from the fifties. However, I'm the only one who can manage to sing with the pseudo-Transylvanian accent that "Monster Mash" requires. This dubious skill makes me the lead singer, despite Steve's protests.

"We need a name for our group," says Randy.

"How about The Warriors?" I ask.

Everybody agrees. We watch westerns.

We sing "Monster Mash" over and over. We want to be famous. We want all the little Indian girls to shout our names. Finally, after days of practice, we are ready for our debut. Walking in a row like soldiers, the four of us parade around the playground. We sing "Monster Mash." I am in front, followed by Steve, David, then Randy, who is the shortest, but the toughest fighter our reservation has ever known. We sing. We are The Warriors. All the other Indian boys and girls line up behind us as we march. We are heroes. We are loved. I sing with everything I have inside of me: pain, happiness, anger, depression, heart, soul, small intestine. I sing and am rewarded with people who listen. This is why I am a poet.

I remember watching Richard Nixon, during the whole Watergate affair, as he held a press conference and told the entire world that he was not a liar.

For the first time, I understood that storytellers could be bad people.

Poetry = Anger • Imagination

Every time I venture into the bookstore, I find another book about Indians. There are hundreds of books about Indians published every year, yet so few are written by Indians. I gather all the books written about Indians. I discover:

1. A book written by a person who identifies herself as mixed-blood will sell more copies than a book

written by a person who identifies herself as strictly Indian.

2. A book written by a non-Indian will sell more copies than a book written by a mixed-blood or Indian writer.

3. A book about Indian life in the pre-twentieth century, whether written by a non-Indian, mixed-blood, or Indian, will sell more copies than a book about twentieth-century Indian life.

4. If you are a non-Indian writing about Indians, it is almost guaranteed that Tony Hillerman will write something positive about you.

5. Reservation Indian writers are rarely published in any form.

6. Every Indian woman writer will be compared with Louise Erdrich. Every Indian man writer will be compared with Michael Dorris.

7. A very small percentage of the readers of Indian literature have heard of Simon J. Ortiz. This is a crime.

8. Books about the Sioux sell more copies than all of the books written about other tribes combined.

9. Mixed-blood writers often write about any tribe that interests them, whether or not the writer is descended from that tribe.

10. Most of the writers who use obviously Indian names, such as Eagle Woman and Pretty Shield, are usually non-Indian.

11. Non-Indian writers usually say "Great Spirit," "Mother Earth," "Two-Legged, Four-Legged, and Winged." Mixed-blood writers usually say "Creator," "Mother Earth," "Two-Legged, Four-Legged, and

Winged." Indian writers usually say "God," "Earth," "Human Being, Dog, and Bird."

12. If an Indian book contains no dogs, then the book is written by a non-Indian or mixed-blood writer.

13. If there are winged animals who aren't supposed to have wings on the cover of the book, then it is written by a non-Indian.

14. Successful non-Indian writers are thought to be learned experts on Indian life. Successful mixed-blood writers are thought to be wonderful translators of Indian life. Successful Indian writers are thought to be traditional storytellers of Indian life.

15. Very few Indian and mixed-blood writers speak their tribal languages. Even fewer non-Indian writers speak their tribal languages.

16. Mixed-bloods often write exclusively about Indians, even if they grew up in non-Indian communities.

17. Indians often write exclusively about reservation life, even if they never lived on a reservation.

18. Non-Indian writers always write about reservation life.

19. Nobody has written the great urban Indian novel yet.

20. Most non-Indians who write about Indians are fiction writers. They write fiction about Indians because it sells.

Have you stood in a crowded room where nobody looks like you? If you are white, have you stood in a room full of black people? Are you an Irish man who has strolled through the streets of Compton? If you are black, have you stood in a room full of white people? Are you an African man who has been playing the back nine at the local country club? If you are a woman, have you stood in a room full of men? Are you Sandra Day O'Connor or Ruth Ginsburg?

Since I left the reservation, almost every room I enter is filled with people who do not look like me. There are only two million Indians in this country. We could all fit into one medium-sized city. We should look into it.

Often, I am most alone in bookstores where I am reading from my work. I look up from the page at a sea of white faces. This is frightening.

There was an apple tree outside my grandmother's house on the reservation. The apples were green; my grandmother's house was green. This was the game. My siblings and I would try to sneak apples from the tree. Sometimes, our friends would join our raiding expeditions. My grandmother believed green apples were poison and was simply trying to protect us from sickness. There is nothing biblical about this story.

The game had rules. We always had to raid the tree during daylight. My grandmother had bad eyes and it would have been unfair to challenge her during the dark. We all had to approach the tree at the same time. Arnold, my older brother. Kim and Arlene, my younger twin sisters. We had to climb the tree to steal apples, ignoring the fruit that hung low to the ground.

Arnold, of course, was the best apple thief on the reservation. He was chubby but quick. He was fearless in the tree, climbing to the top for the plumpest apples. He'd hang from a branch with one arm, reach for apples with the other, and fill his pockets with his booty. I loved him like crazy. My sisters were more conservative. They often grabbed one apple and ate it quickly while they sat on a sturdy branch. I always wanted the green apples that contained a hint of red. While we were busy raiding the tree, we'd also keep an eye on my grandmother's house. She was a big woman, nearly six feet tall. At the age of seventy, she could still outrun any ten-year-old.

Arnold, of course, was always the first kid out of the tree. He'd hang from a branch, drop to the ground, and scream loudly, announcing our presence to our grandmother. He'd run away, leaving my sisters and me stuck in the tree. We'd scramble to the ground and try to escape. If our grandmother said our name, we were automatically captured.

"Junior," she'd shout and I'd freeze. It was the rule. A dozen Indian kids were sometimes in that tree, scattering in random directions when our grandmother burst out of the house. If our grandmother remembered your name, you were a prisoner of war. And, believe me, no matter how many kids were running away, my grandmother always remembered my name.

"Junior," she'd shout and I would close my eyes in disgust. Captured again! I'd wait as she walked up to me. She'd hold out her hand and I'd give her any stolen apples. Then she'd smack me gently on the top of my head. I was free to run then, pretending she'd never caught me in the first place. I'd try to catch up with my siblings and friends. I would shout their names as I ran through the trees surrounding my grandmother's house.

My grandmother died when I was fourteen years old. I miss her. I miss everybody.

So many people claim to be Indian, speaking of an Indian grandmother, a warrior grandfather. Let's say the United States government announced that every Indian had to return to their reservation. How many people would shove their Indian ancestor back into the closet?

My mother still makes quilts. My wife and I sleep beneath one. My brother works for our tribal casino. One sister works for our bingo hall, while the other works in the tribal finance department. Our adopted little brother, James, who is actually our second cousin, is a freshman at Reardan High School. He can run the mile in five minutes.

My father used to leave us for weeks at a time to drink with his friends and cousins. I missed him so much I'd cry myself sick. Every time he left, I ended up in the emergency room. But I always got well and he always came back. He'd walk in the door without warning. We'd forgive him.

I could always tell when he was going to leave. He would be tense, quiet, unable to concentrate. He'd flip through magazines and television channels. He'd open the refrigerator door, study its contents, shut the door, and walk away. Five minutes later, he'd be back at the fridge, rearranging items on the shelves. I would follow him from place to place, trying to prevent his escape.

Once, he went into the bathroom, which had no windows, while I sat outside the only door and waited for him. I could not hear him inside. I knocked on the thin wood. I was five years old.

"Are you there?" I asked. "Are you still there?"

Years later, I am giving a reading at a bookstore in Spokane, Washington. There is a large crowd. I read a story about an Indian father who leaves his family for good. He moves to a city a thousand miles away. Then he dies. It is a sad story. When I finish, a woman in the front row breaks into tears.

"What's wrong?" I ask her.

"I'm so sorry about your father," she says.

"Thank you," I say. "But that's my father sitting right next to you."

THE MILITIA IN ME

Denis Johnson

In July 1992, I went to Alaska to pan for gold, and to live out the happy story, I don't mind admitting, of the American who finds something fundamentally valuable and untouched in earth no person has ever walked on. My first day in Anchorage I made the acquaintance of two men who fascinated me. John lived off the land and well off the grid and on, as he put it, "the cutting edge of freedom" in the hills outside Talkeetna; had built his own cabin, acted as midwife at the births of his four children. His friend Richard prospected in the Bonanza Hills southwest of Anchorage and hunted bears with a compound bow. They'd set up a kind of headquarters in a booth at the Arctic Burger, a coffee shop frequented by Alaska old-timers—they still call it "the Roadrunner" though copyright laws forced a renaming years ago. Openhanded, cheerful men—winning to talk to—these two had come into the city that summer to stump for presidential candidate and ex–Green-Beret-hero Col. Bo Gritz. Not that they cared much for politicians or harbored any great hopes for government. Richard himself refused to pay taxes on his income. The IRS was after him for over a hundred thousand dollars, but he denied them any claim to legal authority, as the sixteenth Amendment had never been properly ratified. "The whole thing's a bluff," he said. He'd gone so far as to have himself deleted, somehow, from the Social Security system——his Alaska driver's license showed, where the familiar number should be, nine big zeroes all in a row.

"Bo Gritz is a true leader," Richard said. "He gave a speech in Colorado and eight thousand men in the audience pledged they'd follow him into battle if it came down to that. That's eight battalions," he pointed out.

And it was time to talk of battalions. Forty-three concentration camps had been built around the country. Under U.N. auspices, foreign troops conducted exercises on our soil; others, whole divisions, waited on the Baja peninsula. Both men believed that somebody had shanghaied the United States, that pirates had seized the helm of the ship of state and now steered it toward some completely foreign berth where it could be plundered at leisure. One of Bo Gritz's military contacts, they said, had verified all this. "The word's gone out, the order's come down: 1992 will see the last presidential election."

My wife and I honeymooned that month, just us two, at Richard's mining operation in the Bonanza Hills. A plane dropped us off, and a plane would pick us up nine days later. Meanwhile Cindy and I lived without any contact with what I had up to then believed to be the world, in a place without human community, authority, or law, seventy miles from the nearest person. We brought a shotgun with us—I'd never before owned a gun, somebody else always handled that stuff in what I'd thought of as the world—and I was surprised to discover that keeping it ready and handy instantly asserted itself as the bedrock requirement of our lives. And other things I'd never thought about became uppermost, matches and tools and, above all, clarity of thought and our ability to improvise —we had to stay focused in our senses, ever mindful of our tasks, because what we'd brought, and who we were, was all we had. At last whatever happened to us could only be *our* fault or bad fortune, and fixing it *our* responsibility. We realized our lives had never before been our own—*our* lives.

I had always lived under the protection of what I've since heard called "the Nanny State": Big Mom, ready to patch me up, bail me out, calm me down, and only a three-digit phone call away.

Just the same, it's a free country. I'd always taken for granted that the government looked after the basics and left me free to enjoy my liberty. Now I wasn't so sure. This little taste of real autonomy excited in me a craving for it. Maybe I wanted freedom from the government's care and protection. Maybe I wanted freedom from any government at all. I felt grateful for people like Richard, who'd run away from home and could get along for weeks at a time in places like the Bonanza Hills.

In the immense solitude of the Bonanza Hills somebody had been reading. In the prospector's cabin we found a few books: *None Dare Call It Conspiracy* by Gary Allen and Larry Abraham, describing the gigantic fraud perpetrated by the nation's Federal

Reserve system. *Racial Hybridity* by Philip Jones, B.A. Also by the same author: *The Negro: Serpent, Beast, and Devil*—a stamp in the flap identified it as the property of the Aryan Nation Church in Hayden Lake, not sixty miles from our home in Idaho. We'd heard of them: eight guys in a rundown compound with a lot of wooden crosses and kerosene, taken seriously by nobody except those who were paid to do so, like the press and the FBI.

When we got back to Anchorage, Cindy and I attended the America First Party's rally for Bo Gritz, a small affair, surely fewer than a hundred people under an awning hastily erected in a light Alaskan rain, city folks and country folks, but mostly country folks, of all ages but mostly middle-aged, eating moose and venison barbecued right there in the small downtown park. There was one black kid present about eighteen, laughing at the world and enjoying the food. Nobody bothered him. Bo Gritz showed up, ate some moose, and made a speech. A man of medium height, barrel-chested and blunt-faced, he looked less like my idea of a warrior than like someone who'd hire himself out to collect delinquent loans. One loan in particular concerned him: He promised, if elected, to instruct Congress to mint a single coin "of the basest, most worthless metal we can find," to which he'd assign the value of one trillion dollars. "And I'll toss it down at the feet of the bankers and say—there, pick it up. That's the national debt. *Paid in full.*" The crowd, small as it was, managed to produce a roar. "It may seem our numbers are small. And they are," he said. "But I'm not worried. Do you know why? Because I've read the book, and I know how it turns out." And just as he said it, some in the audience nodded and said too: *"We win."*

What book? The Bible's Revelation? *The Turner Diaries,* in which provocateurs touch off a racial Armageddon? I didn't ask. And what would we win?—an election, or a war? I didn't ask.

The people I talked with seemed to imply that the greatest threat to liberty came from a conspiracy, or several overlapping conspiracies, well known to everybody but me. As a framework for thought, this has its advantages. It's quicker to call a thing a crime and ask *Who did it?* than to call it a failure and set about answering the question *What happened?*

A year later, I'm traveling the Texas-Mexico border region in a rented car. The border patrol stops me well north of Big Bend National Park—sixty miles north of the border—and the officer asks me who I am and where I'm from and I tell him. "Can we have a look in your vehicle?" "What if I said no?" "Then we'd bring the dog over and he'd tell us we better search the vehicle." "You mean he'd give you probable cause for a search?" "Just your refusal to let us search," the officer says, "would be probable cause for a search."

In the elections last November a number of Democrats ran unopposed in our county. Republicans held on to their offices, but gained none locally. Nearly one-fifth of the people here receive some kind of public assistance—twice the rate of the New York boroughs—and our main industry is heavily subsidized by the federal government. But this isn't some hippie conclave next door to San Francisco. It's Boundary County, Idaho's northernmost district.

Perhaps above all our subsidized industry, logging—with

access roads built free by the federal government and stands of timber in the national forest auctioned off to lumber corporations at a loss to the nation's taxpayers—makes this region a resentful hot zone. We live in these hills, we see them covered with tens of thousands of square miles of a marketable, renewable crop, but the government insists on letting too many of these trees grow up, fall over dead, burn to ash, come to nothing. Resentment makes a blind spot when it comes to extremists— you hate the government? So do we, even if between the two hatreds lies a vast, mainly unexamined, difference.

Three years ago the Weaver family, who lived south of us on Ruby Ridge, ended an eighteen-month siege in a firefight with U.S. marshals. In the first exchange of shots, one of the marshals and one of the Weaver children died. Two hundred federal marshals and FBI agents descended on the town of Bonners Ferry. None of us knew where all these people had come from. They instituted a curfew and banned gatherings, ran up debts in the stores, surrounded the Weaver place, killed Mrs. Weaver while she stood in the doorway of her cabin with her infant daughter in her arms. Bo Gritz showed up and talked her husband Randy and her surviving children into surrendering. The federal agents left town. None of us knew where they'd gone.

Then, too, here live a few folks like me—a city boy grown too neurotic to abide urban life, a lover of the wilderness chiefly for its solitude, but certainly no country boy—surrounded by a forest that would quickly extinguish him were he ever to lose his way in it, working half the day at a computer console and then stepping out to stumble mystified among the greasy barely functioning accoutrements of rural living, snowplows and well pumps and chain saws and pickups, things the local ten-year-olds can take down into piles and reassemble blindfolded. I fish poorly. I've never hunted, mainly for fear I'll shoot myself. And I like the trees, whether standing up or fallen over rotting. I don't like seeing clear-cuts like great big vacant lots in the wilderness. Yet I'm one who's lent sympathy to the militias, the throwback mountaineers, even the Christian Nazis. This is a free country. I just want to be left alone. I thought that's all they wanted, too.

During the eighteen months that Randy Weaver lived under a kind of self-arrest thirty miles away, it regularly occurred to me that if I were a real journalist, I'd be visiting him often and getting the story on him and his family before whatever was going to happen finally happened. But he clearly valued his privacy; and I must not be a real journalist, because I felt compelled to value it, too. What did they want? I didn't ask.

In the sixties I was a pot-deranged beatnik who remained in college mainly to avoid Vietnam. I didn't trust that particular government, but I thought that Washington could fix things if only *we* could take it over. Now I'm in the White House, or somebody a whole lot like me is.

At about three o'clock one morning in October 1994, while you and I were sleeping, Congress passed the Telephone Privacy Act requiring the phone companies to reengineer their equipment, and granting $300 million in federal funds to make the change, so that every phone in the United States of America can be tapped by federal agents from their offices.

• • •

At breakfast one morning, also that October, my family and I read the weekly paper together, captivated by its account of the recent sweep-search of the Sandpoint Middle School. Cops and dogs had locked the children down for three hours while they combed through lockers and belongings. They found a pistol and a bag of marijuana, not a big haul, but the principal was satisfied that he'd managed to "send a message." Indeed he had. My kids attended Mt. Hall Elementary about sixty miles north, and they heard it all the way up here. A couple of questions: What language is that, exactly? And one my son Daniel asked: "How come they didn't just use the intercom?" The response of North Idaho parents to this message was overwhelmingly favorable.

From Section 90107 of the Omnibus Crime Bill: "The President may declare a State or part of a State to be a violent crime or drug emergency area and may take appropriate actions authorized by this section." Such actions include sending in federalized National Guard, and "any Federal agency." Section 180102 authorizes Multi-Jurisdictional Task Forces to be funded with "assets seized as a result of investigations" to be used "to enhance the operations of the task force and its participating State and local law-enforcement agencies."

Ryan runs the surplus store down the road, the kind of surplus store that lives up to all the expectations about North Idaho, dealing in, along with the usual outdoor gear, gas masks, semi-automatic rifles, concealable weapons, literature like *The Anarchist's Cookbook*. I bought all four volumes of *The Poor Man's James*

Bond there and that's all any writer would ever need in the way of reference material on murder, terror, or guerrilla war. I like Ryan. He's a student of the U.S. Constitution, and he keeps a stack of Informed Jury pamphlets on the counter right at the point-of-purchase. Often we talk politics, and we find a lot to agree about—he's become as suspicious of the State as I have. But when I suggested that maybe he'd like to check out the Libertarian Party, he was shocked at the libertarian notion that each person should be allowed to pursue happiness in his or her own way, even homosexuals. "But you could have a township that banned gays, as long as people weren't forced to live there, and as long as you didn't go over and bomb the gay township," I pointed out. "Listen: Do you know what they *do* to each other?" Ryan asked me. "We *would* go over and bomb them."

What about that college beatnik—was he in the government's sights? I wrote away to the FBI for my records a couple of years back. Three months later I got four pages headed *Student for a Democratic Society.* Here and there on these pages can be found bits and pieces, mainly about a demonstration I attended in 1967, at which I was arrested. But for the most part, the paragraphs have been blacked out with a felt-tip pen, and I have no idea what they say.

I'm standing by our mailbox on a two-mile straightaway on Meadow Creek Road between the Purcell Mountains and Deer Ridge, one of my favorites places on earth. In this alpine region the valley's bed is the largest open space I can stand in, four square miles occupied by our family and five others. In the mailbox today I find an envelope bearing no return address, and in the envelope two legal-size typesheets crammed with a six-thousand word tract entitled "BLUEPRINT FOR The FINAL TAKEOVER OF THE USA By 2 ALIEN Jews, Donald Goldberg and Indy Badh-WAR." It describes how the president starts a phony war and then uses demonstrations against this war as an excuse to suspend civil liberties. "Secret, elaborate plans for martial law and for directing military WITHIN OUR BOR-DERS IS already drawn up/distributed . . ."

About once a week I play cards at the Club Bar just across the state line in Troy, Montana. The Club is profoundly Mon-tanan, a patchwork homemade-feeling saloon with a barrel stove and a fight every night and dogs and orphans wandering in and out, and a plywood coffin propped up in a corner. The bar itself is no great shakes. They used to have an impressive one, but in the sixties a powder-monkey for the Highway Department came in during his lunch hour wired with dyna-mite and ordered everybody out, then blew himself up, and the bar too. The establishment's owner, Tony Brown, explains that the coffin is for "the next guy who dies in here."

In the eighties, Tony served as the mayor of Troy, and per-haps by reason of this former prominence the Militia of Mon-tana approached him almost two years ago. In a series of private meetings "right here at this table," he says, slapping the poker table, a group of three men assured him that they intended to protect the rights of citizens and discriminate against none. Tony Brown agreed to book the local high school's auditorium for a meeting of the Militia of Montana.

In the meantime, he read the militia's literature, and he had some questions. "Do you mean to tell me," he asked them, "that if a little faggot boy wanted to lead the charge, like blowing on the trumpet, you wouldn't let him in your militia?" John Trochman, head of the militia, told him no— "Not unless he converted to our religion."

Tony Brown makes his way across the small west end of Troy, Montana, a town with no section on the other side of the tracks—all of Troy is on the other side of the tracks. Tony Brown makes his way to the high school, to the militia meeting, where he's agreed to serve as MC. He cuts through a neighbor's backyard, gets hold of one of the neighbor's hens, and plucks from its back one feather.

Interested citizens, mostly men, have filled the auditorium. At this time resentment against the national government runs high in Troy—the U.S. Forest Service has just floated a list of proposed regulations that make it hard to imagine any human could set foot in the federal forests without transgressing them, and it's rumored also that 30,000 rounds of ammunition have been issued to the officers in anticipation of having to enforce the new rules. Better than two hundred angry Trojans have come to hear what the Militia of Montana has to say about all this.

Tony Brown, holding a chicken feather in his left hand, places his right one over his heart and leads the gathering in the Pledge of Allegiance. He reads Articles I and II of the U.S. Constitution, and the Declaration of Independence, and the Constitution of the State of Montana, and then, by way of introducing Mr. Trochman, he reads a nine-page speech lamenting that "the current state of America is truly alarming to any man who is capable of reflection," a speech all about

Thomas Paine and the Founding Fathers and the Kennedy assassination and the Warren Commission and the forest service and taxation without representation, and about the night in 1773 when American colonists stuck feathers in their hats and dumped out tea in Boston Harbor.

Brown finishes his speech by refusing to endorse the Militia of Montana, and then sticks his feather in his hair and walks out of the meeting, out of the building, back to the Club. Back to the poker game.

"I was the first one to tell those assholes they were assholes," Brown likes to say these days. "But I want it understood—all these extra laws, extra police, extra oppression: I just don't think that's the way to go."

As I watched the TV coverage of the Waco tragedy in 1993, I kept in mind that the trouble there began over the nature of the firearms the Branch Davidians had stockpiled for themselves, over the question whether their weapons were military but legal, or *too* military and forbidden. It occurred to me that the attempt to abridge or deny what people see as a basic human right can result in more misery and carnage even than the people's abuse of that right. I began to feel personally involved in the question. I don't want to see whole families killed in order to protect me from the threat of random violence.

The government's vigilance led it to pass in 1992—by no means an unusual legislative year—1,397 new federal laws and to generate 62,928 pages of regulations protecting me from, among other things, the possibility that I might make a bad deal on a nectarine. Have I checked my nectarines lately? The bureaus employed 125,666 people to write these regulations, return them to Congress, and wait for a response. After sixty days a regulation becomes law.

It is illegal to sell a peach smaller than two and three-eighth inches in diameter. Nectarines are covered, too. But nectarines have no fuzz, and are therefore legal down to a diameter of two and five-sixteenth inches.

But if freedom means self-responsibility—what about the people who can't take care of themselves? My friend, I'm one of those people. Every day I don't bring down something fatal on my head is another miracle. And every day I experience such a miracle, I want another one. Leave me alone. I'm in love with these miracles.

Last summer our family took a cabin in the Canadian Yukon, forty miles from the nearest neighbor. I wanted to live again for a while out from under authority. But the local conservation officer came around regularly just to visit—there wasn't anybody but us to talk to—and also one day an immigration officer showed up and interviewed me and wrote things down about me on a pad. I started to wish we'd gone back to Alaska instead.

The life was basic—wood, food, water, weather. I read books about the U.S. Constitution and the Founding Fathers. At night we listened to the shortwave—the VOA, the BBC, Monitor Radio, and also a couple of Christian Right stations whose constituents had obviously become embroiled in the whole question of what the U.S. government thinks it's doing. Looking in my books, reading of the great people and tremendous ideas that had once found a home on this continent and produced the U.S.A., I wondered, too, about the revisions we've since allowed. This isn't the United States I was taught about in school, and it's not the one the Founding Fathers founded. Meanwhile I listened to Linda Thompson, a fiery critic of everything governmental, babbling on WHRI's *For the People* about bringing down U.S. choppers with .308s, and the more modulated voice of the show's host in response, both voices mourning the death of something even more precious than human life, and above all crying out, of Ruby Ridge, of Waco: *What happened?*

The lamentation stirred my heart. The incomprehensible actions of federal agents at Ruby Ridge and Waco had taught me that people willing to make a stand for their rights run the risk of martyrdom. Always and everywhere that's been the story. But my life long I'd believed the promise that here in America we tell a different story, of a nation created by and for those very people, and no home for bullies and tyrants. A government made, in the words of its first Declaration, "to secure those rights." Not to *grant* them, not to ration, license, or prioritize among them. To *secure* them.

My own unexamined assumption had been that the world's gotten so much more dangerous since the late eighteenth century that only a fool would expect George Washington or James Madison to stand by the original Bill of Rights today.

But I'd forgotten that when they gathered to frame the Constitution they did so in a country full of Tory infidels, just after a revolution, on a continent where several powers vied for rich territory, in a world full of terrorists and saboteurs, in a nation very, very wobbly on its legs. Yet they counted the security of this infant nation less important than the freedom of its citizens—and so they honored the rights of those citizens to speak and think and worship and freely trade, and the right to keep weapons as sophisticated as anything the military could acquire for itself, even to the point of buying a cannon and positioning it on one's front lawn right downtown.

What happened? If I ask the government, if I ask my leaders, they'll say nothing happened. This is still a free country. If I ask the stations broadcasting in the upper bands, the voices from Nashville and New Orleans and Noblesville, Indiana, fading in and out in the ether, they have an answer, but it's an answer to a different question, and it goes like this:

God made the world in eight, not seven, days. Two branches of humanity were fashioned, from one of which descended the Twelve Tribes of Israel; the others, the darker races, God created on a different day. Early in history Sephardic people came down from the north into the Middle East and supplanted the original Jews, drove out the Chosen People, and for centuries these quislings have conspired to rule the earth through the institutions of finance. The true Chosen of God, the descendents from the original Twelve Tribes, are the white race.

Just before the Great Depression the U.S. federal government and the nation's economy itself were hijacked by the Jewish families who run the banks of the Federal Reserve. They seek to own everything and enslave everyone by extending their power over the earth through a one-world government to be developed out of the current United Nations. They foster high-level groups committed to this goal. Anyone who's anyone in U.S. statesmanship, for instance, belongs to the Council on Foreign Relations, and some of them openly espouse the idea of a single world government, though that isn't necessarily the council's stated goal.

These people use the federal income tax, never legally instituted (the amendment fell one vote short of ratification, a fact afterward covered up) to rob us of our wealth. The Federal Reserve prints worthless money and lends it to the nation and gets it back as true value, backed by the good name of the United States, and gets it back with interest.

These ideas have been floating around since before the invention of the printing press. They found a new perch when the Federal Reserve and the League of Nations were formed. People saw them taking a solid shape in the policies of FDR's New Deal, looming large when the U.N. came to be. Who did it? Behind it all, behind all of modern Western history, lurks the Master Conspirator Jew.

The young French nobleman Alexis de Tocqueville traveled the U.S. for nine months in 1831, and in his writings on young America he makes no mention of conspiracy. He found no Jewish plotters. No Secret Service, FBI, BATF. No FDR, no LBJ. Karl Marx, Father of the Communist Conspiracy, had written nothing yet. The Federal Reserve did not exist.

How did America's future look to the Frenchman? "An innumerable multitude of men, all equal and alike, incessantly endeavoring to procure the petty and paltry pleasures with which they glut their lives. . . . Above stands an immense power which takes upon itself alone to secure their gratification. . . . to keep them in perpetual childhood. . . . It covers the surface of society with a network of small complicated rules . . . men are seldom forced by it to act, but are constantly restrained from acting . . . a flock of timid and industrious animals, of which the government is the shepherd . . ."

Alexis de Tocqueville didn't smell a conspiracy, just the natural course of politicking, what we now call "politics as usual," candidates trying any way they can to attach themselves to emotional issues. What do you covet? What do you fear? We'll fix it. Come election day even the national, federal leaders want to be part of my family, putting food on my table, money in my pocket, a zone of safety around my children. That's why so many federal laws duplicate state laws already on the books—the feds want to help run my hometown. The New Republicans call it "micromanaging" a hi-tech phrase that itself just duplicates a couple of old sayings: "All politics is local." Or "Everyone runs for sheriff."

The U.S.A. was meant to be a collection of small governments kept from oppressing minorities and each other by one limited but overarching federal system of laws and courts. But people *prefer* to oppress each other, each one *wants* all the others regulated, and the Feds took a lesson from local politicians who used this basic desire to their advantage by promising to honor it in exchange for votes.

I want to float above the fray, want to be like Walt Whitman, "both in and out of the game, and watching and wondering at it." But when the violence starts, I'm not aloof. I'm in the middle, pulled both ways. When the violence starts, the one in the middle, if he's honest with himself, must feel the guilt for the excesses of both sides.

When I heard about the bombing in Oklahoma City, I felt sick to my soul . . . My God, what have I done?

I believe the State should be resisted wherever it encroaches. But the bombers of that building will demonstrate for us something we don't want demonstrated: There's no trick to starting a revolution. Simply open fire on the State; the State will oblige by firing back. What's harder is to *win* a revolution, and the only victory worthy of the name will be a peaceable one.

Why should I be talking about resisting government? Take it all around, we Americans are the freest people on the planet. Our riches afford us mobility, variety, and opportunity enough to drive us crazy, as well as the time to go crazy in—more and more of all of these as time goes on. Like other systems descended from English law, ours offers certain protections from government intrusion—fewer and fewer of these as history marches forward.

If I'm not on either side when the shooting starts, and I don't like being in the middle, then where do I belong?

I'm one among many, part of a disparate—sometimes better spelled "desperate"—people, self-centered, shortsighted, stubborn, sentimental, richer than anybody's ever been, trying to get along in the most cataclysmic century in human history. Many of us are troubled that somewhere, somehow, the system meant to keep us free has experienced a failure. A few believe that someone has committed the crime of sabotaging everything.

Failures need correction. Crimes cry out for punishment. Some ask: *How do we fix it?* Others: *Who do we kill?*

My family flew back from the Yukon in a plane. I drove home in the pickup across a thousand miles of North American wilderness, sleeping beside streams and moving at my own pace and answering to no one.

Some miles north of Smithers, British Columbia, one of the tires went flat. I kept two spares aboard, but the jack, it turned out, wasn't working, and so I stuck out my thumb in hope of a lift into Smithers. A pickup with Alaska plates stopped a quarter mile up the road, and I ran up there and explained the problem to my rescuers, two young men hauling a big stock-trailer over- flowing with antlers and a self-possessed, unperturbable dog of the sledding type who sat between them in the front seat. "We've got a jack," the driver said, and began backing his rig up along the shoulder toward mine, slowly and expertly—he didn't stick his head out the window, but only eyed the jutting side mirrors.

These two, I saw when they got out to put a jack to my bumper, were country boys from quite another era, guys in overalls and big shoes and blackened jeans and red suspenders, with boyish, wispy beards, like ghosts from the War between the States. The driver was thick and blond and as becalmed as his dog, only more of a golden Labrador, the other man much like a retriever too, the thinnish intelligent kind, and both of them with the true clear gaze of dogs.

"Lot of antlers," I said. They had hundreds piled in the trailer, to the roof. They told me they made furniture out of antlers and drove around anywhere and everywhere, selling it. For the past month I'd been reading about the old days, missing them as if I'd lived in them, and I said, "You sound like free Americans."

"No," the smaller man said, and thereafter did all the talking while the other, the blond driver, changed my tire. "No Amer- ican is free today."

"Okay, I guess you're right. But what do we do about that?"

"We fight till we are," he said. "Till we're free or we're dead, one or the other."

"Who's going to do this fighting?"

"A whole lot of men. More than you'd imagine. We'll fight till we're dead or we're free."

Ghosts indeed. Rebel ghosts wending through the Appalachians to enlist in time for Gettysburg.

"Listen: I'm asking: Just tell me: What do you want?"

"Freedom. We just want freedom."

"But I mean—what happens if you bring down the government? What do you want to replace it with?"

"We'll need strong men, strong leaders. I believe the time will provide them," he said.

"And is that the only way to get it? In a war?"

The young man was chewing tobacco. He had big, kind eyes and his lips worked around his chew. I feel it worth mentioning that he didn't spit in my presence. He said, "Freedom has to be bought with blood."

In that landscape of mountains and empty distances, the statement resonated with profound authority. Blood sacrifice—it's as old as human spirituality itself, it's the thread that binds the Old Testament to the New, that binds in faith the Christian people to the God who bought their freedom from sin with the blood of his only son. But hasn't the price been paid, according to the Bible? Or does it seem we've been abandoned here unredeemed, confused, trying to decipher a strange new text?—a Third Testament cobbled together out of bits and pieces of the other two and interpretations that don't bear much examination. Prophesies of blood sacrifice and a war between good and evil, prophecies not yet fulfilled.

CREEKS OF GALIURO
Craig Childs

I stopped. Swallowed. Looked around my feet, my eyes burning with sweat and light. A hundred and nineteen degrees Fahrenheit, at least. This was the hottest July on record for Arizona. It was in fact the hottest single month recorded in all of North America. If I prayed for rain, the sky would laugh at me. Last time I listened to a radio I heard that forty people had died while trying to cross the border. They had all run out of water.

The creek bed on which I stood, stretching across the boundary of the Sonoran and Chihuahuan Deserts in southeast Arizona, was dry. The air carried no sound. I reached down and, among scorched white stones, picked up the shell of a turtle.

This Sonoran mud turtle had died long ago. The shell's edges flared like a conquistador's helmet. About an inch and a half long, it rested in my palm like a small creek stone, one with hardly any weight to it, as if made of balsa. Inside I could see the ribs, curved and fused to the underside the same way ribbing is built into wooden ships. I returned it to the ground and walked forward.

I am never any good in this kind of heat. I lose track directions, not minding if thorns stab my legs, the same thorns I would have avoided at dawn. I crawled into the narrow shade of a cliff, watching a single cloud, waiting for it to become huge and pendulous, scratching its belly with lightning, splitting open with rain. Instead it huffed into nothing, as if exiting a boiling kettle.

I left from there and walked into the shade of cottonwoods, where I nearly stepped on a rattlesnake. It was a western diamondback stretched inconspicuously across dry leaves, not even rattling from two feet away. I made a sound—something like *whoaholycrap*—and swerved my boot the other way. The snake did not move, did not twitch, did not flick its tongue. I had seen six rattlesnakes in two days—all Arizona blacks and diamondbacks—and as always, they reacted with the firm politeness of a brief, irritated rattle, or they did not react at all. As a rule, I have been treated kindly by rattlesnakes.

Saguaro cacti stood all around the low slopes of the canyon, coming down to the edges of these deep groves of trees. I walked into the brothy darkness beneath alder trees, ducking under some of the larger, more boldly strung spider webs. Inside the shade I found a place to wait, arranging leaves behind my back and leaning against them. I waited for night, six hours away. When shadows went long at about five o'clock, I returned to a place in the bed where earlier I had detected a trace of dampness. I organized a stopwatch, a tape measure, and my notebook on the stream cobbles and watched the spot, which was still moist. At about 5:30 water came out of the ground. It did not spew up, but slowly escaped into the surrounding sand and small rocks. The wet circle grew until water became visible. Then it bubbled out like a small fountain and the creek began.

Many of the desert streams that flow through the summer emerge in this way. They come out at night, as if fearful of the sun, rising through small gravel-filled corridors that connect the stream on top to the subsurface stream flowing far beneath. By midnight, this entire creek bed would be the site of a clean, swift stream. Walking across during the day, you would find this absurd to imagine.

As soon as light strikes leaf surfaces at sunrise, the riparian forest sets its higher metabolism into motion, photosynthesizing and pumping phenomenal amounts of water up to the canopy. The thickly arranged plants along the creek are known as *phreatophytes,* meaning they have no control mechanism for water. They are not true plants of the desert. They take as much water as they can get (a day's worth for a single tree being enough for a few lifetimes of a large cactus), sending it out the leaves, into the heat, making the understory as humid as a New Orleans summer. Instead of flowing across the ground, the creek is hoisted a hundred feet into the air into the leaves of sycamores, willows, cottonwoods, alders, and Arizona walnuts. What is not taken shrinks into the ground and returns to the water table. The surface creek is sucked dry.

As light faded from the trees, the creek saturated the surrounding ground before actually taking depth. I drank it there, at its source, my lips against the rocks. Within an hour it was moving. Here and there a new channel broke forward with swift fingers, liberating the wing of a moth, the doily veins of a decomposed cottonwood leaf, a dead beetle. Then it slowed, testing the route, finding places into which it spilled. Dusk came. The creek gained speed, making sounds, pushing pieces of gravel around, sucking air from the soil. As soon as the creek had about eighty feet of ground, longfin dace, supple little fish about an inch or two long, began darting about. There must have been a hundred of them. They had spent the day in sponges of soaked algae protected under leaf piles, or in rotted pieces of wood where water had collected, surviving in a half-alive torpor as the rocks baked around them. Water beetles, who had hidden in the same fashion, spun into action.

Crouched at the water, squinting to write measurements in the coming dark, I glanced to the darker tunnel of over-hanging trees upstream. Fireflies had appeared. They besieged the tall grass. Their lights were not constant or sharp but rather were ephemeral, green lanterns fading in and out, describing brief paths through the air. Eerie flickers revealed corners and closets within the canopy, and when a firefly neared the ground, a pale green circle of light cast over the twigs and leaves. They were accounted for in my notes, along with the rates of flow from the creek:

> *1st firefly at 7:45*
> *many more by 7:49*
> *dazzling by 7:54*

Finally, in the dark, the gurgling sound of the creek became loud enough that the bottom of the canyon had transformed.

Through a parade of fireflies and the dance of fish and diving beetles, the water had come. Tomorrow, in the sunlight, all of this would again be gone.

I should not give the impression that all the creeks here appear and disappear completely. Like the creek of the fireflies, many have surface water for twenty yards or ten feet or half a mile, with dry stretches between. At night these grow and sometimes connect, and during the day they recede, but not all of them entirely. Small waterfalls can still be found in the deepest shade during the day, and some of the creeks keep miles of water on top day and night.

I had come walking the creeks below the Galiuro Mountains, one of the more remote ranges in Arizona, northeast of Tucson and northwest of Willcox. Depending on what you count, there are well over ten good, running streams here. In the winter they run full steam, bank to bank all the way to the San Pedro River, a river that flows north out of Mexico into the Gila River, which runs south of Phoenix, curving across the state to meet the Colorado River before returning to Mexico. In the summer these small creeks are piecemeal, consisting of wet and dry sections scattered haphazardly through the canyons.

Although the Galiuros reach as high as 7,663 feet, they do not account in size for the amount of water produced in the springs and creeks below. These desert creeks, all around a 4,000-foot elevation, are too numerous. Even larger mountain ranges that feed the surrounding deserts cannot produce this volume of water. For the number of cattle historically grazing this area, about twenty-five windmills would be expected. There are only six. Much of the water is actually a remnant of Ice Age water. Stored and doled out in the increments of small streams, this Pleistocene water slowly drains from aquifers buried in the mountains, joining banks of much more recent runoff water. Radiocarbon dating on the groundwater here places it back ten thousand years, while the oldest water goes back to over fifteen thousand years. Hydrologists call it fossil water.

The Nature Conservancy in 1982 purchased forty-nine thousand acres of private land and government land leases below the Galiuros. Even as a neighboring rancher sued the Conservancy for not grazing cattle on this leased land, the conservation outfit talked the Bureau of Land Management into a five-year riparian and grassland restoration plan for the area. The plan mostly involved doing nothing, letting the place get back about its business. The boldest moves were the removal of cattle that had been grazing the area heavily since the late 1800s, and an experimental controlled burn program. The canyons at the northern boundaries of the Conservancy property are within two federal wilderness areas, which, when combined with the Conservancy's Muleshoe Ranch land, encompass the entire watershed of these desert streams.

For the most part, surrounding ranchers are complimentary of work that has been done at Muleshoe Ranch. Most of these ranches have voluntarily kept their stock below maximum numbers. Because of the ensuing quality of their ranges, after the last three years of hard drought, these ranchers were some of the few to survive without major economic losses.

The ranch manager at Muleshoe, Bob Rogers, is a congenial man in his thirties who no longer deals in livestock. He does not boom his voice, and he scratches the dirt with his work boot in the middle of a conversation. He is far less at ease in political situations than he is repairing fences, a task that had to be done on one fence sixteen times in a single summer after a barrage of floods. Other pieces of land belonging to the Nature Conservancy are of higher profile and have provoked disputes: quarreling with local government or citizens over water rights or grazing or public access or hunting. Muleshoe, on the other hand, is thirty miles down a dirt road that is sometimes washed out. Scientists doing work out here usually vanish into the backcountry for the length of their research. Public visitation is minor. Rogers is pleased with all of this.

He found the only known pair of endangered Mexican spotted owls in the range. Government biologists were skeptical about his claim, saying that sycamore forests with understories of oak and juniper are no good for spotted owls, so Rogers took them there, showed them the birds. He has a good grasp of the land, how to get around. His grandmother was born beside Aravaipa Creek, which crosses the northern point of the Galiuros. Most of his family background is in the ranching business, which he considers himself to still be in. It is only that he is tending to creeks instead of cattle.

"In a canyon like Double R," he said, "cattle will get into the shade and water on a day like this and they won't move. Not for days. Not for weeks. That is why you either have old, massive trees—from before cattle grazing—or only new trees that have grown since we got the cows out." I have noticed this: one sycamore probably over a hundred years old with acres of shade below, then beneath it young, weedy sycamores shooting up everywhere. The trees of in-between age are absent, represented by the time cattle were present.

I spent some time talking with him about the creeks, getting an idea of what the different seasons are like, sorting through his records of flow measurements. We spread maps on the floor at the headquarters, got on our hands and knees. "Now *this* is some lost country," he said, scribbling his finger over a series of canyons to the north. "I don't know where this water comes from. Just doesn't make any sense to me, but it certainly is there. Right *there*," he stabbed his finger down. The creeks of Galiuro befuddle him. So much water in a place where there should be so little.

After spending a week walking the southern canyons, I traveled north, to the place Rogers had called lost country. I started in the morning in one of the canyons, taking note of whatever I saw first: a coiled Arizona black rattlesnake (coming through again later in the day, I found the bare clearing where the snake had shoved pebbles away, leaving its coiled shape on the ground) and a yellow-breasted chat scolding me through the stained-glass light of cottonwood leaves. The creek here ran steadily. It stopped in only a few places, draining into a downwelling zone to reappear elsewhere along the floor, around the next turn. These forests were the thickest I had seen. Dangling throngs of grapevines snared my ankles and I pushed through hedgelike walls of vegetation that blocked the view of the creek. A couple of times I found myself off the ground, suspended on cribs of grapevines, then stumbling out to the desert, into the light, hoping to find a shortcut. The land beyond the thin bands of forest was nude with rock. Saguaros stood here and there, along with numerous leafless ocotillos barren as fence posts. The sky was everywhere, sharp, hot, blue. A soaked bandanna stiffened in three minutes. I fell back into the forest, looking for the creek again.

The air inside was a potent marinade of humidity and heat causing my upper lip to taste like the sea. Any exposed skin became a repository for field specimens, my flesh a sticky net drawn through the brush, my forearms collecting insect wings, spiderwebs, curled bits of leaves and bark, patches of soil, and live ants. Flying insects struggled with their wings pasted to the back of my hands and to my forehead. From in here, the creek sounded like dishes being put away, a purposeful clatter in the distance. I followed the sound and ducked through to a broad pool where a small waterfall entered at the top. Fish, some of them a foot long, flashed and scattered. A rusty-orange dragonfly dodged up and down the stream corridor, its vellum wings making the rasping sound of dry garlic skins.

A spring came in from the opposite side, draining from cracks in a sheer stone wall. Shrouds of maidenhair fern and already-bloomed monkeyflower hung below the spring, dripping ten-thousand-year-old water into a natural trough, which then ran into the pool where the fish had calmed after my intrusion. I held myself up by the trunks of two young willows as I leaned toward the pool. The fish settled mostly in one place, the Sonoran suckers resting heads on each other's tails the way horses lean on one another. The smaller, more stout Gila chub kept their distance, hovering higher in the water than the suckers. The streamlined dace, both speckled and longfin species, hung everywhere, high and low, here and there.

I crouched slowly between my two willow trunks. It never seems to me that fish *swim*. Swimming seems like a mechanical process with articulated parts performing a variety of operations:

the breaststroke, the butterfly, the dog paddle. There are no rigid strokes to a fish in motion. It is more like sailing. If fish had words, they would use *swim* for all of us terrestrial animals struggling through their medium, and something else for themselves.

Fish in the desert, though. It sounds like a play on words, a trick phrase. *A woman without a man is like a fish without a desert.* But these fish are not random, not accidental slips that spilled out of the mountains. They are desert fish, found nowhere else. A number of fish biologists contend that they are, along with the water they live in, holdovers from the Ice Age. There are other contentions that they even precede the last ice age. Streams are threads through time, remaining through numerous climate changes as ice ages and deserts rise and fall. The fish cannot stand up and walk to more suitable habitat, so for the hundreds of thousands of years that the desert lasts, they seek refuge in these final springs and streams, adapting to the particular rigors. I once talked with a biologist named W. L. Minckley, who had found speckled dace in a spring along the higher benches of the Grand Canyon. The only physical link between the spring and any streamflow would be during floods, and that connection consists of impassable waterfalls thousands of feet down toward the Colorado River. This, he told me, led him to believe that the fish were there *before the canyons were cut.* The fish would have lived in that one piece of water for uninterrupted millions of years.

Obviously humans have changed the course for desert fish by interfering with their insular habitats. Extinct in the desert are the likes of the First June sucker, three species of Mexican dace, the Monkey Spring pupfish, Phantom shiner, Las Vegas dace, thick-tail chub, and numerous others. In some cases, especially with the native fishes of the less-studied Mexican streams, the extirpation occurs so rapidly that there has been no time to even document extinctions, ironically similar to what is occurring in rain forests. In Arizona, 81 percent of native fish fauna is presently classified or proposed for classification as threatened or endangered.

There have been cases of native desert fishes being actively poisoned out of waterways to make way for non-native sport fish. Referred to as trash fish, most natives are not fleshy or large enough for eating or do not put up the right kind of fight against a fishing line. I once discussed poisoning with a man who had worked on one of these eradication projects, a man who went on to become the superintendent of Glen Canyon National Recreation Area on the Arizona-Utah border. In his early years he had operated a drip station, one of fifty-five stations that introduced 81,350 liters of the poison rotenone into the Green River and its tributaries in the fall of 1962. The plan was to regionally dispose of the native humpback chub, a now-endangered fish, to make way for bass for sportfishing. "That is how we saw things then," he explained with a regretful but helpless tone, as if telling of war crimes. "We didn't understand."

Minckley, one of the foremost biologists working with desert fishes, said he could not see the remaining few natives of Arizona deserts surviving the next fifty years. Minckley's words were short, gruff. I talked with him in his office at Arizona State University in Tempe, where he is a professor and researcher. His desk was a mess of books and papers. A poster of native fish species hung on the wall. "Western fishes are completely unique," he explained. "There are only a few examples left in the desert anymore. The value of a species is just . . . just . . . so hard to hold onto. These species, these fishes, are sentinels for the system. They go, and you know that the place—the larger habitat—is being decimated. One of the things that pisses me off is that it is not necessary. You don't have to introduce bass into remote streams. The biggest factor for these fishes is the competition with non-natives. Dams are not that much of a consequence. Destruction of riparian habitat is not nearly as big a factor. It's those damned non-natives."

Minckley let out a hard breath and wrenched his left hand over his forehead, having told this story before. "All a native desert fish really needs is a place where nothing preys on its young. I am really getting too old to pussyfoot around with all of this. You've got to be insane to be in this business. We are continually losing."

He lamented the lack of support for desert fishes. People fail to get excited about something so remote and unfamiliar as a fish, even if that failure draws to an end not only a large number of species but an entire form of life. Non-natives are brought into these creeks for sport, and I have been unable to argue my way through a steadfast fisherman on the topic. I started bemoaning this to Minckley, telling him that it is difficult to express the value of a fish, something called a trash fish no less. He closed his eyes, retreating to someplace far away. "I know," he said, grumbled, whispered. "I know I know I know I know."

Consider the sum of all life, the heaped arrays of adaptations flung one after the next into the abundance of forms, each possessing codes pertaining only to its ancestors and its immediate predecessors, teeming organisms hefting around history in their cells, a library of each quirk and evolutionary indecision of the past 3.5 billion years, but only a record in each species of its single divergence from the source, with no register of errors or chance events gone awry because those were discarded to extinction, leaving a peculiar animal honed to a perfect set of symbols and codices, down to the Sonoran topminnow *Pecil-iopsis occidentalis,* perhaps soon to be vanquished from the planet. Protecting species is the same intrinsic gesture as preserving the original documents and constitutions of an entire civilization, or the love letters of grandparents.

Especially among biologists there is a respect for life and its uniqueness that goes almost unspoken, a reverence for the incomprehensible diversity of organisms that has woven itself into patterns across the earth. We, biologists or not, look at these creatures, including ourselves, the same way we observe stars of the night sky—with unspoken questions hanging from our mouths. To be privy to the eradication of a species and to know damn well what is going on is a shame beyond repair.

A recent government meeting was organized to discuss the preservation of certain desert fishes. One of the top policy makers announced that before anything was done that might hinder non-native sport fish in favor of natives, they would have to assess which of the two should take priority. To keep from bursting into a rage, Minckley stood up and walked out.

Roberts at Muleshoe Ranch told me that while walking up one of the creeks he saw a bass shoot by. It was the first non-native he had seen in that creek. Up higher is a stock tank that a family insists on keeping filled with bass for fishing. In floods the stock tank overflows and the bass tumble into the stream. Roberts swallowed and looked at the ground. It is like being told you have cancer.

• • •

To avoid the embarrassment of destroying another species, there have been mad scrambles and last-minute panics. The recovery of the Sonoran topminnow came so late that its habitat was already heavily fragmented and the species had been driven to genetic isolation. The fish that were chosen and reintroduced along numerous creeks turned out to be inbred, carrying no detectable genetic diversity at all. One of the populations in Mexico, one that was not used for reintroduction, was found to have strong genetic diversity, higher fecundity, and higher growth and survival rates. The reintroduced population from Arizona, basically engineered by humans who drove them into detached habitats, was already a dud ready for extinction.

There have also been subtle, illegal maneuvers to preserve these fish. In 1967 Minckley hauled two species out of a spring in an ice chest and transplanted them into a creek. For such a simple act, it was more consequential than many budgeted, staffed, and researched restoration attempts made since. At the spring he had found several species of native fish: the Yaqui chub, the Sonoran topminnow, and the Yaqui sucker. The Yaqui chub, *Gila purpurea,* was at the time uncomfortably near to extinction. He said, "I filled up a cooler with water, grabbed a hundred chub and female topminnows, then hauled ass up to Leslie Creek and let them loose. Somehow they took hold."

At the time there were no specific laws about transporting native fishes, but Minckley's move was somehow regarded as illegal, and a decade later government land and wildlife managers openly frowned on his actions. Ironically, his act prevented the extinction of the Yaqui chub. Shortly after he had transplanted these fish, the spring, which had become the final refuge for the species, completely dried. The fish he had transported in his ice chest became the only remaining population and are now the genetic stock of the Yaqui chub that have been reintroduced across southern Arizona.

I traveled fifteen miles north until reaching a creek directly below the crest of the Galiuro Mountains. A canyon burrowed into the desert, carrying a length of dark, fat pools and short waterfalls. The forest was no haiku, no simple arrangement. It was a mess. Flood debris and alders. Alders grew so thick that I had to place my two hands before my face, or walk backward, my backpack parting the way until the way became too tangled, and parted me. I had left the last canyon and traveled fifteen miles farther north, walking into a majesty of cliffs. Smooth walls and buttresses jetted seven hundred feet to either side, where chambers rounded into places to sit and great curves of rock. The alders thickened. Their leaves are more numerous and darker-colored than those on any other riparian tree, their branches starting near the ground and crowding each other to the oblivion of the canopy. I stopped trying to walk the edges and came down to the water, pushing my way through the stream, fish slapping my shins, water to my crotch. I pushed away vines and branches, breaking with my thighs the trapeze webs of orb weaver spiders.

The alders were so abundant due to a large flood that came through a decade earlier, spitting the remains of cottonwoods, sycamores, and willows into the San Pedro River. The alders were the first to come back. They returned with a vengeance.

Floods get rid of things, cleaning the creeks. Along with

tearing out the forests, floods dispose of non-native fish. One thing natives have over these non-natives is that they can survive incredible hardship. Floods come down like rolling loads of cement. In Aravaipa Creek north of here, which carries one of the largest assortment of native fish, half of the creek's entire water output is discharged over twenty-two days of the year. A quarter of the year's water appears within three and a half days. An autumn flood on Aravaipa sent the creek fifty feet above its normal waterline, and more than half of the riparian forest was destroyed. Most aquatic insects were wiped out. Researchers returned to find that the fish had hardly even moved, that the populations kept roughly the same proportions, as if the flood had been nothing to them but a shrug.

The razorback sucker has a peculiar hump of muscle on its back, shaped like a top keel, located close to the heart to deliver immediate bursts of swimming power against overwhelming currents. As one fish biologist told me, floods mean nothing against this one muscle. While other native species—aquatic plants, invertebrates, and amphibians—must often repopulate a previously flooded stream in the form of seeds, eggs, or airborne adults, fish are often still there.

Consider the proportions. A two-inch dace and a fifty-foot wall of water, boulders, shattered cottonwood trees, and mud. The flood subsides. The dace has not moved. A researcher named Gary Meffe, working at Arizona State University, planted Sonoran topminnows and non-native mosquitofish in a Plexiglas flume. The mosquitofish has wiped out topminnows throughout most of Arizona, largely by preying on juveniles, but tends to disappear after heavy flooding in narrow canyons, while topminnows remain. This piqued Meffe's curiosity.

When he sent a pulse of high water down his flume, the native topminnows quickly faced into the current, taking nearly motionless positions along the sides or near the bottom of the flume, wherever frictional drag gave the water a slight pause. Mosquitofish panicked and darted anywhere. If they oriented into the pulse it was with hesitation. They would not hold their places, flashing from side to side or turning completely around, their bodies catching different currents, their tails tucking into eddies and pulling them off course. They were flushed out of the flume. Even newborn topminnows snapped to the correct position and stayed there when a pulse came down. The mosquitofish had no genetic memory of water behaving like this, while native fish hovered in the eddies and shear zones, hunkering down, refusing to move or even twitch their fins in the wrong direction.

Few environments in the world are in such a constant state of violent expansion and contraction as this. If these streams were forests, they would vanish suddenly, understory and all, leaving nothing but hard ground, then reappear from nowhere. Devastating fires would charge through, sometimes several times in one year. The common assemblage of rabbits, elk, and bears would never do in a forest like this. An entirely new means of life would have to be invented.

On the other end of the spectrum from floods are the retreat and disappearance of the streams, sometimes daily, sometimes once a year. Rather than avoiding retreating sections of stream, some beetles and water bugs seek out these habitats in search of prey. Predator densities rise quickly. Raccoons and coatis scoop beleaguered fish out of the last pools, and black-hawks drop from the canopy to find whatever else has been stranded. The stresses and cycles of desert streams are uncountable. If not floods, then drought. At one desert stream in the last stages of drying, researchers saw eight predacious water bugs fly into two pools and consume twenty fish within a matter of a few hours.

Fish scattered ahead of me as I slid through the water. They schooled around each other, darting beneath tree roots. These were all natives. This canyon has yet to see a non-native. Dragonflies flitted and poised on the ends of twigs and snatched prey from the air. A researcher had walked into one of the nearby canyons last summer studying these insects, finding a tropical damselfly, *Palaemnema domina,* that had never been seen in the United States. In canyons west of here he captured three species of damselfly that had never been recorded anywhere in the world. Down in the rich forests along one of these Galiuro creeks he cataloged twenty-five species of damselflies and dragonflies, some with zebra-striped abdomens, others with colors scripted into their wings. With these creatures hovering in and out, the place verged on primeval.

I worked around root-strapped boulders, pushing through the water. Every few minutes I caught glimpses of the desert outside where saguaros perched across the walls. Towers of rock had pulled away, leaning out as if about to fall and bridge the canyon. These were censored views, framed by so much greenery that it seemed unlikely that there was any world beyond here at all. The sun could not get directly inside the forest, so the place became a steaming greenhouse, the air strong as horse breath.

A wind shoved through at 2:30, launching a fresh and unmistakable smell. Rain. Cold rain and hot rocks, the smell of a summer storm. There was not much of the sky to see, but there were certainly no clouds. I kept moving, trying not to wish too hard for rain, not to disappoint myself. Every summer the storms come as each desert inhabitant waits down here. We all watch the growing clouds after months of sheer heat until we are leaning toward them. Then one day they break open. The desert is deluged, flooded, reborn. The storms are insanely powerful with wind and rain. For months we wait for this.

After half an hour a thunderstorm moved over the canyon rim, lumbering in like a floating city. Thunder came through with low, gravely echoes off the walls. I looked up. *My god,* I thought, I prayed, *pummel us down here. Ravage us. Please.* This had been, in fact, the hottest July recorded across the entire Northern Hemisphere. We needed rain down here.

I found a fifty-foot boulder in the stream and climbed its back to where I had a clear view of the canyon and the heavens above. It was like standing on a glowing woodstove. The boulder sent heat straight through my body, up my raised arms to the sky. The clouds were dark with water, bulging down as if about to rip open. A few drops of rain fell. Fat drops. I closed my eyes, turned my head upward. One hit my cheek. My first rain since sometime in the late winter or the spring. But that had been a different kind of rain. So much desire in the summer desert. So much goddamned, furious desire. I was begging out loud, holding my hands up.

It did not come. The drops ended. Thunder lost its sharpness to distance. The boulder was still hot, having evaporated each drop, not letting them stain the surface for more than two seconds. I crawled off the boulder feeling self-conscious. I had made a fool of myself begging at the sky.

The sun returned, baking the roof of the forest. As I walked, spiders danced frantically in my hair and down my forehead. Grapevines unfolded around me, slinging off their host trees or their boulders. Pools turned emerald with depth and I bent over to plunge my head in, flipping my hair back so that water ran down my spine. Primrose flowers grew in the gravel, some of them a foot taller than myself.

When dusk came I unloaded gear onto rugs of fallen leaves where I would make my camp. The forest had become disturbingly dark. I glanced up, my ground pad in hand. I did not move as I looked through the offhanded crossing of branches, leaves, and vines. Dark, closed places like this make me uneasy. It is not the wild beasts or the idea of a lunatic with an ax. It is not facing my dreaded interior self. It is the informality, the thoughtlessness, the brooding wisdom, the endlessness, the closure of darkness. More than that, it is the thing in darkness I cannot name. I was once called in by an adventure travel magazine where a number of writers at a table were asked to do a piece on their fears in the wilderness. Someone said she would take spiders, and everyone laughed sympathetically. Another person said heights, and another being lost, both of which elicited noble nods and *mmm* sounds. I said dark, and not one of these outdoor folk said anything. They all looked at me to see if I was kidding. "Dark," I said. "You know. *The Dark.*" They all kept looking at me.

I stayed in the forest for a few minutes, reasoning with myself. Then I packed and climbed out. I went up only two hundred feet, scrambling in the loose rock around prickly pear cactus, before dropping my gear again. It was easier to breathe up here. Hard, definite edges and blocks replaced the boiling, fleshy shapes of the forests. It was not dusk, as I had thought. Orange sunlight embedded the cliff tops. The nest of solid green below sounded like an aviary. No matter how loud the birds became, they still seemed secretive, hidden in the trees around the water. I kicked away the larger rocks and lifted off the balls of cholla cactus. There I could sit and look down into the stirring, breathing forest. I finally stretched back, pulled off my clothes, and covered my body with a sheet.

Sometime in the night a brilliant white light branded my eyelids. I woke. There were no stars, only a black sky. The air smelled wet. The breeze, liquid. My hands were clutched over my chest and I did not move them. In fact, I tightened them, bracing for what would come next. It sounded like a block of marble cleaved open with a sledgehammer. The sky broke in two with thunder. Echoes pounded back, thrumming against my spine.

Lightning shot to the southeast. The air exploded again. Lightning then fell all around, snagging on the higher terrain. Scraps of lightning showed from behind rock towers. I counted the canyons by how many echoes of thunder were returned. Four pulses of thunder: four canyons. Then I heard the tapping. Rain began to fall. Another bolt of lightning. The rain increased, dabbing my face, making the sound of bean-filled rattles. I could hear it up on the cliffs, rain sheeting against rock. Rain dimpled my sheet, then sopped the fabric against my skin. I kept my hands folded on my chest. Water ran like tears out of my eyes, into my hair, through the rocks and into the forest. The creek grew by just that much.

My prayers. I remembered my prayers.

SPIRIT-FRIED NO-NAME RIVER BROWN TROUT: A RECIPE

David James Duncan

ike Christ (aka ∝), and unlike most of the rest of us, a pan-fried trout is utterly forgiving. If you use too high a flame, the skin takes the abuse and the flesh is still delectable. Too low a flame and it still makes decent sushi. Even overcooked for hours in British Babette's Nightmare simmer-it-to-mush style, the structural integrity of muscle that spent its entire life fighting river current is nearly impossible to reduce to goo.

Secret ingredients? There are none. Indispensable ingredients? There are two. The first? Honest butter. Forget margarine, forget olive oil (the cultural dissonance!), forget *I Can't Believe It's Not Coagulated Petroleum With Yellow Dye!*®, forget cholesterolic and caloric paranoia, period. Wild trout frying is not a meal, it's a rite. You are preparing to eat an animal that gave up its beautiful river and only life for your pleasure. Pleasure ought, therefore, to be maximized. Open your palate to the trout's flavor and your heart to its riverine essence, and that essence will charge through you like spring runoff, flushing every artery you've got. It is never "heart smart" to refuse to open your heart. Butter aside, there are no Trout Frying Commandments. Almonds, garlic, and cornmeal offer interesting counterpoint if you like fried almonds, garlic, and cornmeal; needless distraction if you don't. The flesh under discussion requires no trick additives. If you open your heart and use enough butter, a trout fried in a dredged-up chrome fender over an acetylene torch is worth eating.

Due to the chef-friendly equation between ease of prep and splendor of result, the trout is considered by many to be an easy fish to fry. It is not. The reason it's not is that butter is only one of the two essential ingredients, and the other is frequently overlooked. What is the mystery ingredient? *The trout itself.*

The cause of this shocking omission is the corporate-spawned delusion that those blotchy, cellophane- and styrofoam-swaddled, dented-Grumman-canoe-colored fish-corpses at the local chain supermarket are, as the label claims, "trout." Don't believe it! The supermarket product is mass-manufactured, half-embalmed pond-spawn. Raised on obscene industrial pellets, "toned" by flaccid, poop-flecked waters, these hapless victims of genetic Mcdiddling bear as much resemblance to wild river trout as does a drug-bloated, shit-smeared, feedlot moo-cow to a wild bull elk. *True trout frying cannot take place until a food-worthy species has been identified and a choice specimen taken.* Trout frying can begin, in other words, only with the catching of a *wild* trout, which can be obtained only after a journey to clean wild water. We have of necessity moved, in a single paragraph, from a tube-lit, corporate-owned refrigeration unit to the most unspoiled lake, river, or stream within range of your home. This is what I call

"Progress"! We're still not quite ready to catch a fryable fish. But we are at least now safe to begin considering their true variety.

Trout species vary from drainage to drainage, as Highland Scots and Indian tribes once did and by choice still do, and as any conceivable long-term, slow-time, sustainable inhabitant of the "Americas" will one day do.

Even the same one trout species takes on surprisingly different characteristics and flavors from river to river. The reasons for this are myriad, sometimes holy, and far beyond the scope of a single human mind, let alone a single human recipe. Suffice it to say that in my little home niche here in western Montana, I catch seven kinds of wild trout (the brook, the Mackinaw, the cutthroat, the rainbow, the bull, the cutthroat-rainbow hybrid, and the brown); that two of these are native to these waters, four introduced from elsewhere, and one (the hybrid) a little of each; that all seven are well able to sustain themselves without human assistance if human ignorance and avarice give them half a chance; and that it is this self-sufficiency that has earned the best of them the beautiful designation "wild."

But, ah, Industrial America! Of the seven local species, the indigenous bull trout is endangered, the indigenous West Slope cutthroat threatened, and the introduced Mackinaw lousy eating, so the first two I release and the third I culinarily ignore. I'm so stunned by the blazing colors of the occasional brookie I catch that I'm as likely to kill it as I am likely to kill a mountain bluebird or western tanager. And almost every time I set the hook to a bread-and-butter rainbow or hybrid cutbow, it pirouettes skyward and so does my heart, so that by the time I land it I'm as likely to kill and eat it as I am to kill and eat a member of the Joffrey Ballet.

Six of seven species landed, six of seven released, and my frying pan still empty. The reader begins, perhaps, to see the difficulty in obtaining that second Trout Fry Essential. Who wants to kill and eat beauty? Who wants to kill and eat one's dance partner? I am one of those people who finds the American rodeo clown a wildly more romantic figure than the Spanish bullfighter, since rodeo clowns not only refuse to mince and posture, but practice—with far bigger, far more dangerous bulls—the art of catch-and-release. I am also, however, one of those people who, like trout themselves, eats flesh. In honor of this unanimity, I now turn, with all the appetite that's in me, to the seventh and last local wild-trout possibility: the brown.

Our Montana brown trout—like most nineteenth-century arrivals—began the long journey westward by crossing the Atlantic in ships. There were two distinct immigrant families. I call them the McBrowns and the Brauns. The more silvery, red-spotted Loch Leven McBrowns originated, like a lot of Montanans (the clans Craighead, McClay, McGuane, Maclean, Doig, Duncan, etc.) in Scotland. The more buttery-colored, orange-spotted Brauns hail from Germany. And to this day, if you gently squeeze the living bellies of either, they let out a croaking sound that brings Scottish broguery and *Deutsch* umlauts to mind.

What I love best about McBrowns and Brauns, though, is not the Old World heritage or remnant dialect: it's the fact that these fish, unlike most European introductees to this land, did not follow the Pioneer/Plunderer, Industrial Robber Baron, Missionary Zealot, or Racist Cracker models. *Mirabile dictu,* brown trout chose the Native American model. From the moment of their release upon this continent, the McBrowns and Brauns opted, belly-croak brogues and umlauts notwith-standing, for sly, adaptable, indigenous ways. And indigenous-ness, by *Gott,* is what they got.

Moving from oak barrels into America's sweet rivers, lying deep and still when in doubt, brown trout set out not to invade their new continent but to *belong* to it. They carved out a niche among the competing species. They achieved balance with the food supply. They learned to sidestep the pantheon of predators. They learned to migrate elk- or Indian-style to beat the harsh seasons. They survived river-stopping ice-ups, riverbed-scouring ice-outs, multiyear droughts, hundred-year floods, irrigation overallotment, placer and open-pit mines, 75,000 American dams, generations of polluters, generations of political representation by river-molesting nudniks, genera-tions of bombardment by cow-asses uncountable, generations of bombardment by Sportfishing Huns.

Despite all such assault, they thrive. There are rivers, streams, and spring creeks all over America that have, in a single century, become as impossible to imagine without their wild browns as the waters of the Pacific Northwest were once impossible to imagine without their salmon. There is no veteran fly fisher con-versant with the various salmonid species who does not consider browns the Coyote of North American Trout. The McBrown's and Braun's swift transition from Highlander and Deutschlander to ineradicable American Native bypassed the usual Outlander Phase. It took a *fish* to do it, but brown trout are living proof that a gracious and native harmony—to the European immigrant who daily seeks nothing else—is attainable not just in theory, but in body, tooth, and soul.

Another thing to love about browns: There are private "game ranches" in many states, Montana included, where you can hand over a MasterCard, borrow a rifle, use the roof of your luxury sedan to steady your sights, shoot a terrified, fence-bound deer, elk, or buffalo, climb back in the sedan, order the beast professionally gutted and cleaned if your shot killed it—professionally executed, gutted, and cleaned if it didn't—then order a haunch of it cooked to specs, on site. For the right kind of money you may even be able to order your haunch professionally pre-chewed. So what a pleasure to report that *there is no analogous way to purchase or pretend to dominate or sink your pointy teeth into a wild brown trout.* Brown trout are not for sale. For 99 percent of their lives they're not even visible. Hiring an ace angler to kill one for you is socially difficult and legally illegal. And hiring a professional fishing guide to lead you to one suitable for eating is an excellent way of enticing the guide, who is almost certainly a poker-faced, closet brown-trout worshiper, into making sure you get skunked.

The wild brown is, then, as egalitarian a quarry as happiness itself. To catch in order to fry in order to eat one of these indigenous beauties, even the most prodigiously portfolioed oligarch in America has to slip into a Gore-tex fartsack and stagger out into a cold, wild river, where, with his brain the size of a canteloupe and fiscal grasp of continents, he'll find the Coyote of Trout, with its brain the size of a peppercorn, anything but willing to rise up and die.

• • •

Even for those of us who live here, plying the rivers for browns over the course of a Montana summer is no way to keep steady meat on our tables or healthy egos on our ids. Brown trout are delicious—to my palate, the tastiest species of my legal local four. But of the local trout species, they wear the most perfect camouflage, have the teeth most likely to cut through a leader, prefer the snaggiest lairs, and almost invariably, when hooked, head for the nearest sunken tree. They have the keenest eyesight and greatest paranoia about what's going on up onshore. They're often nocturnally voracious but uncatchably ascetic by day. Upon achieving trophy size they turn cannibalistic, nearly immunizing them to the efforts of us insect-imitating fly-slingers. And when they *are* rising, they have the subtlest of rise-forms, making them the most difficult trout to locate and stalk. As a result, those who would consistently catch browns must own more than a pedestrian itch to wet a line. Of fly fishers especially, these fish demand not just interest but obsession. Not a pretty obsession, either. In order to become one of the rare maestros who can deceive these beasts at will, one must immerse oneself for years and to the eyeballs in the sort of obsessive fish-speak I've been scribbling this whole past paragraph—

unless one happens to know a wicked secret: *Even the oldest and most sagacious of browns grow temporarily crazed—by sex.* No fooling. Every mature brown trout that swims makes a spawning run in fall. This seasonal change of metabolic and existential purpose transforms the Coyote of Trout into the most imbecilic of impulse shoppers. It's a tragic but all-American malady: you can sell a spawn-minded brown damned near anything.

I'd heard stories, before moving to Montana, about how aggressive browns grow in October. Being from the Northwest coast, I imagined a belligerence akin to that of salmon, who purposefully stand guard, after arriving at the spawning grounds, around their redds. There is no similarity. Like all but the kinkiest humans, a brown wants no other species of creature in its bed of love except other browns. Unlike most humans, the brown considers its *entire visible world* to be this private bed, remains open-eyed and armed (to the teeth) round the clock, and at the sight of trespassers aims to kill. It's a strange behavior to transpose into human terms. If my wife and I were to become the sexual equivalents of brown trout tonight, our foreplay would consist of attacking and swallowing seven pet chickens, five goldfish, a guinea pig, a Dalmatian, a pony, and a horse. *Vive la différence!*

I know a gin-clear creek, near a highway I often travel, that meanders through a quarter-mile-long meadow too pretty to pass by. I called it Three Fish Meadow, because the eight or ten times I'd plied it, I caught an average of three pan-sized trout, none of them browns. One crisp day in early October, I stepped into the same meadow, obeyed an impulse to tie on a fat orange jack-o'-lantern of a fly called an October Caddis, cast it into a pool-table-sized pocket behind a wheelbarrow-sized rock, and immediately hooked a nice brown. After landing and releasing the fish, I cast into the same little pocket—and instantly hooked another good brown. This happened five more times. Each of the seven browns raised hell in the pocket, crashing into and dragging line across its cohorts. Each subsequent fish nevertheless savaged my pumpkin fly. Continuing up through Three Fish Meadow, I caught and released twenty-six trout averaging thirteen inches. All but two were sex-crazed browns. The meadow, in spawning season, needs a new name.

I remember, midway through the meadow, a female brown who had claimed as her boudoir a side-channel so shallow I never thought to fish it, and so nearly stepped on her as I came hiking along full speed. *Yet she didn't spook!* At the sight of a seventy-two-inch human splashing down upon her with a hundred- and-eight-inch fly rod in hand, this fourteen-inch creature shot to the foot of her bedroom-sized glide, did a one-eighty, then zipped straight back at me, *as if to scare me off by charging.* If she'd been a few inches longer, it might even have worked!

Since I didn't bolt, the horny she-trout halted in eight inches of water not four feet to my left, and proceeded to glower up at me. I tried to glower back, but her eyes began to unnerve me. *If I lay some eggs in a nest in the gravel here,* she seemed to be thinking, *will you swim over 'em and do your part?*

Deciding we both needed a reality check, I choked up on my fly rod like a baseball hitter who's been given the bunt sign and dropped my big orange fly, *PLONK!* right on top of her head. This was not fly fishing. This was terrorism. I was doing to the little trout about what Brom Bones did to Ichabod Crane in *The Legend of Sleepy Hollow.* A sane trout would, like Ichabod, have fled for miles. My flirtatious friend grabbed the pumpkin fly as if it were a tossed bridal bouquet. I began laughing so hard I lost her—a relief to us both. But talk about sexual aggression! The Chinese ought to be grinding up October browns instead of elkhorn to restore wilted Eros.

Much as I enjoyed catching those browns, and much as I would have further enjoyed eating a few, I encounter a moral quandary with regard to the brown trout's seasonal nincom-poopery: What fly-fisherly honor is there in catching and eating a creature whose peppercorn outsmarts our canteloupes forty-eight weeks out of the year, by simply waiting for the sex-drunk four weeks when it couldn't outsmart a fly-fishing Orvis shop mannequin? What honor is there is matching wits with and deceiving a normally inspiredly elusive creature while it lan-guishes in a lovesickness so severe that a fourteen-inch spec-imen considered *me* a potential mate? Many of us could whomp Shaquille O'Neal at one-on-one basketball while *he* was having sex, too. Is this cause for pride? When a brown in the throes of its own mania to create life slashes my fly in late autumn, it is not a fly-fishing conquest by me: it's a biological conquest of the brown trout by the brown trout itself.

That said, I must make a confession. When it comes to fly fishing, I'm an addict, hence a pretty low-rent guy. My impulse to fish is so strong that I'll admit it: it's *fun* for me to attach my fly to a brown trout's biological conquest of itself. What I must ask myself and all honest fly fishers, though, is whether there is a more and a less honorable way to proceed with this low-rent malady of ours. Is there a sustainable way for us, and for the sex-stoned brown, each to pursue our very different addic-tions and live to tell the story?

I believe so. I believe the sustainable solution is a recipe: I dis-covered, one day in late fall, that it is not only possible but enormously pleasurable to spirit-fry and eat a brown trout, then release it unharmed. It happened like this:

One October day I slipped into my waders, drove to a certain never-to-be-named brown-trout river, hiked down to a certain logjam, dropped a fly in the eddy behind this jam, lost sight of my fly when it drifted behind some willows, heard a slurping sound behind the willows, raised my rod at the sound, watched the rod slam downward, and felt the angry headshakes of a solidly hooked fish.

Those headshakes excited me for three reasons. First, I recognized them to be the headshakes of a brown—my fry-pan favorite. Second, judging by the slow authority of the shakes, this brown was sizable: I pictured salmon-sized trout steaks sizzling in *Le Creuset.* Third, the logjam it was hiding in happened to be a logjam I'd built myself earlier in the summer, by chain-sawing and dismantling a dry-docked upstream jam and walking its logs a quarter-mile downstream to this deeper site and getting hung up en route in half-drowned, abandoned barbed-wire fences and driving into Missoula and cruising the hock shops and finding an ancient pair of bolt cutters and dickering the guy down to twelve bucks and driving back to the river and cutting and coiling and removing drowned barbed-wire fencing till I got my hands punctured and shins dinged up and logs right down where I wanted them. This jam was, in other words, an act of indigenous fly-fishermanly madness. And the wild animal on my line was evidence that Mother Nature had noticed my madness, and approved of it.

A big brown in summertime, hooked in the very same place, would have bolted into the logs and snapped my line in short order. The October brown, however, shot directly away from the logs into the snagless center of the run, where nothing good could possibly happen to it, and proceeded to veer from side to side, not as if looking for escape, but as if looking for something to attack and kill. Typical spawning-run brown behavior. I worked my way through willow brush to the hole's tail-out, forded the little river, waded back up to the pool, and waited for the big brown to come up with a new idea.

It never did. It came up with desire, anger, beauty, size, and that was it. After five or six minutes of furious veering, it tired. I led it down to the tail-out, eased it into the shallows in front of me.

I looked at the brown. The brown looked at me. I saw by the oversized, totemic jaws that the fish was a male. I took him in my hands, turned him gently on his side, measured him against the marks on my fly rod: twenty-two inches. Filleted out, quartered, and fried with almonds, he'd sate my entire family. Released, he would create his own.

The little stones in the stream were bronze in the October sunlight. The brown, against those stones, was brilliant yellow, white, and gold. His pelvic fins, translucent amber, were the size of silver dollars. The orange spots scattered down his side shone, as Richard Hugo once said, "like apples in a fog." He was so old he'd developed a gaze like a cougar, a redtail, an eagle. One does not capture an animal like this every day. I was able to pluck out the fly, right him in the water, keep my grip loose so as not to harm him. I was not able to let him go.

I dropped to my knees in the water beside him, my waders fending off the cold. The current swirled around half of me and all of the brown, coming in small, uneven surges that gently rocked my body; it felt like riding a quiet horse. Though I held him captive, the brown stayed perfectly in rhythm with this horse. Since he faced upstream, I turned that way too, and looked in the direction the brown trout was looking. Ours was an eastward-flowing stream. It was evening. The sun was turning orange before us in the west. Mountains veed to the water on both sides of the river, the northward-sloping ridges green and white with pines and new snow, the southward-sloping ridges yellow with last summer's grass. As the flow swirled down toward us, reflected sun turned its surface into a blinding sheet of orange-flecked silver. As the silver came closer, reflected sky turned it into broken shards of blue. Closer yet, the blue vanished, the water went as clear as air, and the sunlit stones beneath us became a bed of shining gold. All this beauty, all these riches—and I was *still* not sure what I would do with my brown.

Then I noticed, right in front of us, a fresh-dug, trout-length excavation in the bed of gold. It was his redd. Or hers. His paramour's. And as I stared at this redd, beaten into the stones by a seemingly departed female trout's body, I realized for the first time in my life just who the animal in my hands would truly be making love to. Not to his mate. Hardly to a mate at all. She'd dug the redd, laid her eggs. But he would never touch her. All he would ever touch was this water and these stones. He was making love, as was his mate, to the blinding silver, the broken blue, the shining gold.

I touched his side with my finger. A drop of milt spilled from his vent and vanished downstream. He was in the throes, even as I held him. I saw why I'd considered spawning browns stupid. I saw it was I who was stupid. I saw that, at a certain time of year, the rhythm of the river becomes impossible for these creatures to resist: that the mere act of swimming, mere caress of cold water, becomes a long slow copulation; that their entire upstream journey is an arduous act of sex. The dip in the gravel, nest of eggs, spraying of milt, was just the culmination of that weeks-long act. I looked again at the mountains veeing down toward the water. The gravel beneath us was made of fragments of those mountains, the current flowing past made of their melted snows. The brown trout I held was making love to the mountains and snow.

I realized that, in consuming this fish, I'd be consuming part of everything that made him. I realized that everything that made him was precisely what, or who, he was making love to. I realized that this same everything is who we, too, are made of; who we, too, are submerged in; who we, too, daily eat; who we, too, seek to love and honor. The trout in my hands let me feel this. He was, through no intention of his own, a spiritual touchstone. And one takes such stones not to stomach, but to heart.

One doesn't want to kill beauty, one doesn't want to kill a dance partner. But one doesn't want to let them go, either. I held that brown way longer than I should have. Held him till my hands began to burn. I've said it before: I must say it once more: *there is a fire in water. There is a flame, hidden in water, that gives not heat, but life.* I held a trout, and my own two hands, in that fire. The cold flames ran through and past us. And I was fed, I was sated, I'd had all the nourishment and flesh I needed when at last I opened my heart, opened my hands, and let my beautiful brown trout go.

BRIDES OF PLACE
Ellen Meloy

Steep thyself in a bowl of summertime.

—Virgil, *Minor Poems*

Solstice Daybook, June 21

Four descriptions of nature writing: The literature of loss, an elegy, a lamentation. An "antidote to despair." The antibodies to doom, words and experiences that remind us of our vital connections to the natural world so that we might repair and revere them. My favorite: Writers write because they can't shut up.

The rising sun bathes me in a slow, languid blush. My fleece blanket heaps up around my ankles in a sorry puff of rejection. Even at this early hour the red sandstone walls are a magnet for heat; I can feel them pull the sunlight across my skin. Beyond my bed a small stream shimmers its spirit over a ledge of slick-rock. A *Uta stansburiana* passes my sleep-gnarled hair in such a prim strut that I swear it is wearing two tiny pairs of spike heels on its four tiny lizard feet. From somewhere nearby come the chewing noises of a large herbivore. The home terrain of Colorado Plateau canyon country is familiar but my sleeping place uncertain. (I arrived in the dark, in a thicket of cricket sound, and went to sleep.) I know the day—summer solstice, my birthday—but not the time. Things rock-solid change places with thoughts tenuous, then change back again.

To be this old seems a terrible thing. At least I think I should feel terrible.

Here is what I am thinking: A body is never final. Mine still functions despite a lingering backache, which may be a boulder under my pad or an injury suffered in the past winter when a white horse reared up in a Lone Ranger maneuver and, unlike the masked man, I left the saddle and hit frozen ground flat on my back, *fwump,* like a raw chuck roast slapped down on a stainless steel table.

I am thinking that some of my women friends talk less of happiness or of Whitmans metaphysical exuberance or clearcut forestry and more about their gynecological histories. Others are running out and having their ankles tattooed. Their memories turned to porous sludge, graying men and women obey daily schedules embedded in compact electric notebooks, they swig gringo balboa or whatever they call the smart herb that obviously cannot help me because I have entered old age without ever living the New Age, too dim-witted to know what to ask for from the bright young vegan with the pierced tongue at my local health food store, assuming I can *find* my local health food store and can communicate with someone who has driven a gold spike through her taste buds. My contemporaries mature into wisdom, reflection, and abject panic. They are attending church in droves because they realize they are going to die.

I lie on the ground in a sweet, wild canyon and think that it is somewhat pleasant, actually quite a relief, not to be smart anymore, to let a few flies orbit my cranium in an indolent buzz. On the solstice, the dawn of long summer light, I roll over onto a dense cluster of dried-up, blackish pellets and this is what I think: I am having a midlife crisis on top of a pile of sheep dung.

The chewing herbivore is a mature desert bighorn ewe. She browses a blackbrush and watches me. I sit on the forehead of a cow's skull and watch back. At a greater distance three more ewes feed on a talus, superbly balanced and agile on the steep slope. Some of them have black tongues, others have pink tongues. Only one of the ewes has a lamb. All of the sheep have gentle faces and the legs of a troop of weightlifting ballerinas.

If you look for desert bighorns, you will not find them easily. Even hard-rock patience can end in their absence from where you think they are. Writer Peter Steinhart believes that these elusive creatures live in "seams of time," that "their thoughts run to realms so remote that they lift bighorns right out of the material world." I am inside the seam with five of them. I am getting old. The sheep have become rare enough to raise the specter of their vanishing.

Of Eurasian origin, North America's Ovinae subfamily crossed the Bering land bridge during the Pleistocene and, south of Alaska, evolved into the distinct species *Ovis canadensis.* The species reached its southern limits in the provinces of northern

Mexico. Desert bighorn distinguishes the sheep that live in Mexico and the arid Southwest from the more abundant, adaptable mountain bighorn, denizen of the intermountain West and northern Rockies. Biologists group four races, or subspecies, under the term "desert bighorn." One of these races adapted to local environments in the Great Basin and Utah's canyon country: *Ovis canadensis nelsoni,* the hosts of my birthday party.

Maps that speculate on the desert bighorns historic range a century ago show broad puddle shapes that cover plateaus, badlands, and low, rocky hills. Today's remnant herds reside in habitat the size of water droplets—reduced in number, sparsely distributed in isolated mountain ranges and broken canyon country, the most remote reaches of their once expansive territory. The causes invoke a familiar mantra: habitat loss, human encroachment, fire suppression, diseases from domestic livestock. Then the story grows sadder still.

The ewes and lamb around me exercise a remarkable and dangerous fidelity to place. They feed in defined territory and frequent water sources used by generations. From the older ewes the young learn where to forage, quench their thirst, bed down, mate, give birth, seek escape, and die, all of it usually within range of an ancestral water supply. The bighorn became a *desert* bighorn by forming a relationship with its environment—dry, austere, unpredictable—and encoding *home* into its genes. It ended up smaller and shorter in leg than its hulky mountain cousin, with bigger horns that help regulate body temperatures in desert extremes and a metabolism that accommodates drought. With influence from geographic separations, such adaptations evolved into hereditary differences and diversified the species.

The press of modern culture tends to homogenize biological diversity. Those life forms best suited to a changing world, the most aggressive and adaptable species, some would say the least poetic, survive: poison ivy, catfish, the mummichog, a topminnow that can live in the dirtiest water imaginable. The quirky ones, the brides of particular habitat, the place-faithful, may find their biological lineage at a dead end. In favor of the generalists we have chipped off nature's specialists, the late-comers and the homebodies. Environment-specific variations on a main genetic theme, a subspecies is a young evolutionary, so to speak, and among the most recent to differentiate. They can be very local. Commonly, they are the first to become extinct. In small numbers, confined to a single patch of landscape and reliant on a precarious niche, the risks escalate. Infections, usurpation of water, or other misfortunes could result in catastrophe.

My locals, among them the solstice ewes, comprise a population of about forty sheep. Laws and biologists protect them and other bands in the Southwest. For now their numbers hold steady. Perils surround them in a land they can no longer safely inhabit, a demarcation that amounts to an asylum. The sheep remain loyal to their beautiful and fateful desert. It is their entire universe.

The ewes jerk their busy jaws over scraggly shrubs and chew. They remain wary of me but not alarmed. They strolled into my bedroom, aware that I am some sort of prolapsing prefossil and ought to be permitted to stay that way. Nevertheless, I must walk away soon and let them browse in peace. They know their escape route and will use it. Escape usually means an uphill scramble to a higher vantage point and the casting of a farewell look over their shoulders. Or they might vanish into thin air, as I have seen wild sheep do, leaving me alone with blue sky and their likenesses, pecked a thousand years ago on the varnished sandstone cliffs around me by aboriginal hunters, people who surely loved the shape, the power, the meat of this magnificent creature. In this region the frequency of bighorns in rock art is second only to the prints of human hands.

I have purged the suffocating mope, the incipient snap of aging brain cells, and given myself over to the sheep. The ewes lose themselves in their own sensations, perhaps the succulent flavor of a fourwing saltbush leaf on their thick tongues or an itch behind the ear, relieved with a stroke of a hind foot and a head shake. I pull a leaf from a saltbush and taste it: salty with a pungency that feels like porcupine quills up the nose.

If anything compels me to write about the natural world, it is that many wilderness worshipers are so busy choking on awe or so depressed by the triumph of greed over preservation that they forget nature can be absurdly funny. I thrive on the quirks and puzzles and mazes, the raw material for paradox and pleasure. Around wild ungulates I behave in a nonsensical manner. I invite pathological color experiences. Sand amuses me. I am addicted to cottonwood sex, to the S&M of a hedge-hog cactus with a maniacal sheath of spikes topped by a velvet bloom of delirious scarlet, to the loneliness of someone who steps out of a crushingly social world to seek, where there are few humans, the riddles of what it means to be human, knowing well that the riddles end up unanswerable, knowing that sealed into a solitary world, my only companions might be a band of wild sheep. And when I laugh, I begin to feel the dreaded creep of hysteria, lyricism edged with pain. Have I noticed that I might be laughing my head off *at a funeral?*

A great deal of nature writing sounds like a cross between a chloroform stupor and a high mass, in Latin, on a hot day, surrounded by bleeding plaster icons. Words penned to the "wild" chronicle a failing purity, where no land or seascape is untouched and all that is truly wild is lost. In the real world, I think, more and more the profane inhabits the sacred. Even I use words like "clear-cutting" and "gynecology" in the same breath. I write a book about a river and cannot tell if it is a love story or an obituary or both. On another desert river, miles and miles from any town, I find a barrel of toxic herbicide, discarded with a facile and illegal carelessness into a resplendent dance of sunlight on water. As I bury my face in the voluptuous innards of cliffrose petals on a remote mesa, a low-flying, kelp-colored military jet passes over with a roar so thunderous it nearly makes my ears bleed. Today is my birthday, and during its twenty-four hours nineteen species will become extinct.

Look into the eyes of a domestic sheep and you will see the back of its head. Look into the eyes of this bighorn, the black, curiously horizontal irises set in amber orbs, and you will see a lost map to place, a depth that we may extinguish before it touches us. The bighorns' tenacity to this paltry remnant of wildland inspires as well as frightens me, for like them I cannot abandon the geography that feeds my every breath. The creative process, too, can be nothing less than an indestructible fidelity.

Between the sheep and me, our prospects diverge radically: my mortality, their extinction. If the sheep fall below the numbers needed to replace themselves, biologists would bring in

desert bighorns from game farms or different stock. Nevertheless, there would be an extinction, though not of the desert
bighorn. This band's ancestral fiber of desert woven into living
tissue—hundreds of years of wild faith to *this* wild place beneath
their hooves—would shred, unraveling the seams of time.

The sheep browse no longer but stand quietly with eyes that
seem to look inside themselves. The little *Uta,* the side-
blotched lizard in the high heels, parks her four-inch body on
a warm rock, her eyelids at half-mast and a rather queasy look
on her face. She has caught and eaten three fat black flies. She
feels how I would feel if I had swallowed three turkeys. A swal-
lowtail alights on my knee, then on my hand. I cup the butterfly in both palms and open them as if they were wings. A
soft breeze makes the butterfly tremble. In the breeze: wings
closed. In the stillness: wings open. We are a joined pulse. The
butterfly stays with me all morning, flitting about as if it were
my birthday gift.

Diminished by the intensifying heat, the stream has nar-
rowed to a thin ribbon across the red slickrock. I press my forehead into its cool sheen. I shall try to age with grace rather
than sorrow. I shall inquire about that smart tea, gecko
bermuda, ginglo biboola. I shall never ride white horses. The
solstice light stretches before me, and I know I shall fill it. In
the words of poet Mary Oliver, "I would like to do whatever it
is that presses the essence from the hour."

It pleases me that the sheep do not move, for I could not
bear that farewell look over their shoulders if they scrambled
away. The lead ewe remains close by. She and I are a couple
of old ladies in an asylum, our heads stuck stubbornly in a

precarious niche, clinging to an instinct to inhabit this far-flung, prickly place as if it were to be forever. It is our entire universe. As Steinhart said of the bighorn, I would like someone to say of me, *Her thoughts run to realms so remote they lift her right out of the material world.* Among my species this is not an asset but a liability, and I have paid dearly for a reckless devotion to roofless places of mind and body. At last I have reached an age where I know it is useless to resist.

MY LANDLADY'S YARD

Dagoberto Gilb

It's been a very dry season here. Not enough rain. And the sun's beginning to feel closer. Which, of course, explains why this is called the desert. Why the kinds of plants that do well enough in the region—creosote, mesquite, ocotillo, yucca —aren't what you'd consider lush, tropical blooms. All that's obvious, right? To you, I'm sure, it's obvious, and to me it is, too, but not to my landlady. My landlady doesn't think of this rock house I rent in central El Paso as being in the desert. To her, it's the big city. She's from the country, from a ranch probably just like the one she now calls home, a few miles up the paved highway in Chaparral, New Mexico, where the roads are graded dirt. She must still see the house as she did when she lived here as a young wife and mother, as part of the city's peaceful suburbs, which it certainly was thirty years ago. She probably planted the shrubs and evergreens that snuggle the walls of the house now, probably seeded the back- and front-yard grass herself. And she wants those Yankee plants and that imported grass to continue to thrive as they would in all other American, nondesert neighborhoods, even if these West Texas suburbs moved on to the east and west many years ago, even if the population has quadrupled and water is more scarce, and expensive, than back then.

So I go ahead and drag around a green hose despite my perception that *gold,* colorless and liquid, is pouring out onto this desert, an offering as unquenchable and ruthless as to any Aztec deity (don't water a couple of days and watch how fast it dries away). Superstitions, if you don't mind my calling them that, die hard, and property values are dependent on shared impressions. I'm not ready to rent and load another U-Haul truck.

With my thumb over the brass fitting and squeezed against the water, I use the digits on my other hand to pluck up loose garbage. You've heard, maybe, of West Texas wind. That explains why so much of it lands here on my front yard, but also a high school is my backyard: the school's rear exit is only a dirt alley and fence away from my garage, and teenagers pass by in the morning, during lunch, and when school lets out. I find the latest Salsa Rio brand of Doritos, Big Gulp Grande cups, paper (or plastic or both) bowls with the slimy remains of what goes for cheese on nachos from the smiley-faced Good Time Store two blocks away, used napkins, orange burger pouches, the new glossy-clean plastic soda containers, waxy candy wrappers from Mounds and Mars and Milky Way. Also beer cans and bottles, grocery-store bags both plastic and paper, and fragments from everything else (believe me) possible.

I'm betting you think I'm not too happy about accumulating such evidence. You're right. But I'm not mentioning it to complain. I want the image of all the trash, as well as the one of me spraying precious water onto this dusty alkaline soil, to get your attention. Because both stand for the odd way we live and think out here, a few hundred miles (at least) from every-place else in the United States.

My green grass in the desert, for instance. My landlady wants thick, luxuriant grass because that's the way of this side of the border, and this side is undeniably better, whatever mis-conception of place and history and natural resources the desire for that image depends on. It's not just her, and it's not just lawns. Take another example: a year ago about this time, police cars squealed onto the asphalt handball and basketball courts on the other side of the school fence to regain control of a hundred or so students lumped around a fight, most of them watching, some swinging baseball bats. What happened? According to the local newspaper, the fight broke out between a group of black students, all of them dependents of Fort Bliss military personnel (as their jargon has it), and a group of Hispanic students. "Hispanic" is the current media term for those of descent from South of the Border. Even around here. Which is the point: that even in this town—the other side of the concrete river considered the official land of Spanish-language history and culture—the latest minority-language terminology is used to describe its historic, multi-generational majority population. With the exception of one high school on the more affluent west side of town, Anglos are the overwhelming minority; at the high school behind my backyard the ratio must be ten to one. Though Mexico has been the mother of this region, and remains so, it's the lan-guage and understanding of The North that labels the account of the school incident: "Hispanic" students, black dependents of GIs.

If green grass is the aspiration, the realization of an American fantasy, then the trash is from the past, the husks of a frontier mentality that it took to be here, and stay, in the first place. Trash blowing by, snared by limbs and curbs and fences, is a display of what was the attitude of the West. The endlessness of its range. The ultimate principle of every man, woman, animal, and thing for itself. The meanness required to survive. The wild joy that could abandon rules. The immediacy of life. Or the stupidity of the non-Indian hunter eating one meal, then leaving behind the carcass. Except that vultures and coyotes and finally ants used to clean that mess up. The remains of the modernized hunt don't balance well in nature or its hybrid shrubs, do not biodegrade. And there are a lot more hunters than before.

Trash contradicts the well-tended lawn. And in my neighborhood, not all is Saint Augustine or Bermuda. Hardy weeds sprout and grow tall everywhere, gray-green century plants shoot stalks beside many homes. El Paso is still crossing cultures and times, the wind blows often, particularly this time of year, the sun will be getting bigger, but the pretty nights cool things off here on the desert. Let me admit this: I'd like it if grass grew well in my backyard. What I've got is patchy at best, and neglected, the brown dirt is a stronger color than the green. So the other day, I soaked that hard soil, dug it up, threw seed grown and packaged in Missouri, covered it with peat humus from Menard, Texas, and I'm waiting.

ABOUT THE CONTRIBUTORS

Edward Abbey is the author of numerous novels and books of essays, including *The Monkey Wrench Gang* and *One Life at a Time, Please*. He worked many years as a fire lookout and park ranger in the Southwest. He died in 1989 at his home in Oracle, Arizona.

Sherman Alexie is the author of several volumes of poetry as well as the short-story collections *The Toughest Indian in the World* and *The Lone Ranger and Tonto Fistfight in Heaven*, which he adapted into the screenplay for the award-winning film *Smoke Signals*. He lives in Seattle.

Jimmy Santiago Baca is the author of the memoir *A Place to Stand*, which won the International Award, and the poetry collection *Winter Poems Along the Rio Grande*, among other books.

Mary Clearman Blew is the author of *Writing Her Own Life: Imogene Welch, Rural Schoolteacher*, a biography of her aunt, and *Balsamroot: A Memoir*, among other books. She lives in Moscow, Idaho, where she teaches creative writing at the University of Idaho.

Craig Childs is the author of *Crossing Paths: Uncommon Encounters with Animals in the Wild* and *Stone Desert: A Naturalist's Exploration of Canyonlands National Park*, among other books. He has been a frequent contributor to National Public Radio and lives in Crawford, Colorado.

David James Duncan is the author of the novels *The Brothers K* and *The River Why*. His collection of essays, *My Story as Told by Water*, was a finalist for the 2001 National Book Award. He lives with his family in Montana.

Gretel Ehrlich is the author of *The Future of Ice: A Journey Into Cold* and *A Match to the Heart: One Woman's Story of Being Struck by Lightning*, among other books. She has worked on ranches in Wyoming and divides her time between California and Wyoming.

Dagoberto Gilb is the author of the short-story collections *Woodcuts of Women* and *The Magic of Blood*, among other books. He has been a frequent contributor to National Public Radio and lives in Texas.

Denis Johnson is the author of several poetry collections as well as the novel *Angels* and the short-story collection *Jesus' Son*, which was adapted for a movie of the same name. He lives in northern Idaho.

William Kittredge is the author of *Hole in the Sky: A Memoir*, which won the PEN West award for nonfiction, and *The Best Short Stories of William Kittredge*, among other books. He grew up on a cattle ranch in southeastern Oregon and taught creative writing at the University of Montana for many years. He lives in Missoula, Montana.

Patricia Nelson Limerick is the author of *The Legacy of Conquest* and *Desert Passages*, among other books. She was the recipient of a 1995 MacArthur Foundation fellowship. She lives in Boulder, Colorado, where she teaches history at the University of Colorado.

Thomas McGuane is the author of the novels *The Bushwhacked Piano* and *The Cadence of Grass*, among numerous other books. He lives on a ranch in Sweet Grass County, Montana.

Larry McMurtry is the author of the novels *Lonesome Dove* and *The Last Picture Show*, among many other books. He has written numerous screenplays and operated bookstores in Washington, D.C., and Archer City, Texas, where he now lives.

Ellen Meloy is the author of *The Last Cheater's Waltz: Beauty and Violence in the Desert Southwest* and *Raven's Exile: A Season on the Green River*, among other books. She passed away in November 2004 at her home in Bluff, Utah.

Sharman Apt Russell is the author of *Hunger: An Unnatural History,* and *An Obsession with Butterflies: Our Long Love Affair with a Singular Insect*. She teaches writing at Western New Mexico University and Antioch University and lives with her family in southwest New Mexico.

Leslie Marmon Silko is the author of the novels *Ceremony* and *Gardens in the Dunes*, among other books. She was the recipient of a 1981 MacArthur Foundation fellowship. She grew up on the Laguna Pueblo Reservation in New Mexico and now lives in Tucson, Arizona.

Rebecca Solnit is the author of *Hope in the Dark, River of Shadows: Eadweard Muybridge and the Technological Wild West*, which won the 2004 National Book Critics Circle award for criticism, and *Wanderlust: A History of Walking*, among other books. She lives in San Francisco.

Wallace Stegner is the author of the novel *Angle of Repose* and the essay collection *Where the Bluebird Sings to the Lemonade Springs*, among many other books. He taught creative writing at Stanford University and died in 1993 following an auto accident in Santa Fe, New Mexico.

Jack Turner is the author of *Teewinot: A Year in the Grand Tetons*, among other books. He taught philosophy at the University of Illinois before leaving academia and becoming a mountaineer. He lives each summer in Wyoming's Grand Teton National Park.

Terry Tempest Williams is the author of *Red: Passion and Patience in the Desert* and *The Open Space of Democracy*, among other books. She is serving as the Annie Clark Tanner Fellow in Environmental Humanities at the University of Utah in Salt Lake City. She lives in Castle Valley, Utah.

PERMISSIONS

ACKNOWLEDGMENTS

The germination of this book started as far back as my reading of Norman Maclean and Richard Hugo, two exquisite poets of place whose influence has been incalculable. William Kittredge provided a map of the literary terrain in previous anthologies, and in his wise suggestions for this book. Eric Magnuson and Joshua Boltuch were valuable sleuths. Toby Cash Richards had the faith to hire a greenhorn to spot wildfires in New Mexico, a job that allowed me to read all summer on the government dole. Martha Ross was a voice of encouragement and a sharp reading companion. Ruth Baldwin turned all the necessary cartwheels to make this project feasible; she cannot be thanked enough.